MAINLINE RAILWAY STAMPS

TRANSPORT
PHILATELY
SERIES

MAINLINE RAILWAY STAMPS

HOWARD PILTZ

PEN & SWORD TRANSPORT

AN IMPRINT OF PEN & SWORD BOOKS LTD.
YORKSHIRE – PHILADELPHIA

First published in Great Britain in 2018 by
Pen and Sword Transport
An imprint of
Pen & Sword Books Ltd
Yorkshire - Philadelphia

Copyright © Howard Piltz, 2018

ISBN 9781473871908

The right of Howard Piltz to be identified as Author of this work has been asserted
by him in accordance with the Copyright, Designs and Patents Act 1988.

A CIP catalogue record for this book is available from the British Library.

Typeset in Cormorant Infant by Pen & Sword Books Ltd

Printed and bound in India by Replika Press Pvt. Ltd.

Pen & Sword Books Ltd incorporates the Imprints of Pen & Sword Books
Archaeology, Atlas, Aviation, Battleground, Discovery, Family History, History,
Maritime, Military, Naval, Politics, Railways, Select, Transport, True Crime, Fiction,
Frontline Books, Leo Cooper, Praetorian Press, Seaforth Publishing, Wharncliffe
and White Owl.

For a complete list of Pen & Sword titles please contact

PEN & SWORD BOOKS LIMITED
47 Church Street, Barnsley, South Yorkshire, S70 2AS, England
E-mail: enquiries@pen-and-sword.co.uk
Website: www.pen-and-sword.co.uk

or

PEN AND SWORD BOOKS
1950 Lawrence Rd, Havertown, PA 19083, USA
E-mail: Uspen-and-sword@casematepublishers.com
Website: www.penandswordbooks.com

CONTENTS

DEDICATION

It is with great pleasure that I dedicate this book to my wonderful wife Christine who has been by my side for over 46 years and without whom I would never have been so happy.

And Chardi.

INTRODUCTION

or this second book in this series on public transport subjects featured on postage stamps, once again the author will combine two of his life long hobbies and look at the principal railways around the world.

For those that read the first book in this series, the following is very much a necessary repeat, setting the scene for the love of stamps and railways.

The two sides

Collecting stamps brings a wonderful new view of the world that the collector, celebrated in the more formal title of the philatelist, is led through an amazing world of knowledge, where the inquisitive mind can ponder some mysteries of bygone times. Why, you may ask, do British postage stamps never, but NEVER boast their country of origin, preferring instead to use an elegant bust of the current monarch such as the work of the celebrated artist and sculptor Arnold Machin O.B.E (1911-99) that has appeared on every British postage stamp for over 50 years? Or why Swiss stamps bear the enigmatic title 'Helvetia', and as if that isn't difficult enough, then where are some far-off lands that these days only appear in our history books? Go south a tad, one might be told, to find Southern Rhodesia, or for that matter just a little more thought might be needed to give us the answer for that evocative name Tanganyika.

Likewise, someone with a worldly interest in transport may find that the hobby will lead him – or her – all over the world, if not literally, then as a by-product of studying the subject. There are a great many transport professionals that have worked on several different continents throughout their working lives to bring the benefit of their skills to areas one might consider under-developed in the areas of public transport. Personally, the author has spent many years as an enthusiast of most forms of public transport and has been to places that until the advent of cheap air travel seemed quite outlandish. Whilst he has never been to Indonesia, he has read, enthralled, of the fire-breathing dragons that abounded there; however, he has been to a lake on Vancouver Island on Canada's Pacific coast where lived the world's two largest flying boats regaling in the name of *Mars*, whilst it seemed to him at the time – he was 14 – quite exciting, but utterly easy in 1959, to talk himself onto the inaugural KLM Viscount flight from Manchester to Amsterdam only to find there was no return flight home that day (memories of the heart-clutching scream from his Dad over the phone will never fade: 'You're WHERE?') or a flight, not much later but this time with permission – and paid for – to go plane-spotting alone to the Paris Air Show. Not many years later, he visited the USA to look for the last gasps of two iconic forms of American transport – PCC trams in Newark, NJ, and the Pennsylvania Railroad GG1 electric locomotives. I could also go on a little too long about getting rather merry drinking the local brews in places like Prague, Lisbon or the countryside around Brussels whilst chasing trams.

Coming Together with Works of Art

At first sight, it might seem a little odd that one should wish to combine these two totally disparate hobbies, but by good fortune the author happens to have a liking for both subjects and a long time ago began to appreciate that in stamps one could find the wonderful combination of transport history told within a glorious gallery of miniature works of art. See through the ages how the reproduction techniques on stamps have developed from simple monochrome etchings such as this 1948 stamp from America.

Interestingly, apart from a very few definitives of the 1890s and 1900s, it was to be 1963 before a British stamp would appear with more than one colour; not even the UK's 1953 Coronation stamps boasted more. The accepted appearance developed first to two or

three colours and then as with everything else towards the end of the twentieth century, convention went out of the window as we saw full colour art-work and the use of photographs and, quite often in these days of digital photography, fairly heavily manipulated ones at that.

What's in this collection?

There will be several different formats that the reader will find mentioned in this book, and there follows a brief summary for the novice philatelist:

Mint stamps: unused stamps, un-marked on their face and with the gum on the back still intact. It used to be the habit of collectors to stick gummed, paper hinges to the back of their stamps for mounting in an album. The damage that this does for serious collectors has discredited this practice and one will often find these days the initials MNH (Mint, not hinged) within the description of a particular stamp or set of stamps.

Used stamps: As the terminology states, postage stamps that have been used for the purpose they were designed for, indicating that the due fee for the service required has been paid, and stuck on the envelope or parcel as proof. Hence they bear a post-mark (sometimes referred to as a 'franking' or 'cancellation') to indicate the office of cancellation and will undoubtedly have no gum on the back but traces of the paper they had been stuck to. Apart from its rarity value, a collector will look for how heavy the post-mark appears on the stamp and how well the backing has been removed, a thinning of the stamp itself or loss of any part of the face or the perforations will render the stamp valueless, scrap, or – where it is a particularly rare example – seriously devalued.

Definitives: What one could describe as the regular, run-of-the-mill stamps that one would get on a day-to-day basis.

Miniature Sheets: or mini-sheets, are often produced by the issuing postal authority using one or more stamps with a border that might be an extension of the illustration.

Presentation packs: Here we have one of the philatelist's best friends, for not only is there usually one, pristine and mint example of each stamp in any particular issue but they are presented behind a clear film, hinged so that the stamps may be withdrawn if one wishes, and then within a card wallet often containing sometimes quite copious details of the event celebrated as well as technical information, and then all within a cellophane envelope for virtually indefinite preservation.

Classic Locomotives of Scotland

Look at this Pack issued by the Royal Mail in 1994. Apart from four stamps featuring on typically Scottish railway subjects, they are presented as a mini-sheet that itself depicts the well-known Glenfinnan Viaduct on the West Highland line between Fort William and Mallaig, today well known for its appearance in the Harry Potter films.

First Day Cover (FDC): If the Presentation Pack is not your thing, then join the many collectors of the FDC, as its name implies, posted and franked on the first day the stamps go into circulation and so gaining a certain cachet. The envelope, or cover, may be a product of the issuing post office and cancelled with a special, carefully applied franking, but that is by no means certain and quite often you may find that a specialist dealer or the organisation involved may have produced their own cover, obtained the stamps in advance and even having a hand in designing the special franking.

Specialist Covers: These are covers that are not designed for use on the first day of issue of a particular stamp or set of stamps. An organisation, maybe with an eye on the commercial opportunity, will produce a specially printed envelope to commemorate an event even if no special stamps have been issues, use a postage stamp that may or may not be of particular relevance, and possibly apply a special franking. Often very attractive and collectable, but of value only within a small circle of collectors.

PHQ Cards: 'PHQ' stands for Postal Headquarters but here refers to reproduction of stamps on post-cards. All items published by the British Post Office are given a number that is prefixed by the letters PHQ. The first card issued was the 3p **W.G. Grace** stamp from the set commemorating County **Cricket**, issued on 16th May 1973. This card was numbered PHQ 1 and the numbering sequence has continued to the present day. There are several sets that replicate stamps illustrating our hobby.

Railway Letter Service: The Railway Letter Post was created on 1 February 1891 by agreement between the Postmaster General and 75 British railway companies of the era. The original railway letter fee, in addition to the normal Royal Mail postage, was 2d (0.83p). More recently, modern day railway preservation organisations have seen a commercial opportunity and examples of their stamps are illustrated in this book.

What is *not* generally in the author's collection are stamps produced where there is quite obviously no intention to satisfy a need to provide a postal service in the issuing country. There are, however, a few cases breaking that rule, and illustrated are examples of stamps produced for postal authorities in the West Indies by a magazine publisher! As you will see, the end results are worthy of inclusion due to their exemplary quality, and of course one has to admit that in a great many cases, the railway letter service stamps produced by today's preserved railways were principally produced for sale to collectors.

It is, perhaps, the author himself who has had the biggest journey of exploration, bringing together the stamps and researching the background of the stamps shown and described in this book, and it is only right that the author acknowledges the tremendous assistance given to him by the publishers and its staff in producing such an attractively laid-out book to show to its greatest extent the subjects. So, dear reader, follow me now on a rather circuitous tour of our world with the aid of the artist and his fascination with transport through the medium of the humble postage stamp.

MAIN LINE RAILWAYS

For this second book in this series on public transport issues featured on postage stamps, once again the author will combine two of his lifelong hobbies and looks at the principal railways around the world on standard gauge tracks that encompasses the majority of the western world's major railway arteries. The book will also illustrate railways on other gauges of track where they constitute a country's major arteries, and in particular many of Africa's railways used the 'Cape Gauge' of 3ft 6in, worthy of inclusion here particularly as some of South Africa's Beyer-Garratt engines claimed to be the world's biggest and most powerful outside the US. It is not an exhaustive survey encompassing every country and every issue; for that one needs to refer to major catalogues issues by such well-known authorities as Stanley Gibbons Plc.

There have been many and varied reasons why postal authorities have issued stamps featuring railway subjects varying from inaugurations to major anniversaries or just national pride, the latter often from the former Eastern-bloc countries but that is not by all means all.

The Royal Mail in the UK has certainly not ignored railways, especially in later years and the author will visit probably more of his native country's stamps than most other countries, but he's biased. The author often looks in his albums to try to understand why sometimes a particular country will be represented by bulging sections whilst others may be represented by but one or two stamps, so follow the story around the world in roughly an eastern journey, learning about some of the national histories on the way and admiring the work of some extremely accomplished artists that mean philatelists and rail-lovers together can enjoy many beautiful miniature works of art.

THE BRITISH ISLES

The Royal Mail was first established in 1516 making the organisation just over 500 years old, It provides the principal postal services today but is no longer owned by the UK Government, being a publicly-quoted company on the London Stock Exchange, hence its title today is followed by the initials Plc. Nevertheless, every British postage stamp for over 50 years has born the 'authority' of the Monarch's head, the work of the celebrated artist and sculptor Arnold Machin O.B.E (1911-99).

Another name that was associated with British postal services for some time was the General Post Office that encompassed postal services and telecommunications until 1969. Eventually, these two sides were split up, although today those of a certain age will well remember the initials GPO still often used to refer to a post office.

Although the 'penny black', the first British postage stamp, was issued in 1840 it wasn't until August 1975 that the first stamp appeared that featured railways, in this case to celebrate the 150th anniversary of the inaugural train to run on the Stockton & Darlington Railway, as we can see hauled by George Stevenson's locomotive – *Locomotion* – as featured on this First Day Cover. Choice of locomotives featured on the other three stamps represented examples from each of the next 50 years up to the HST diesel trains of the 1970s, surely amongst the world's most successful trains, remaining in first line express duties up to today, over 40 year later, and still the yardstick by which more modern stock is measured.

The next issue that the author has chosen to feature and titled 'Famous Trains' was issued in January 1985 and according to the booklet within this presentation pack was inspired by the 150th anniversary of the

CORNISH RIVIERA

CHELTENHAM FLYER

ROYAL SCOT

GOLDEN ARROW

FLYING SCOTSMAN

formation of the Great Western railway in 1835 for the construction of the London to Bristol line. No apology is offered for featuring the work of the late Terence Cuneo, CVO, OBE, RGI, FGRA, in this book as well as the first book in this series as he was probably the world's pre-eminent artist in the field of railways, and here we see five wonderful works by the master that were commissioned by the Royal Mail. There are two views of Great Western trains as well as one each from the other railways that made-up the Big Four companies prior to Nationalisation in 1948. PHQ cards to the usual post-card format do much greater justice to these beautiful images.

Another 150th anniversary was celebrated in 2013 and this time it was for London's Underground that first carried passengers from Paddington to Farringdon in 1863. The tunnels were only just under the surface of the capital's streets (the sub-surface lines that today cover the Metropolitan, District and Circle lines), built by the cut-and-cover method and used steam engines to power the trains. The first stamp in this series illustrates the large stations that were possible on these lines. Further stamps take the story from the earliest deep-level lines that were

built using men with rudimentary tools working within huge wooden shields, views of the restricted size carriages and their interiors towards the ultra-modernity of the new Jubilee Line's station at Canary Wharf in the regenerated Docklands. The Presentation Pack illustrated is a mine of information covering all aspects of the building and running of this famous facility that at the time carried more than a billion passengers per year. (Latest figures published by Transport for London put that at 1.37 billion! We hope this is not all at once!)

Allowing all propriety to go out of the window, we can allow ourselves a little levity by enjoying stamps that could well be aimed at our younger generation, hopefully drawing their attention to joy of stamp collection, for who could have anticipated British postage stamps featuring

Thomas the Tank Engine

"Goodbye, Bertie," called Thomas

James was more dirty than hurt

"Yes, Sir," Percy shivered miserably

They told Henry, "We shall leave you there for always"

Thomas the Tank Engine in the more formal days of the monochromatic fashions of the 1953 Coronation stamps? 'Bust my Buffers!' some would say, but the world of Thomas and his creator is beautifully covered in depth within this presentation pack issued in June 2011, as well as the very attractive stamps that are in fact photographs of scenes set-up for the series of films produced for television in the 1980s with the story so memorably told by the former Beatle Ringo Starr (or more formally Sir Richard Starkey, MBE).

In the author's first book covering Narrow Gauge railways, the subject of Railway Letter Service stamps was covered in some depth as it was these railways that have been to the fore-front of the story. The Talyllyn Railway was the first line to be taken over and run by enthusiasts and was the first to resurrect the practice of providing a letter service in the preservation era. Looking to preservation lines based on the standard gauge or main lines, it has proved a much bigger challenge in choosing which ones to illustrate here. According to the Heritage Railway Association website, there were 108 operating railways and tramways as well as another 60 steam centres that are members of that Association in 2017, so the choice is vast to say the least. Those that have been chosen here are but a representative selection, especially as many railways do not operate of genuine Railway Letter Service and therefore as such their stamps are classified as mere labels and not what could be considered stamps by serious collectors. Another problem is the quality of these items, that can vary from the crude up to those that are comparable with the products of the Royal Mail.

The Bluebell Railway is a volunteer-run line running from the Sussex village of Sheffield Park to join up with the main-line at East Grinstead and is proud of its position as the UK's first preserved standard-gauge passenger railway. Commencing operation 1960, it is today one of Sussex's greatest tourist attraction. This mini-sheet illustrates

BLUEBELL RAILWAY LETTER SERVICE

'BLUEBELL SPECIAL' PASSES KETCHES FARM HALT EN ROUTE TO SHEFFIELD PARK ON 11th MAY 2005

Taken from a photograph by David Phillips. Design by Edwin Craggs of Moorside Publishing Ltd. Printed by Wyke Printers Ltd, Hull.

surely the quintessential nature of the line, a country branch connecting a number of country towns and villages with the main line.

Another country branch line saved from extinction by preservationists is the Mid-Hants Railway in Hampshire. Just like the Bluebell Railway and several of the other preserved lines in the UK , this line has adopted a popular name and in this case it is the Watercress Line; after closure by British Railways in 1973, the first trains under the new ownership ran in 1977. One of the first stamps issued under the formal Railway Letter Service was this one depicting a most elegant product of the railway industry in

MID-HANTS RAILWAY

Railway Letter Stamps

Full Sheet Value £1.50

the Victorian era, the T3 class 4-4-0 locomotive No.563, built by the London & South Western Railway in 1893. On retirement, it became part of the National Collection and preserved by the National Railway Museum at York although controversially, in 2017 it was gifted to one of the Watercress Line's contemporaries in that part of the country, the Swanage Railway in Dorset.

Also part of the British Isles is Ireland and the southern

portion being the independent Republic of Ireland, or Eire in Gaelic, with a long railway heritage. The main lines of the island as a whole have an unusual track gauge of 5ft 3in that originated as a compromise between several different gauges adopted by the early pioneers. Much as in the British Mainland, we find several independent lines of the island gradually coalesced into one state-owned railway company in each of the Republic and the Six Counties, a colloquial name for what is now known as Northern Ireland, that part that remained part of United Kingdom when Partition separated the island in 1921. In the Republic that was Coras Iompair Eireann, known usually by the initials CIE that remains today responsible for almost all public transport through various subsidiaries including Iarnod Eireann that markets itself as Irish Rail.

This set of stamps issued in 1984 to mark the 150th anniversary of railways on the island illustrates many aspects of Irish railways from the island's first line, the Dublin & Kingstown opened in 1834 and ironically using the standard gauge of 4ft 8½in. Also included are express locomotives from the two principal railways after the unification of the many independent lines, and a modern electric multiple unit of the DART (Dublin Area Rapid Transport) that today includes the Dublin & Kingstown

Irish Railways
1984

line, although today Kingstown is renamed Dun Laoghaire and is the principle terminal for ferries from Great Britain.

On the mini-sheet border, we can also see not only a contemporary USA-built diesel locomotive but also a train from the eccentric Listowel & Ballybunion Railway that connected the two towns in County Kerry using the Lartigue monorail system. Actually, three rails were supported by a series of A-frames that required carefully balanced trains, effectively twin locomotives and carriages where passengers and especially livestock was often required to occupy opposite sides! Although the original railway ran from 1888 to 1924, today a replica line has been built as a tourist attraction.

The second illustration shows another minisheet issued in 2017 that brings the story up-to-date showing modern trains in railway stations which, like in a great many countries throughout the world, boast some of the Republic's finest architecture.

EUROPE

L eaving the British Isles, it is perhaps fitting to look quickly at some Railway Letter Service stamps issued to mark the 1994 opening of the Channel Tunnel, connecting Folkestone in Kent with Sangatte on the other side of the Channel in northern France. Eurotunnel are the managers and operators of the rail-only tunnel that sees high-speed trains connecting London principally with Paris and Brussels. Le Shuttle services provide transport of cars, coaches and trucks through the tunnel, whilst freight trains transit the tunnel connecting large swathes of Europe with the UK.

These stamps were produced in conjunction with Benhams, conveniently based in Folkestone and who, together with the associated Buckingham business have produced several covers for the philatelic fraternity. Buckingham's produce a great many attractive covers for railway lovers and are recommended for people like this author that enjoy the relationship between most forms of transport and stamp collecting.

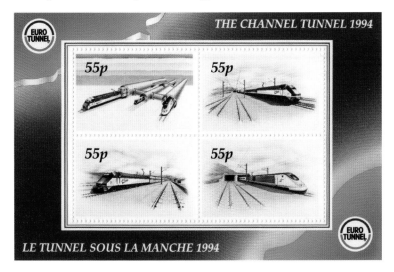

FRANCE

France doesn't have the iconic head of a British Monarch to grace their stamps but instead has Marianne as we see in this simple definitive stamp showing a dancing lady, known to every Frenchman and woman as a national symbol of the French Republic, a personification of liberty and reason and present on the official logo of the Country and its coins right up to the present day Euro. Her origin is a national enigma, thought by many to represent a female allegory.

In his youth, this author saw images of Marianne on just about every French stamp he saw and took it be as iconic as the Queen's head that still stands proud on all British stamps, but the French artists have shown us the direction taken on most stamps issued in France until the inevitable modern productions that often show less taste than the producers' ability to use photo-manipulation, and a selection of miniature works of art are shown here, usually to celebrate an aspect of progress on the railways, a particular favourite of the author being this delightful product of the difficult Second World War days and what the French know as an 'Engineer' showing the great regard these men were held in, with protective goggles in a modern locomotive cab, with an older locomotive added for comparison.

This First Day Cover illustrates just how informative they can be, and here we see one produced by RATP (the Paris bus and Metro operator) for one of a series of stamps issued by France Poste showing various celebrated engineers, in this case "the father of the metro" Fulgence Bienvenüe.

This is a typically French portrait, as well as including the characteristic entrance to a Paris metro station emblazoned 'METROPOLITAN' in full, and a franking from the town of his

birth at Uzel Pres L'Oust with the number 22 indicating the postal number of the *department* or county, in this case Cotes d'Armor.

Although the Japanese were first to show the value of high speed trains working on dedicated lines, France came a close second and today the TGV (*Train a Grand Vitesse*) name is just as synonymous as the Japanese Shinkansen, and the French *La Poste* have issued several stamps to celebrate the ever-growing network.

BELGIUM

Moving north-east brings us to a country with a proud but difficult modern history, having been fought over in two world-wars. Going back further, we learn of the country's claim as the cradle of the industrial era fuelled by huge natural resources. Like many countries in the western world, this has declined seriously since the rise of the Far Eastern economies and today, cities such as Charleroi present a tragic scene of abandoned industry.

One of Belgium's more significant heavy industries was the manufacture of railway equipment and especially locomotives bearing makers' plaques from such names as John Cockerill and Societe Franco-Belge immediately come to mind and here we see examples of railway locomotives old and new on a beautiful mini-sheet issued in 2017, a combination of the art of the engraver and photographer.

THE NETHERLANDS

The country celebrated for Dutch Masters, canals and cheese stands high in the author's esteem for the friendliness of its people, probably going back to the end of the Second World War when Great Britain went to massive efforts to supply emergency food aid for the starving

population. The Dutch are masters too of the sea, as so much of the country is Polders or land reclaimed from the sea.

The Dutch railway system – *Nederlandse Spoorwegen* – known more usually as NS, is a dense railway network connecting virtually all major towns and cities. The first line was opened in 1839 between Amsterdam and Haarlem, and expanded by 1847 to The Hague and Rotterdam. Originally built to a broad gauge of 1,945 mm (6ft 49/16in), it was converted to standard gauge in 1866, and now extends to a network of 3,223 route km.

The first two pairs of stamps celebrate the centenary and 125th anniversary of the network but also give the philatelist a good idea of the changes over the years in stamp design, particularly when we see next this block of stamps issued in 2005 which bears the insignia of TPG POST, the state-owned postal service at the time.

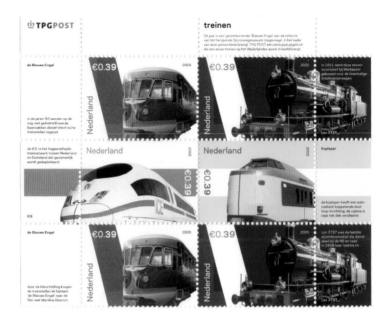

GERMANY

The history of this proud nation and its huge railway system has already filled many volumes so the author will confine himself to using the postage stamps to illustrate a few notable events down the years and the first being this very simple little stamp from 1969 showing a model of Germany's first successful locomotive *der Adler* (German for eagle) that was built by Stephenson's of Newcastle in 1835 for the Bayerische Ludwigsbahn (Bavarian Ludwig Railway)

that ran between Nuremberg and Fürth.

An equally historic event is illustrated by the next stamp, issued in 1979 to mark the centenary of the world's first electrified railway line, The stamp is actually a copy of a well–known photograph showing the first demonstration by Werner Von Siemens and his business partner at the time Johann Georg Halske using a 155volt supply from a centrally mounted power rail. For modern-day health & safety experts it is noteworthy that neither photograph nor stamp show any sign of railings to prevent unintended electrocution.

Move forward to 2006 and here is a set of photographic images issued to show the modernisation and progress of the nation's railways.

The 1932 Fliegender Hamburger (or Flying Hamburger) was Germany's first diesel powered train used between Berlin and Hamburg.

Then we see the 1936 Henshel-Wegmann Zug (or train), a one-off steam locomotive and train built to show that steam could perform as well as the brash new ideas and was used between Dresden and Berlin.

The third of these stamps shows the impressive outline of one of the 1957 class VT 11.5 diesel multiple units built by Deutsche Bundesbahn (DB) in 1957 and used for Trans Europ Express services. Perceived as flagships of the DB rolling stock, they carried first-class seating only and ran from 1957 until 1972 and thereafter on German inter-city services.

Finally we are brought thoroughly

up-to-date by this image of ICE, an InterCityExpress train developed for Germany's expanding high-speed lines. The train illustrated is an ICE3 built by Siemens in 2000 for speeds of up to 330kph (210mph) and used principally between Frankfurt and Cologne.

AUSTRIA

Like the nation as a whole, the history of Austria's railways is inextricably linked with Hungary as part of the Austro-Hungarian Empire formed in 1867. The main-line railways on the Austrian side of the border were run by The Imperial Royal Austrian State Railways, (kkStB) created in 1884 but in 1923, some years after the dissolution of the empire it was replaced by the state-owned Österreichische Bundesbahnen (Austrian State Railways, or ÖBB).

With such a large percentage of the country being mountainous, it is not surprising that all main lines are electrified and the author has chosen to illustrate the system with a recent stamp issued in 2017 to mark the centenary of the Brenner Railway that connects the country with Italy, from Innsbruck to Verona using the Brenner Pass.

The locomotive shown is a member of the articulated freight class 1020 or 'Crocodile' style built in 1940 so characteristic of Austrian and Swiss systems where great power is needed to pull large trains on the twisting and climbing passes of the Alps. The last member of the class was withdrawn in 1995.

Graphically showing the terrain of the country is this 2005 stamp showing a railcar of the independent Montafonbahn, a 12.7km branch line that has connected Schruns and the lower Montafon with Bludenz in the Voralberg State in the extreme west of Austria since 18 December 1905. The railway has the distinction of being the first electrified line in the Austro-Hungarian Empire.

As mentioned in the first book in this series on narrow gauge railways, Post AG, the Austrian postal authority, have the facility to produce stamps using images provided by the public called Personalisierte Marke (or personalised brand) and this third illustration shows one such stamp depicting a double-deck electric multiple unit used on the Vienna-Salzburg service.

SWITZERLAND

The Introduction to this book posed the enigma – why do Swiss stamps bear the title HELVETIA? Helvetia is the female national personification of Switzerland, officially Confœderatio Helvetica, the Swiss Confederation. The allegory is typically pictured in a flowing gown, with a spear and a shield emblazoned with the Swiss flag, and commonly with braided hair and a wreath as a symbol of confederation. The name is a derivation of the ethnonym Helvetii, the name of the Gaulish tribe inhabiting the Swiss Plateau prior to the Roman conquest.

This beautiful country is renowned for its neutrality, its banking and its mountains, and its railways that run with unequalled efficiency that every other transport operator aspires to. Its population speak principally different languages – French, German and Italian, depending in which Canton they live in, although actually there is at least one other language, Romansh, believed to be a descendant of Latin and spoken in the Graubünden Canton. Such a wide number of languages produces problems for national organisations such as the national railway operator Swiss

Federal Railways German: Schweizerische Bundesbahnen (SBB), French: Chemins de fer fédéraux suisses (CFF), Italian: Ferrovie federali svizzere (FFS) or the postal authority: Swiss Post (French: La Poste suisse, Italian: La Posta Svizzera, German: Die Schweizerische Post, Romansh: La Posta Svizra) is the national postal service of Switzerland, a public company owned by the Swiss Confederation. Hence you will see railway locomotives on the national system bearing the initials SBB.CFF.FFS, although postage stamps have to be a little more pragmatic with their wording.

This First Day Cover celebrates the 150th anniversary of Switzerland's first railway, a 17km line from Zurich to Baden in 1847 and the stamps shown feature a Class Re.460 electric locomotive built 1991-6 by SLM, the Swiss Locomotive & Machine Works in Winterthur, a 1935 'Red Arrow' electric set, a 1930 Pullman coach, and German built locomotive Limmatt of 1847, Switzerland's first locomotive.

Two further stamps illustrate mountain lines: Firstly celebrating 100 years of the Jungfraubahn, part of a system of local lines that ascend from Interlaken to the summit of the Jungfrau, at 4,158 metres (13,642 ft) one of the main summits of the Bernese Alps. Together with the Eiger and Mönch, the Jungfrau forms a massive wall overlooking the Bernese Oberland

and the Swiss Plateau, one of the most distinctive sights of the Swiss Alps. Some years ago the author was told a story that makes remembering the names of these peaks easier: The Mönch (Monk) stands between the Eiger (Ogre) and the Jungfrau (young lady).

The next shows a 2017 stamp and a fragment of its surround mark the 125th Anniversary of a rack-railway engine operating on the Brienz Rothorn Bahn, a tourist line that climbs from Brienz, at the eastern end of Lake Brienz, to the summit of the Brienzer Rothorn. The railway is 7.6 kilometres (4.7 mi) long, is built to 800 mm gauge (2 ft 7½in gauge), and uses the Abt rack system. Unusually for Switzerland, the line is not electrified, and most trains are operated by steam locomotives built in the 1890s. Exceptionally, a further four were built by the same manufacturer in the 1990s!

Worthy of inclusion is this post-card bearing a beautifully graphic photograph of vertical boiler locomotive No.7 of the Vitznau-Rigi Railway, and the first locomotive to be built by SLM. For the 125th anniversary of both SLM and the line in 1983, this unique steam locomotive was restored to

operating condition in 1996. After two successful summer seasons with daily operation on both the Vitznau and the Arth line, it was handed back to its owner, the Swiss Transport Museum in Lucerne. The stamp was also issued for the celebrations at the same time

SPAIN

Known to most Europeans for its sun, sea and beaches, this country is best known to railway fans for the unusual gauge of its main-line railways, generally quoted as 5ft 6in or more accurately as 1668mm, the Iberian Gauge. A Parliamentary committee of 1884 prescribed 1674mm but this was subsequently reduced slightly to coincide with that of neighbouring Portugal. This broader gauge has, however, left its legacy through to recent years when meeting the rails of France and even for through services further afield and great ingenuity has been required to avoid trans-shipment of freight and forcing passengers to change trains. Changing the rolling-stock's

bogies has recently been supplanted by wheel-sets with adjustable gauge where wheels are physically moved on their axles.

The first set of stamps shown here represents the stamp-engraver's work at its best to produce some beautiful images issued in 1958 to mark the

17th International Congress of Railways held that year in Madrid. The steam locomotive shown is a member of the celebrated 242F class of Express Passenger locomotive with the unusual – for Europe – wheel arrangement of 4-8-4 and built by La Maquinista Terrestre y Maritima SA of Barcelona in 1955 and one (no.2009) has been preserved in the Madrid Railway Museum.

Also illustrated in this group is an early example of the Talgo train. Formed in 1942 and an acronym for **T**ren **A**rticulado **L**igero **G**oicoechea **O**riol, (Alejandro Goicoechea and José Luis Oriol being the founders of the company) the firm has specialised in low profile articulated coaches each running on a single axle, more often than not powered by locomotives of standard profile as here. Popular in Spain, the company has recently been looking at the British market.

Since 1992, the Alta Velocidad Española (AVE) service of high-speed rail in Spain has been operated by Renfe, the Spanish national railway company, at speeds of up to 310 km/h (193 mph) and these lines and their trains are built to run on the commonly accepted Standard Gauge. Happily, the AVE initials also spell out the Spanish for bird, a lovely play on words.

HUNGARY

Another enigma for the unwary, though possibly not a totally unknown title but just where, or what, is Magyar? One learns that the Magyars were a people that originated in the Urals and migrated westwards to settle in what is now Hungary in the ninth century and brought with them their language. The name is thought to have come from 'Megyer', a prominent tribe in that area. After the Second World War, Hungary fell under the influence of the Soviet bloc until that collapsed and the nation is now once again independent. Whilst not appropriate to this publication, readers may well find studying this country's history remarkably informative and rewarding.

The national railway system, the Magyar Államvasutak, or generally referred to as MÁV and its railways have been featured in the country's stamps probably more often than is the average. The author has chosen first a set of four stamps issued in 1946 to mark the centenary of the country's railways, when the country was, like a great many other countries, licking its wounds after the Second

World War.

The currency quoted – *ap* or *adópengő* - was a temporary unit issued in January 1946 and only used by government agencies to stabilise the financial system. It was replaced by July the same year by the forint, still in use today. In view of the time-scale, not surprisingly these stamps are very simple using a single colour but nevertheless these are particularly attractive examples of the printer's art.

The 10,000ap stamp features *Heves* of 1846, not one of the first engines as no images of the 1845 engines built by Cockerill of Belgium appeared to have survives. Next is a 424 class 4-8-0 locomotive first built in small numbers by the railway itself but with the start of the Second World War, a further 216 were built and the class became the backbone of passenger and freight trains for many years. Less successful was the pair of V44 electric locomotives built in 1943 by the Ganz Works of Budapest as experimental engines. Unfortunately, the one shown here succumbed to an air-raid. Finally in this set is a single unit railcar built again built by Ganz in 1935 using a Jendrassic high-speed but lightweight diesel engine for use on cross-border expresses between Budapest and Vienna, the first international service to be worked by a railcar.

For comparison, shown here is a stamp issued in 2016 by Magyar Posta, the Hungarian postal authority, and shows the M40 class locomotive known as 'humpy' for obvious reasons, first built 50 years ago by Ganz-MÁVAG, a merger of two established locomotive and tramway builders. Although some of the M40 engines have been retired many do still remain in service.

SERBIA AND BULGARIA

The author has chosen to combine the stamps from both these countries for both sets illustrated here celebrate the 125th Anniversary of The Orient Express, renowned by authors and travellers the world-over for its opulence and intrigue. However, oddly, both countries differ on the year to mark! Serbia chooses 2008 whilst Romania has it as 2010. The train was created in 1883 by Compagnie Internationale

des Wagons-Lits (CIWL) and began operating that year between Paris and Constantinople, or what we now know as Istanbul (Turkey), and passing through Bucharest (Bulgaria). Belgrade, in Serbia, didn't see its first arrival until 1919 having come a different route and hence the amended title Simplon Orient Express. Nevertheless, both sets of stamps illustrate beautifully the nature of the train.

ISRAEL
Yet another enigma for us all is Israel's inclusion in this chapter, but the country always prefers it that way as most of the time the population looks west for its commerce and tourism. After all, the country takes part in the Eurovision Song Contest – sufficient argument for this author who visited the country in the mid-60s and found the railway system in a very poor state and largely starved of capital and customers as was not unusual in that time, but today, as the country's economy and with it road traffic grows, so the demand on the railways has driven substantial rehabilitation and growth. Today there are over 1100kms of standard gauge lines, diesel powered and with many principal services using typically European-style double-decked carriages. The flagship project of Israel Railways

First Locomotive
in the Holy Land

Locomotive of the
Jezreel Valley Train

Locomotive at the time
of the
British Mandate period

Locomotive of
Israel Railways

is the construction of a high-speed rail line from Tel Aviv to Jerusalem. The line will begin as an extension of the current railway to Ben Gurion Airport and Modi'in, and will terminate in a new underground station beside the Jerusalem Central Bus Station. Electrification is also planned and new locomotives are on order.

The Israel Postal Company (and its predecessor) has been at the forefront in producing attractive stamps with the added assistance for philatelists and the public alike that relevant detail is usually given in the margins and we see this feature is the 1977 'Railways in the Holy Land' issue, but you need to excuse the gaudy colours.

UKRAINE

With the fragmentation of the Soviet Union that the West first saw by the collapse of the Berlin Wall in November 1989, Ukraine became independent on 24 August 1991, with its capital Kiev. Excluding the Crimea region that was annexed by Russia in 2014, the state-owned railway system extends to over 23,000kms of 'Russian'-gauge

track – 1520mms or just under 5ft, with the majority of the main lines electrified principally at 3kv dc.

The country's postal authorities have long been keen to celebrate its railway's heritage including locomotives, rolling stock and station, and from 2008-13, it issued a series of stamps illustrating many of the railway's modern rolling stock and the author has tried to show a small selection of these attractive stamps.

RUSSIA

remains the world's largest country even after the dissolution of the Soviet Union in 1991. The country has been included in this chapter as even though less than 25 per cent of its area is in Europe, that encompasses 77 per cent of its 110million inhabitants. It was on December 25 1991 that the Soviet hammer and sickle flag was lowered for the last time over the Kremlin, thereafter replaced by the Russian tricolour. Earlier that day, Mikhail Gorbachev resigned his post as president of the Soviet Union, leaving Boris Yeltsin as president of the newly independent Russian state.

The earliest stamps in the Soviet Union featuring railway subjects date from 1922 and it became the habit of Soviet as well as other eastern European countries within the Soviet Bloc to celebrate achievements in railway and other technological advances by frequent stamp issues.

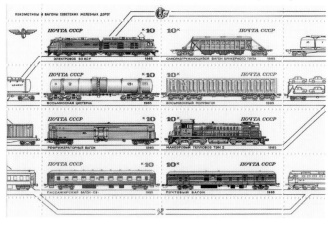

The first mini-sheet shown is from 1985 and covers various aspects of contemporary modern rolling stock. The uninitiated should be aware that the initials CCCP are in fact in the Cyrillic

alphabet; its translation into western languages is SSSR – Union of Soviet Socialist Republics.

In 2001, Russian Post issued this mini-sheet and FDC to celebrate the 150th anniversary of the country's railway between St. Petersburg and Moscow.

The Moscow underground system is famous for its lavish stations and they have been the subject of several issues of stamps, including these examples from a set issued in 1947 that show the Stalinskaya station (45k) and Mayakovskaya station (60k), whilst in the Russian era this 2005 mini-sheet also shows modern rolling stock.

These four stamps were issued in 2015 to illustrate the various styles of uniforms worn by railway personnel between 1843 and 2015.

The Baikal–Amur Mainline (BAM), traverses Eastern Siberia and the Russian Far East, at 4,324km (2,687miles) long BAM runs about 610 to 770km (380 to 480 miles) north of and parallel to the Trans-Siberian railway. It was built as

a strategic alternative to that route especially along the vulnerable sections close to the border with China. The BAM's costs were estimated at $14 billion, and it was built with special, durable tracks since much of it was built over permafrost.

This First Day Cover was issued in 2014 supposedly to mark the 40th Anniversary of the line's completion but there appears no definitive date of completion due to the mammoth hurdles needed to be leapt over in order build the line, not forgetting the military intervention. The artist that produced the stamp and cover has certainly succeeded in capturing the bleak nature of the route.

AFRICA

EGYPT

This is appropriately where we start our look at the railways of Africa as it was here that the continent's, and indeed the Middle East's, first railway line was opened between Cairo and Alexandria in stages starting between 1854 and 1856, a distance of 130 miles. Today, the Egyptian National Railway operates over 5000km of standard-gauge lines, principally radiating from Cairo to the Nile Delta area and Mediterranean coast, but also running south to Luxor and Aswan.

The first stamps illustrated were issued in 1933 for the International Railway Congress held in Cairo that year and show a representative collection of locomotives from the earliest days and all built in Great Britain.

Then we come to a single stamp issued in 1959 that

provides the collector with another enigma for the initials UAR no longer appears on any maps, but was a short-lived union between Egypt and Syria between 1958 and 1961. This stamp was issued to celebrate the industrialisation of the country.

TUNISIA

On the Mediterranean coast this is, like most countries to the north of the continent, an Arabic speaking country, but whilst most of its neighbours are some of the biggest countries in the area (Egypt roughly 1million sq.km., and Algeria at nearly 2.4million sq.km), Tunisia is relatively small at only a little over 160,000 sq.km, with its capital of Tunis on the coast. Like many other countries in northern and central Africa, Tunisia came under the

influence of European expansionists when colonisation in the eighteenth and nineteenth centuries was fashionable and in Tunisia's case after centuries of conflicts, the French controlled the country from 1881 to 1957 when the country gained independence, so with the development of railways in that era, unsurprisingly, French influence was to the fore and today The Société Nationale des Chemins de Fer Tunisiens (SNCFT) remains the company's official title when not using Arabic script and although there are nearly 500kms of standard gauge track in the north of the country, over 1600kms of metre gauge track is used in the central and southern areas.

This set of stamps issued in 2015 and shows much of the French influence already mentioned, in particular Le Lézard Rouge or Red Lizard, a tourist train running through the Selja Gorge, a steep-walled canyon in the center of which lies the Selja Wadi. Originally this train was built in the early twentieth century for the Tunisian Bey, or Monarch and as such was preserved.

ALGERIA

The Société Nationale des Transports Ferroviaires, abbreviated SNTF is the national system of Algeria, today stretching to in excess of 3500km of track in the north of the country with the capital Algiers roughly in the centre of the network.

Throughout this series of books, the author has tried to avoid stamps not produced as receipts for postal services. Many countries and postal agencies have used stamps as a revenue streams producing often colourful illustrations of trains from all over the world – just look at the section on The Gambia whilst here we see an example of one of a huge series produced by a magazine publisher but it has been included for its artistic merits and tremendous illustrations of a series of unique Algerian locomotives and published under the banner of the Caribbean island Grenadines of St. Vincent.

This is one of 29 Beyer-Garratt locomotives constructed between 1936 and 1941 by the Société Franco-Belge de Materiel de Chemins de Fer at Raismes in Northern France, operated until the Algerian independence war caused their withdrawal in 1951. They were designated 231-132BT using the French nomenclature, were streamlined and featured Cossart valve-gear, mechanical stokers and 1.8m (5ft 11in) driving wheels, the largest of any Garratt class. On a test in France, one of these achieved a speed of 132 kilometres per hour (82 mph) – a record for any Garratt class (or any articulated class). Indeed, a classic amongst the breed.

THE GAMBIA
Possibly the oddest country to be featured in any book discussing railways. The Gambia is a long, thin country (approximately 225kms east-to-west and a maximum of

about 50kms north-to-south) on the western extreme of the continent, for there was no national railway of any sort in the country, so for the nation's postal authority to produce this series of four stamps is another enigma to add to several in this book.

It would appear that the artist also betrays his country of original (if that was The Gambia?) for all exhibit some quite odd interpretations of the fellow African nations' railway engines. The Author is happy to include these attractive stamps as it reminds him of his good friend Nobby, sadly now deceased, who was a prolific builder of railway models to his own design and gave them the collective name of The Gambia Railways to thwart the 'Rivet-counter', that annoying person with the habit of always trying to criticize other people's work.

GHANA

is another African nation to emerge from centuries of colonial control. Going back as early as the eleventh century, numerous kingdoms and empires emerged of which the most powerful was the Kingdom of Ashanti. Beginning in the fifteenth century, numerous European powers contested this region for trading rights, with the British ultimately establishing control of the coast by the late nineteenth century. This single stamp issued in 1948 is typical of British stamps produced for its colonies and bearing the head of George IV and showing one of the reasons why Britain and its contemporaries were so keen to establish their presence – natural resources, in this case manganese.

Following over a century of native resistance, Ghana's current borders were established by the 1900s as the Gold Coast and this became Ghana at independence on 6 March 1957.

The Ghana Railway Corporation today provides the principle railway

connections on a track gauge of 3ft 6in, also known as Cape Gauge, between the Capital Accra and the city of Kumasi, as well as to Awaso and the port of Takoradi and there is an agreement with Chinese interest to upgrade the whole system at the time of writing.

This series of stamps was issued to mark the 75th anniversary of the system and as well as sumptuous rolling stock shows *Amanful* a diminutive tank engine built by Hudswell Clarke of Leeds in 1922, one of eight supplied by the Crown Agents for work around the country's docks. A further stamp in the series shows another typical British produce of the era – an English Electric diesel locomotive using that manufacturer's engine from the same family as powered so many other exports and classes of engine bought by British Railways.

ANGOLA

immediately brings to mind one of those terribly sad periods that seem to afflict so many nations either as

they struggle to emerge from domination by another power, or as the various factions within that state struggle for control. The country was a colony of Portugal until 1975 but it wasn't until 2002 that civil war finally abated and today the country has a stable government and a flourishing economy built largely on vast reserves of minerals and oil.

This mini-sheet illustrates the country's Portuguese era in 1970 for the century of stamps in the country and shows not only one of the first generation jet airliners – a Boeing 707 of the Portuguese airline TAP (Transportes Aéreos Portugueses) – but also commercial shipping of the era and another Beyer-Garratt articulated locomotive that became so synonymous with the later days of African steam locomotives. This stamp oozes the Garrett's ability to haul prodigious loads, work on relatively light track and round sinuous curves. The initials on the tank-sides are CFB, Caminhos de Ferro Benguela. The railway line roughly followed the old trade routes between the ancient trading centre of Benguela on the Atlantic coast, the central Angolan plateau and the mineral wealth of the then Congo Free State. The line thrived but the Civil War that followed independence from Portugal caused great damage and reduced a once hugely successful artery to little more than a few miles of track to Lobito 34km up the coast. By 2015, the line, now in State control, was rehabilitated using Chinese labour and money to once again access mineral wealth in the Congo.

SOUTH AFRICA

featured in the first book in this series on the Narrow Gauge as of course another country using the Cape Gauge or 3ft 6in gauge track but indisputably the principal lines of this country are more appropriately classified as main lines by any standard, running to in excess of 20,000kms

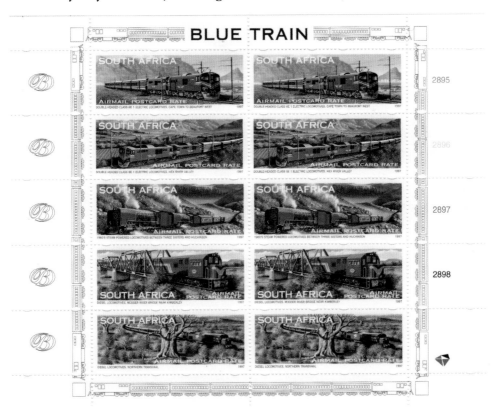

of lines.

Again as in the Narrow Gauge book, the country's postal authority has issued several mini-sheets illustrating aspects of rail transport and here we see a 1997 issue promoting the Blue Train, which runs from Cape Town to Johannesburg. The Blue Line has frequently been named the best luxury train line in the world, and the 1,600 kilometres (990 miles) run is a popular tourist attraction for South Africa.

TRANSKEI

found on stamps will cause some head scratching as it did for the author. The South African government set up the area as one of the two homelands for Xhosa-speaking people in Cape Province, the other being Ciskei; it was given nominal autonomy in 1963, but following a troubled existence, the state was dissolved and the area became part of the Eastern Cape province in 1994.

A set of stamps was issued in 1989 showing scenes in the homeland and trains using stock from the Spoornet organisation (previously part of South African Railways and Harbours Administration,)

ZIMBABWE

is a landlocked country formally known as Southern Rhodesia to the North East of South Africa, with its capital Salisbury. The struggles for independence and majority rule are not for these pages but eventually stability came in 1979, its capital becoming Harare. The country is best known for its dramatic landscape and diverse wildlife, much of it within parks, reserves and safari areas. On the Zambezi River, the Victoria Falls make a thundering 108m drop into narrow Batoka Gorge, and many are the iconic photographs of trains crossing the Victoria Falls Bridge on the border between South Africa and Zimbabwe with the falls behind and the scene is illustrated for us with this set of stamps bearing the date 12 May,1937, the Coronation of King George IV.

Also shown is a portrait of Queen Elizabeth, later to be known as the Queen Mother. These stamps are particularly noteworthy at this time for being printed in two colours.

MADAGASCAR

This island lies roughly 500kms from the African mainland, its capital Antananarivo (previously known as Tananarive) and with a population of about 25million souls that speak the Malagasy language, hence the name on these stamps. The Kingdom of Madagascar traced it ancestry back to the nineteenth century but the monarchy collapsed in 1897 when the island was absorbed into the French colonial empire, from which it gained independence in 1960, although to this day democracy has been shaky. Ecotourism and agriculture are the island's main source of revenue. Its railways are split into two separate lines, the northern system of several connected lines no longer carries passengers but is a freight hauler connecting the capital to the port of Toamasina although restored Micheline railcars (a series of rubber-tyred trains developed in France in the 1930s by various rail companies and rubber-tyre manufacturer Michelin) as shown here operate occasional tourist services. A more southerly line from Manakara on the coast running inland does have a frequent passenger service.

MAURITIUS

an Indian Ocean island nation some 2000kms off the east African coast is one of those beautiful places known for its beaches, lagoons and reefs. The mountainous interior includes Black River Gorges National Park, with rainforests, waterfalls, hiking trails and wildlife like the flying fox. Capital Port Louis has sites such as the Champs de Mars horse track, Eureka plantation house and eighteenth-century Sir Seewoosagur Ramgoolam Botanical Gardens. The currency in use is the Mauritian Rupee shown as Rs on these stamps.

Railways on the island began in the 1860s, a network was quickly built and it soon provided service to most of the island. It was a key factor in the social-economic development of Mauritius during its period of operation but after the Second World War the system declined due to alternative modes of transport and closed in 1964.

The series of stamps shown here were issued in 1998 and gives some remarkable views of the island's character.

ASIA

The world's largest and most populous continent with an estimated 4.4+ billion people (2016 figures) extending from eastern Europe through Russia, China and including the Indian sub-continent, so there is an immense choice for this book.

INDIA

is the most highly populated nation on the continent after China; at the last count (2016) it stood at over 1.3 billion, an astonishing figure. In a nation where the average wage remains very low, public transport is vitally important and images of trains covered by humanity in all conceivable places are legion. Indian Railways is a state-owned system and in a recent year carried 8,107 billion passengers, transported 1,101 billion tons of freight, had 7,216 stations and 1,331,000 employees! What must never be forgotten when looking at the railways of the Indian sub-continent is the British influence stemming from British rule or Raj from 1858 until 1947, and its legacy is the railway system and amongst other things the red-tape that today still governs so much of the area's way of life.

Until quite recently, Indian Railways used three distinct track gauges, the principal lines being 1,676 mm (5ft 6in) whilst over 17,000km of metre-gauge railways have largely been converted to the broad gauge. Many lesser and local lines adopted 2ft or 2ft 6in gauge tracks and they have been covered in the first book in this series.

The first stamps shown here, issued in 1976, show a selection of locomotives from some of the forebears and constituents of today's empire. The 2 rupee stamp shows the first of eight engines ordered from Britain's Vulcan Foundry Workshops of St. Helens in Lancashire that would become India's first engines, 2-4-0 passenger locomotives

डब्ल्यू. डी. एम 2 WDM 2
1963

25 भारत
INDIA

एफ़/1 F/1
1895

50 भारत
INDIA

डब्ल्यू. पी. /1 WR/1
1963

100 भारत
INDIA

जी आई पी नं.1 GIP No1
1853

200 भारत
INDIA

for the Great India Peninsular Railway of 1853, a company established by British Act of Parliament in 1849 with headquarters in Bombay (now Mumbai) on India's west coast. Next we have the F/1 locomotive of 1875, the mostly widely used locomotive on the Indian Railways before Independence. The first was built by Dubs & Co of Glasgow but most, including that shown here, were built at the Ajmer Railway Workshop and the class was finally withdrawn in 1985. A contemporary of this type, the SP/S class, 4-4-0 locomotive of 1912 and built by the Vulcan Foundry is exhibited at the Museum of Science and Industry in Manchester's city-centre. It came from Pakistan where it found itself in 1947 at Partition following Independence.

The 1 rupee stamp shows one of the great products of Indian industry – the WP/1 class of Pacific (4-6-2 wheel arrangement) express passenger locomotive, in this case built as recently as 1963. Independence in 1947 fostered fresh suppliers and the first prototypes were built in the Unites States and subsequently 300 modified engines came from various suppliers including the Chittaranjan Works in West Bengal. In service, these locomotives, as well as many other engines of the era were heavily embellished with decorations by their regular crews. The final stamp of the series shows one of the most numerous Indian locomotives at the time, the class WDM2, an indigenous class of powerful, mixed-traffic diesel locomotives capable of hauling trains of up to 2250 tons.

Next is a very colourful stamp issued by the Country's Department of Posts in 1996 to celebrate the Silver Jubilee of India's National Railway Museum at Chanakyapuri, New Delhi, frequently on tourist trails and comparable to any in the world.

Unquestionably the brightest set of stamps in this volume (although unfortunately due to its size it has been necessary to reduce its dimensions to fit the page) is this mini-sheet issued in 2009 containing four stamps showing the wonders of the country's architecture as seen in some of the principal railway stations. In the twenty-first century, the use of photographs on stamps is becoming more common.

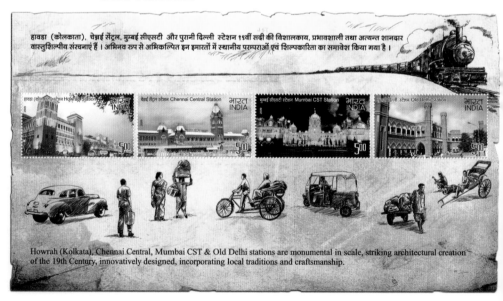

Howrah (Kolkata), Chennai Central, Mumbai CST & Old Delhi stations are monumental in scale, striking architectural creation of the 19th Century, innovatively designed, incorporating local traditions and craftsmanship.

CHINA

is a truly astonishing country that due to its isolationist mantra for so very long is still little known and understood by the Western world. Having developed one of the world's earliest civilisations, until recently based largely on an agricultural economy but since the introduction of economic reforms in 1978, China's economy has been one of the world's fastest-growing.

Known formally today as the People's Republic of China in recognition of the country's Communist ideology, its population is the world's greatest at 1.4billion. Road transport in these circumstances came late to the greater population so railways were a greater importance. The author has chosen two sets of stamps to illustrate Chinese railways, the first from a set issued in 1979, then in 1996 a set of four, and finally a single stamp

卡登實業股份公司承印

issued in 2011, all with a similar theme running through them, of modernisation and growth.

TAIWAN

also calls itself The Republic of China and this can easily confuse the unwary. Today, the island, formerly known as Formosa, has an area of just over 36,000 square kilometres and has a thriving railway system run by the Taiwan Railways Administration.

The island is justly famous in railway circles for its Ali-San logging line, now a haven for tourists and this is covered in the previous book in the series on Narrow Gauge railways. The island's independence is not secure

due to the mainland Administration's sovereignty claims, which is an enormous shame as the island is renowned for is attractive setting, well-illustrated here by two set of stamps featured here, the first from 2011 featuring branch lines, and the second of 2015 aimed at railway tourism.

HONG KONG

today consists of the island of Hong Kong and, separated from it by the Pearl River estuary, the Kowloon Peninsula and the New Territories. The immense commercial success of Hong Kong grew during British administration but in 1997, sovereignty passed to The Peoples Republic of China that controls the area as a 'special administrative region'. The importance of the trading nation grew as a result of its confluence of the far-east shipping lanes and the trade in opium!

Today, Hong Kong is one of those places on the Author's bucket list of things (or places) to do before he dies, although as the years march on this becomes more and more unlikely! The bright lights, huge skyscrapers that leave wonderful twinkling reflections in the water at night, the hoards of milling people, the food (one of the author's greatest delights) and the trams (another). And whilst trams are not part of the remit in this particular book railways certainly are and this mini-sheet issued in **2010**

celebrates the railways that inter-connect the various parts of Hong Kong and also now crossing into China itself.

INDONESIA,

is made up of about 13,000, mostly volcanic, islands, and is home to hundreds of ethnic groups speaking many different languages and a population in excess of 260 million people, the world's 4th largest. It is known for beaches, volcanoes, and jungles sheltering elephants, orang-utans and tigers as well as Komodo Dragons (although it is believed the fire-breathing variety are now extinct!). The island of Java has the country's largest population and also the capital, Jakarta.

The majority of Indonesia's railways are on Java, used for both passenger and freight transport although there are networks on Sumatra, Kalimantan and Sulawesi, that the Indonesian Government hope join-up into a much larger network.

This mini-sheet used to illustrate this country was issued on the occasion of the National Exhibition of Philately held in Bandoeng in 2013.

PENANG and PERLIS

are two names one has to look very carefully for as they no longer feature on stamps. South of the major parts of the Asian Continent, beyond Myanmar and Thailand, the Malay Peninsular stretches south to Singapore, Indonesia and eventually Australia.

These stamps represent some lovely engraving probably done in Great Britain for two of the many states and Sultanates that came under British Administration between in the eighteenth century and the creation of the Federation of Malaya in 1948 and eventual full independence in 1957.

Many of these nominally independent states had their own stamp issues that tended to be identical stamps using the image of the local head-of-state and insignia, and the author has seen examples of these railway images from Kelantan, Selangor, Trengganu, Johore, Malacca and Negri Sembilan, there are doubtless more. These two illustrate scenes from the East Coast Railway from Gemas railway station, in Negeri Sembilan and Tumpat railway station, in Kelantan. An identical stamp from Penang features a portrait of Queen Elizabeth II.

These various states gradually coalesced to form the Federation of Malaya on 31 August 1957 and finally took the style Malaysia in 1963 with its capital Kuala Lumpur, but without the significant element Singapore to the south that went its own way. 2010 marked the 125th Anniversary of rail transport in the region and these four stamps and one minisheet were issued showing much of the history and current fleet of Keretapi Tanah Melayu, the national railway operator.

Malaysian currency is the Ringgit (abbreviated to RM) divided into 100 cents (sen).

JAPAN

is an island nation in the Pacific Ocean off East Asia known for its dense cities, imperial palaces, mountainous national parks and thousands of shrines and temples. Tokyo, the capital, is known for skyscrapers, shopping and pop culture. The country's population stands at 127 million (2016) and Japan Post, a government-owned corporation until 2007 when it was privatised, runs postal services. It was the nation's largest employer with over 400,000 staff, one in four of all government employees.

Japan Post (and its predecessors) have been prolific producers of postage stamps illustrating railways in fact the first one appears to date from 1942, the height of the Second World War. However, the first stamps shown here are two separate issues from 1974, the first pair of two early locomotives (including the country's first engine, built in the UK) whilst the second two illustrate more modern steamers working hard.

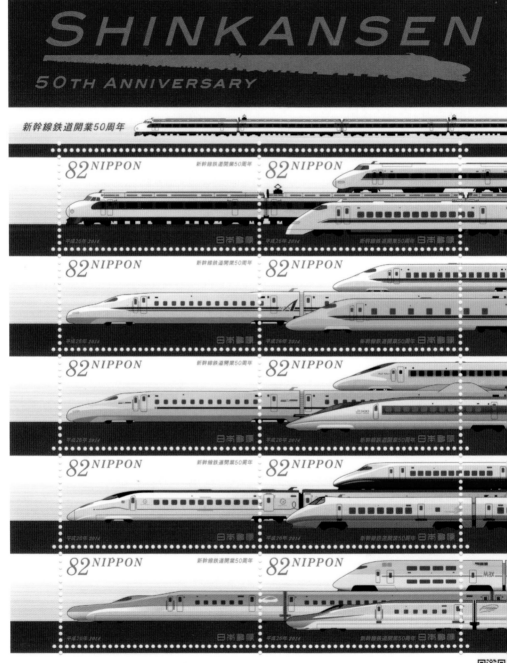

Then finally this recent mini-sheet was issued in 2014 to mark the 50th anniversary of the introduction of the Shinkansen, the world's first high speed train that today connects all the major centres of population including the main islands of Kyushu (with Okinawa's subtropical beaches), Honshu (home to Tokyo and Hiroshima's atomic-bomb memorial) and Hokkaido (famous for skiing). As a rule, the author prefers not to collect stamps that were not primarily designed for postal use, but these are exquisite items probably intended purely for the collector; for our use they are highly educational. A power car in the UK's National Railway Museum, York represents the first trains illustrated.

THE PACIFIC REGION

AUSTRALIA

continues our southerly journey; a British colony since the late eighteenth century but today officially the Commonwealth of Australia, it is a sovereign state with capital at Canberra, and a member of the British Commonwealth.

To describe the nation's railways I am delighted to be able to quote from this beautiful little booklet *Great Australian Railway Journeys* issued by Australia Post in 2010. 'Australian Railways cross the continent east-to-west and south-to-north, covering great distances over often isolated and difficult terrain.' Not only does this little gem provide an insightful potted history of the nation's railways, but then also includes four mini-sheets of, in

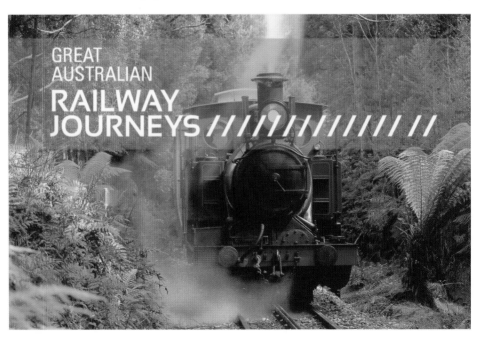

total, 13 postage stamps illustrating The Indian Pacific and The Ghan trains plus the Kuranda Scenic Railway and Tasmania's West Coast Wilderness Railway. And to top it all a further four postcards of further scenes from each of these railways. All at an absolute bargain price of 12.95 Australian Dollars or something like £5 in UK currency. Not surprisingly, these booklets demand a significant premium today.

Track gauges in Australia display significant variations, which has presented an extremely difficult problem for rail transport across the continent for over 150 years. As of 2014, there was 11,801 kilometres (7,333 miles) of narrow-gauge railways, 17,381 kilometres (10,800 miles) of standard gauge railways and 3,221 kilometres of broad gauge trackage. In the nineteenth century, each of the Colonies of Australia adopted their own gauges. However, with Federation in 1901 and the removal of trade barriers, the short-sightedness of all these different gauges became apparent and it was to be 94 years before all mainland state capitals were joined by one standard gauge.

There were some fine locomotives in Australia and this set of stamps from 1993 illustrates some of them well. Interestingly, these are the first included by the author

that are self-adhesive, marking continuing progress in the production of the postage stamp. Titled 'Western Endeavour' we see a New South Wales Government Railway class C38 on that train. These 'Pacific' locomotives were produced by Clyde Engineering in the state being introduced in 1943. Regarded in their home state as one of the most iconic steam locomotives in Australia, the C38 class of locomotive has inspired a passionate following amongst railway enthusiasts and the general public and several are preserved.

The Class S loco *Edward Henty* is shown powering 'The Spirit of Progress' express between Sydney and Melbourne. The Victorian Railways S class were also 4-6-2 'Pacific; express passenger steam locomotives built by the owners Newport workshops to operate this prestigious service between 1928 and 1954 and assigned to the high-speed route on the broad gauge (5ft 3in) line and they remained the VR's most prestigious locomotive class until the advent of diesel electric locomotives in the early 1950s. Edward Henty (1810-78) was a Sussex born son of a banker and made a name for himself when he came to Australia as the first permanent settler in the Port Phillip district (later Victoria).

Finally for Australia is this charming quartet of stamps illustrating the diversity of railway stations throughout the nation from the obvious British influence on Maryborough Station in the Victoria town of that name about 165km northwest of Melbourne. The station has all the appearances of a cricket pavilion at Quorn, South Australia and is home to the Pichi Pichi Railway, a preserved line on the lines of the British Bluebell, and the open Normanton, Queensland station, far to the north of the state and probably better suited to the ambient temperatures of the area.

NEW ZEALAND
was once a British colony much as Australia. The first settlement was by Polynesians that developed the distinctive Māori culture still to be found today. Representatives of Britain and local Māori Chiefs signed the Treaty of Waitangi in 1840 that lead to British sovereignty over the islands. In 1841, New Zealand became a colony within the British Empire and in 1907 it became a Dominion, effectively independent and still a member of The British Commonwealth.

New Zealand's first railway service began between Ferrymead and Christchurch On 1 December 1863 and since then, rail has developed on both islands and has

passed through privatisation in several forms to today's Government control under the name KiwiRail covering both freight and passenger services. Track Gauge is 'Cape Gauge', 3ft 6in.

This First Day Cover was issued by The New Zealand Post Office in 1973 and has captured the characteristics of these typically British colonial steam engines very well, ranging from the Class W tank engine 192 of 1889 that was the first steam locomotive built in New Zealand at the Addington Workshops in Christchurch, and now preserved. At the other end of the scale, the Class Ja express passenger locomotive no.1274 was the final engine built in the country and it too has been preserved.

THE AMERICAS

CANADA

At just over 9million sq.km, Canada is the second largest country behind Russia but with only just over 35million inhabitants is sparsely populated so connecting up such widely separated regions using railways was the natural choice. Unlike most railways world-wide, the initial growth was spurred on by the single purpose of combining the various states into one nation. In 1871, British Columbia on Canada's west coast was lured into the Confederation with the promise of a transcontinental railway – the Canadian Pacific Railway – within 10 years. The 'Last Spike' was driven on 7 November 1885 at Craigellachie, B.C., and the first passenger train left Montréal 28 June 1886, arriving in Port Moody, BC, on 4 July.

The development of railways in the 19th century revolutionized transportation in Canada and was integral to the very act of nation building. Railways played an integral role in the process of industrialization, opening up new markets and tying regions together, while at the same time creating a demand for resources and technology. The construction of transcontinental railways such as the Canadian Pacific Railway opened up settlement in the west, and played an important role in the expansion of Confederation.

The Canadian National Railway is today the largest Canadian railway, having been created in 1918 by a Government keen to stabilise railway finances and it took over several bankrupt lines including the Canadian Northern Railway in 1918 and the Grand Truck Railway in 1920 but in 1995 the business was privatised and today both the CPR and CN are two giant freight haulers in both Canada and the United States. Like its contemporaries in the United States, it found passenger traffic becoming

uneconomic and continuing cut-backs forced the Country's Government to create Via-Rail in 1977 to provide inter-City services as it still does today.

Canada Post, or until the late 1960, Royal Mail Canada, has issued many stamps on railway subjects, the first being this single stamp in issued in 1951 depicting an early steam train of the (US) Western Railroad of Massachusetts and an up-to-date CN diesel locomotive. Undoubtedly a stamp of its era; monotone, diminutive and the engraving of a true romantic.

The Mini-sheet issued for the National Philatelic Exhibition in Montreal in 1984 shows some typical North American locomotives but also reminds us that officially Canada is a bi-lingual nation with French being the mother tongue of about 7.2 million Canadians (20.6 per cent of the

Canadian population, second to English at 50 per cent) according to Census Canada 2016. Most native speakers of the French language live in Quebec, where French is the majority official language.

1986 saw the issue of stamps bearing the images of some very hefty locomotives, one from the Canadian Nation whilst the other, of course, belonged to the Canadian Pacific being a Selkirk or 2-10-4 type locomotive of which 36 were built by Montreal Locomotive Works, in 1929. At 340 tons, they were the heaviest non-articulated locomotives in the British Empire. In 1928, the Canadian Locomotive Company completed the first of two experimental diesel locomotive, 9000/1 that were Canada's first

diesel locomotives and intended to operate as a pair. They had 4-8-2 wheel arrangements and were fitted with Beardmore V12 engines each producing 1330b.h.p. (how times have changed!). During the Second World War, the Canadian Government, becoming concerned that Japan's forces were looking east towards the North American mainland, put armour plates on 9000 and used it with a mobile military armed train. Following the conclusion of the war, 9000 returned to passenger work but tragically was scrapped in 1946.

Also in 1986 came this stamp bearing the enigmatic image of a rotary snowplough, surely one of the more enduring images of Canadian railways.

UNITED STATES

If one feature of American life marks itself apart from the rest of the world it is that their railway system (and their airlines) are entirely private enterprises, national or local (Federal or State) administrations have encouraged many, and given them subsidies and state contracts but there has never been a state airline or railway, at least apart from under-cover operations and until the founding of AMTRAK that in parallel with Canada's Via-Rail was set up by the Federal Government in 1971 to rescue the dwindling passenger services from closure by the big railway companies.

The Baltimore and Ohio Railroad was the first common carrier and started passenger train services in May 1830, initially using horses to pull the primitive carriages, principally stagecoaches on rails. This 1952 stamp celebrated the 125th anniversary of that railway's initial charter and shows one of those first trains, and *Tom Thumb*, the first American-built steam locomotive to operate on a common-carrier railroad. It was designed and constructed by Peter Cooper (1791-1883), an American industrialist, inventor, philanthropist, and candidate for President of the United States) in 1830, to convince owners of the B&O to use steam engines; it was not intended to enter revenue service. It is especially remembered as a participant in an impromptu race with a horse-drawn car, which the horse won after *Tom Thumb* suffered a mechanical failure. However, the demonstration was successful, and the railroad committed to the use of steam locomotion and held trials in the following year for a working engine. The author

wonders if the artist responsible for this stamp was trying to illustrate this race. The diesel locomotive in this stamp should not be ignored, a very early EMD E-unit, the locomotive that transformed motive power in America from steam to diesel.

The burgeoning growth that followed was as a result of financial institutions and individuals recognising the potential benefits of connecting the vast areas throughout the country, and of course, the financial return. Even the American Civil war, 1861-65, encouraged further lines to assist transportation of men and munitions, and shortly afterwards the first trans-continental railroad was completed 1869. Right up until the latter end of the twentieth century, fortunes would seesaw until today just a small number of major companies survive hauling vast quantities of freight coast-to-coast. Gone are the Pennsylvania and the Santa Fe (or more correctly the Atchison, Topeka and Santa Fe Railway) and in their place we have the Union Pacific, the BNSF (Burlington Northern & Santa Fe) and the CSX. Canadian National and Canadian Pacific also have a significant presence.

Stamps too have been prolific in their coverage of railways. The United States Postal Service (USPS; also known as the Post Office, U.S. Mail, or Postal Service) is an independent agency of the United States federal government that traces its roots back to 1775, and is responsible for providing postal service in the United States. It is one of the few government agencies explicitly authorized by the United States Constitution. The first US stamp to feature a railway related subject dates from 1869 and claims to show a Baldwin Steam Locomotive but chosen for illustration next is this item from 1950 that, like the 1948 stamp shown in the introduction were very minimalist fashion of the time, simple etching in one colour on a thin paper, and this time is titled 'Honoring Railway Engineers of America' although this Brit will forgive the 'Americanisation' of some spelling!

Casey Jones, or Jonathan Luther 'John' 'Casey' Jones (1863-1900) was from Jackson, Tennessee, an American railroader who worked for the Illinois Central Railroad (IC). He was killed on April 30, 1900 when his train collided with a stalled freight train in Mississippi. His dramatic death while trying to stop his train and save the lives of his passengers made him a hero; he was immortalized in a popular ballad sung by his friend Wallace Saunders, an African-American engine cleaner for the Illinois Central.

From 1987 comes this postcard used as a First Day Cover bearing one from a set of five stamps, all illustrated alongside, featuring early American locomotives, the larger size of the card allowing one to wallow in the work

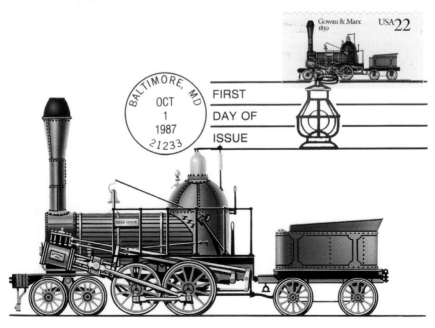

of the talented artist that produced them. The Gowan & Marx engine was a 4-4-0 freight locomotive built in 1839 for the Philadelphia and Reading Railroad, and named after the two gentlemen that financed Moncure Robinson who designed the revolutionary locomotive that caused a sensation when it was launched in America;

In this book's Series Introduction the author touched upon being able to see the giant GG1 electric locomotives of the Pennsylvania Railroad and in 1999 one of these locomotives appeared in a set of 5 stamps depicting some of the more famous named trains.

We see the *Daylight* of the Southern Pacific Railroad, the *20th Century Limited* run by the New York Central to Chicago, the *Hiawatha* from the Milwaukee Road, and the *Super Chief* advertised as the 'train of the stars' and emblazoned with the well-known 'war-bonnet' of the Santa Fe Railroad. Notice how every

opportunity was taken by these independent organisations to promote *their* brand, *their* express train, you almost feel assured of meet someone famous on the *Super Chief*. British Airways managed something similar with their Concorde service across the Atlantic but somehow one feels that red-tape would get in the way of any of Britain's well-known railway senior executives today.

But for the author the one that stands out is the 'Congressional' run by the Pennsylvania Railroad and hauled by one of America's most iconic locomotives – the electric GG1, a class of 139 electric engines built for the PRR between 1934 and 1943 by General Electric and the PRR's Altoona Works. The GG1 entered service with the PRR in 1935 and later ran on successor railroads Penn Central, Conrail and Amtrak. The last GG1 was retired by New Jersey Transit in 1983 and were noteworthy for hauling vast tonnages with barely a glimmer of problems on the electrified networks in the country's north-east for 48 years including the testing years of the Second World War.

Finally, and worthy of

inclusion for their miniscule size but great spread of production (1981-90) are these simple little cartoons covering many subjects as well as railways, for use in coin-operated vending machines, the later coloured examples also made available in sheets.

MEXICO

to the south couldn't be more different to the United States. Its principal language is Spanish and although a great many north of the border also speak that language, in Mexico it is spoken to the exclusion of English, almost as a mark of the country's independence. The country is known for its Pacific and Gulf of Mexico beaches and its diverse landscape of mountains, deserts and jungles, whilst ancient ruins of its Mayan and Spanish colonial history are scattered throughout the country.

The author has not found Mexican stamps that tell any sort of story of the country's railway history though the Ferrocarriles Nacionales de México, the country's state owned system covers the country well and has a long history stretching back to 1837. Today, apart from independently

operated tourist services, the FNdeM concentrates on freight traffic.

A quite beautiful stamp is illustrated, issued in 1973 and featuring a fascinating painting by the Mexican landscape artist Jose Maria Velasco (1840-1912) and showing a British built Fairlie articulated locomotive on the Mellac viaduct between Mexico City and Vera Cruz

PANAMA

These two stamps, issued in 2002, have been included as the author finds them probably the cheekiest he has seen: 'The finest and shortest transcontinental in the world', noting that the country is merely 77kms long at the Panama Canal, linking the Atlantic and Pacific oceans. This 'transcontinental' railway crossed difficult and treacherous country and was built at great human cost between Panama City and Colon that opened in 1855. The

locomotives illustrated here are believed built by the Portland company. After a lengthy period out of use, the line has been reinstated since 2001 carrying both passengers and freight.

CUBA

Offshore in the Caribbean, the island has a long tradition of colourful postage stamps and its railway themed stamps are no exception. This set of six stamps issued in 1967 to mark the 150th anniversary of Cuba's railways is a worthy example but quite unusual in not only showing images of previously issued stamps but also, in the case of the 3c stamp showing the scene of a great railway disaster!

Never before has the author seen this on a stamp, and here we have it twice. The author has been unable to elicit information of the nature of the incident or the two gentlemen illustrated, believed to be railway clerks.

VENEZUELA

on the northern coast of the South American continent is itself something of an enigma, a large country of over 31 million people and whilst oil rich the population have found themselves in poverty and not very pleased about it.

In 1993, the country hosted the Pan American Railway Congress Association (PARCA) and issued a series of ten stamps depicting the various stages in the history of Venezuela's railways, the Instituto de Ferrocarriles del Estado, or State Railway Institution, the country's postal authority even taking the opportunity to add appropriate slogans on the sheet margins such as 'the most cost-effective and economical means of transportation for users' whilst beside another is 'the safest means of transport'. Unfortunately, the inscription on the early green locomotive is a little adrift, the identity of the engine defied the author's research but the line quoted started around the year 1890.

Resolución Nº 112
del 31.03.93
Deposito legal
CF-123933

 26506

El medio
de transporte
que consume
menos energía.

El medio de
transporte más
eficiente
económico y
humano.

El medio de
transporte más
rentable y
económico para
países y
usuarios.

El medio
de transporte
más seguro.

El medio
de transporte
que emite
menos factores
contaminantes.

El medio de
transporte
que menos
stress produce.

Un medio
para reducir
la congestión
vehicular.

Un medio
para reducir
el consumo
de recursos
naturales
no renovables.

Cuidemos el planeta : es el único que tenemos.

GRAFICAS ARMITANO

XIX Congreso Panamericano de Ferrocarriles.

El ferrocarril : gran amigo del medio ambiente.

Ferrocar - Venezuela

Valor de la hoja Bs. 504

ARGENTINA

is a massive South American nation encompassing Andes mountains, glacial lakes and Pampas grassland, the traditional grazing ground of its famed beef cattle. Reflecting Spanish colonisation in the sixteenth century, Argentina is the world's largest Spanish speaking nation.

Argentinia's earliest railways were built on several gauges, 5ft 6in (1676mm), standard gauge and metre gauge, an inconvenience that persists today. Built-up by the Second World War to over 47,000 km (29,200miles) of network, it was one of the most extensive and prosperous in the world, however, with the increase in highway construction, a sharp decline followed leading to the break-up in 1993 of Ferrocarriles Argentinos (FA), the state railroad corporation. The privatised remainder proved unpopular and following a major disaster at Once in Buenos Aires in 2012 the Government decided on re-nationalisation and investment resulting in the founding of Nuevos Ferrocarriles Argentinos in 2015.

These four stamps were issued in 1988 to coincide with Prenfil '88, the 1988 World Philatelic Exhibition, held in Buenos Aires that year and show beautiful artwork of some of the country's characteristic railways. The oldest locomotive is the 2-6-0 locomotive *Yatay,* built by the Scottish company Neilson & Company, one of a batch of

Prenfil '88   ₳ 1 + 0,50

REPUBLICA ARGENTINA

CASA DE MONEDA · 1988   COCHE MOTOR ELECTRICO · 1914   J. M. FOURET Dib.

Prenfil '88   ₳ 1 + 0,50

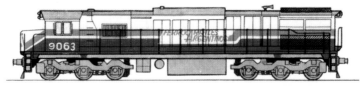

REPUBLICA ARGENTINA

CASA DE MONEDA · 1988   LOCOMOTORA GT-22 · 1988   J. M. FOURET Dib.

Prenfil '88   ₳ 1 + 0,50

REPUBLICA ARGENTINA

CASA DE MONEDA · 1988   LOCOMOTORA YATAY · 1888   J. M. FOURET Dib.

Prenfil '88   ₳ 1 + 0,50

REPUBLICA ARGENTINA

CASA DE MONEDA · 1988   LOCOMOTORA B 15 · 1942   J. M. FOURET Dib.

32 built for the standard gauge British company North Eastern Railway in 1888 and preserved in working order. The fine Class B-15 'pacific' locomotive inscribed *Estado* and built in 1942 belonged to the Argentine State Railway, a State-owned company established in October 1909 and absorbed into the Ferrocarriles Argentinos in 1948. The FA's big diesel is an EMD (of America) GT22 Series, first introduced in 1972 after the rise in popularity of six axle locomotives. This particular loco is one of 34 built under licence by Astarsa (Astilleros Argentinos Río de La Plata S.A.), another 40 came directly from EMD. Finally, this elegant wooden bodied carriage is part of an electric multiple unit set belonging to the Central Railroad and again established by British interests to the broad 5ft 6in gauge, and was part of the first railway electrification between Retiro and Tigre in 1916 on the Buenos Aires suburban network.

CHILE
a long and slender country that sits on the western Pacific coast of the continent stretching for about 6000kms from its northern border with Peru until the very southern tip near Punte Arenas and with Argentina forming its eastern boundary gives us the final stamps to be shown in this book. The arid Atacama Desert in the north of the country contains vast mineral wealth, principally copper but also guano, a highly effective fertilizer due to its exceptionally high content of nitrogen, phosphate and potassium, nutrients essential for plant growth and principally bird-droppings! The country's north eastern border is with land-locked Bolivia and two railways shown on this pair of stamps served the dual role of giving Bolivia access to the sea at Arica and Antofagasta, but also tapping the resources of the Atacama.

The mountainous terrain of the Andes Mountains proves a challenge on both lines and various methods of articulation have been used to provide sufficient power,

shown here by Esslingen of Germany and North British in Scotland. They were issued to mark the 75th anniversary in 1988 of the Patrimonio Ferroviario (Chilean Government agency for the protection of the nation's railway heritage).

Other anniversaries celebrated are these Chilean stamps of 1994, the $100 one (the Chilean peso, at the time these notes were written valued at about 600 to the US dollar) showing 100 years since the foundation of the city of Villa Alemana where Chilean railway development began. Villa Alemana ('German Town' in English) is a city in Chile's central area near Valparaiso and founded by Italian and German immigrants. Appropriately the $250 stamps marks the 250th anniversary of the founding of Copiapó that lies about 800 km north of Santiago by the Copiapó River and is the capital of the Atacama region.

COLLECTING

hat makes us collect stamps? Come to think of it – what makes us collect anything? Is there a hoarding instinct in some of us, or all of us? A squirrel hoards nuts for the lean months whilst at times of national stress we've all seen supermarket shelves emptied quickly, but stamps? Or playing cards? The author has collected various genres of transport models for decades, buses, trains and aircraft in big numbers, but why? There are private collectors of works of art, the value of their collections are not

necessarily monetary but just as likely emotional, and probably not with an eye on an investment. others will see collecting as a way of reliving their childhood, or an aspect of their life most dear to them.

Parents and grandparents will be familiar with children's obsession with collecting cards, maybe of footballers and here we see the excitement of the chase, to obtain the vital last or rarest one to show off to their school friends and perhaps here we will find the psychology of collecting stamps; the pride in building up a collection, the hunt for the rarity or an 'error', a specialisation in itself that can vary enormously from a spelling mistake (embarrassing but not unknown) to missing colours or type.

Like the collector-cards we saved in our youth, stamp collecting may well start with the fascination of issues

from across the globe or from previous eras. A kindly aunt's birthday or Christmas present may see our first album with pages for a great many of the world's nations, and possibly an envelope of mixed stamps, sometimes unused – mint – or maybe used and still on a fragment of the envelope. In this photograph of The Nelson album. we see just such an item, un-dated but this teenage owner has made notes on the contents dated 1953-5. The hunt has begun, to piece together the perceived history of that collection as we are led by the album with the stamps scattered in all probability all over the dining-room table or the lounge carpet and before long the craving developed, to add to this collection and then to multiply the number of albums needed to accommodate the growing collection until eventually order will need to be established. At that time, the likelihood is that there will be some sort of concentration or specialisation, perhaps on specific countries or regions, or themes such as the subject of this series of books.

A great many stamp collectors concentrate on the country of their birth or home and build-up a comprehensive history of that nation's stamps into a portfolio of immense prestige that may even include text to provide a commentary or catalogue number. Another speciality is the study of the perforations that surround each stamp for ease of separating from the sheets, their size and hence the number on each edge, and to damage these devalues the stamp as much as a rip or thinning of the paper itself due to careless removal from its backing or the previously mentioned hinges. As postal authorities modernised and became more mechanised, stamps had watermarks added or phosphor strips which bore vital information. And then there is the collector with an eye on the investment for undoubtedly a great many stamps reward the serious collector very well and there are organisations that offer advice for the committed investor. Reading one of the established magazines on our subject will enlighten some and surprise others.

LOOKING AFTER STAMPS

That such a big industry, or some would say, profession, has grown out of the love of a little piece of paper with gum on the back might be hard to credit but the obsession with the minutiae of the subject can sometimes seem out of all proportion.

Our Aunt's birthday present gave the young and budding philatelist the encouragement to either glue those precious stamps within the dotted squares provided or with wisdom found the little clear hinges that preserved them at least temporarily in place but today both these habits are discredited as they affect the stamp itself, for today the serious collector goes to incredible lengths to preserve each individual stamp in as near as possible the condition it left the printer in. First of all, one should never touch the stamp itself; grease and other contaminants will over time degrade the surface whilst clumsy figures can quite easily crease or tear the delicate paper and perforations, so acquisition of specialised tweezers like the pair shown here are a good idea, then take the trouble to look at the various types of album available.

Most will be ring-binders, ready to accept the many different pages available. Some of these pages will have clear strips of varying depths to keep stamps secure but visible whilst others are available pre-printed with details of the country of origin and the specific issue to which it refers and it only remains for the owner to place his treasured morsel of paper behind special clear envelopes cut to size and ready for attaching to the designated space. Many will produce his or her own leaves, suitably annotated and presumably preserved in beautiful albums bound in leather. Many collectors exhibit their work at well-known exhibitions in city venues across the globe and their work is often lauded amongst their peers.

Finally. The collector must remember the bible of the stamp world – the catalogue. Here one will find a huge coming-together of stamps one wouldn't otherwise dream of, listed in copious detail by country and date to give a

firm basis to any collection. Usually a value will also be provided, although one has to treat these with a little caution, as this is totally dependent on condition and the vagaries of market forces. Dependent upon the detail and how up-to-date one needs to be these can be acquired for a few pounds or up to several hundreds for the most comprehensive, that from Stanley Gibbons stretching to several volumes at a cost running into the hundreds of pounds and whilst these are up-dated regularly only the obsessive or professional will want to replace them regularly.

C000179720

A Chance in a Million?

Scottish Avalanches

Bob Barton and Blyth Wright

SCOTTISH MOUNTAINEERING CLUB

Published by the Scottish Mountaining Trust

First published 1985
Reprinted 1988
Second edition 2000

ISBN 0 907521 59 2

A catalogue record for this book is available from the British Library.

Front Cover: Checking the scarp slope below the cornice on Aonach Mor (Alan Hinkes)
A full depth avalanche on the Great Slab of Coire an Lochain (Allen Fyffe)
Probing for avalanche victims (Steve Penny)

Rear Cover: Heavy snow on Ledge Route, Ben Nevis (Malcolm Creasey)

Production by Scottish Mountaineering Trust (Publications) Ltd

Design by Tom Prentice and Aileen Scott

Graphics by Tom Prentice, from artwork by Dudley Evans

Scanning by Digital Imaging, Glasgow

Printed by GNP Booth, Glasgow

Bound by Hunter and Foulis, Edinburgh

Distributed by Cordee, 3a DeMontfort Street, Leicester LE1 7HD

Details of more than 30 Scottish Mountaineering Club guides to hill walking, scrambling and climbing are available from the Publications Manager, c/o Cordee or by visiting our website at www.smc.org.uk

A Chance in a Million?

Contents

Preface

This new edition of *A Chance in a Million?* is long overdue. Since the first edition in 1985, the study and forecasting of avalanches in Scotland has changed beyond all recognition, largely due to the existence of the Scottish Avalanche Information Service.

The interest shown in the Scottish situation both by the academic world and by European and other avalanche agencies, has greatly enlarged our perspective and shattered much-cherished illusions regarding the nature of Scottish snow conditions. This evolution has been a fascinating and at times, gripping experience.

Our thanks are due to the many individuals who have provided the raw material for the anecdote and information in this book, and to Tom Prentice for his help and encouragement in preparing the book for publication.

Bob Barton, Blyth Wright

Units of measurement

Metric units of distance are used in this book except in anecdotal accounts, where the original Imperial units have been retained. Windspeed is described in miles per hour since this unit is still in meteorological use and is more easily related to practical experience in Britain, than is metres per second. Temperature is given in degrees Celsius (Centigrade).

Fig. 1.1 *The inn sign at Lewes, Sussex, depicting the disastrous 1836 avalanche*

I A Short History

Avalanches in the Glens, Dales and Valleys

The exceptional snowfalls of February 1999 saw a return to the Alps of the catastrophic avalanches which have plagued those mountains since the days of their first inhabitants. Present-day expertise in avalanche forecasting, prevention and protection restricted the number of casualties, but nonetheless, the cost in human lives and suffering, as well as material damage, was severe.

Fortunately, the different topography of the Scottish mountains minimises the possibility of this kind of event and the recorded history of Scottish avalanche tells of no such major tragedies as take place in the Alps. Even the relatively populous Highland glens of the pre-Clearances period seemed to have gone unscathed by avalanche.

Indeed, no Scottish incident compares with the disaster which overtook the English village of Lewes in Sussex in 1836. On December 27 that year, a huge avalanche descended from the comparatively short slope above the village, destroying several cottages and killing eight of the inhabitants. Their communal grave remains to testify to the event, as does the name of a former inn, The Snowdrop, now an antiques shop (Fig. 1.1).

Few other examples exist in Scotland or England of catastrophic avalanches invading populated areas, although some accidents have happened to inhabitants of hill regions. In the Cheviots, on January 27, 1820, Thomas Turnbull, a 42 year-old shepherd of Milkhope in upper Coquetdale, was buried six metres deep by an avalanche which channelled in to a narrow valley. His body was not recovered for some weeks.

Bridging the gap between the Lewes incident and the first mountaineering avalanches of the next century, an avalanche occurred on February 27, 1888, beneath Whinstone Lee Tor in Derbyshire. It was large enough to bury two brothers, Frank and Willie Walker of Riding House, Derwent. Frank had a foot protruding and was rescued alive after being found by dogs – Willie Walker was less fortunate and was dead when found, buried "yards deep" in the debris.

Scotland's first recorded fatal avalanche antedates the Lewes event by many years. Five men died in this, the notorious 'Loss of Gaick', which remains today the only occasion when a Scottish avalanche has destroyed a human habitation, albeit a seasonal and remote one. The principal in this tragedy was John Macpherson, a retired Captain of the 82nd Regiment and, at the time of the accident in 1800, the tenant of the farm of Ballachroan near Kingussie and of the Forest of Gaick.

Macpherson enjoyed a certain unpopularity in the Badenoch area because of his previous exploits as a highly successful recruiting officer. Perhaps because of this, as well as his dark complexion, he was known as the 'Black Officer' or 'an Othaichear Dubh' and was popularly supposed to be in league with the Devil.

Whatever his affiliation, the Black Officer died in the opening days of the new century, about January 4, 1800, along with his hunting companions James Grant, Duncan Macfarlane, Donald Macgillivray and John Macpherson. They were overwhelmed, probably as they slept, in a small cottage near the site of the present Gaick

Blyth Wright

Fig. 1.2 The memorial stone below the Pass of Gaick

Robertson, escaped the avalanche by diving behind a boulder, but his dog was carried away and killed.

A great aura of myth and legend surrounds this event and local opinion was quick to assign supernatural significance to many aspects of the story. This makes interesting comparison with the similar attitudes of Alpine villagers towards avalanche disasters. They too, commonly regarded such happenings as inevitable and unforeseeable, either as Acts of God, or the work of evil spirits. Some climbers and skiers in Scotland apparently still adhere to this fatalistic philosophy!

The magnitude of the Gaick avalanche must have been altogether exceptional by Scottish standards. At least two accounts mention that debris was scattered to a distance of between 400 to 500 metres. This would mean that the avalanche completely blocked the floor of the glen at that point. Large avalanches are quite frequent in Scotland, but in the sparsely populated glens of modern times few threaten the homes of their inhabitants.

One exception occurred in February 1994, when the owner of a house near Ballinluig in Tayside was surprised when the field behind his house avalanched, smashing in two doors and filling his living room with snow to the depth of about a metre.

Even more dramatically, on December 18, 1993, in the White Corries ski area near Glen Coe, five members of staff were driving in a piste machine below the Cliff-Hanger chairlift, when a large avalanche burst out of the adjacent gully known as The Canyon. The avalanche picked up the piste machine, carried it backwards for 200 metres and was about to overturn it, when it spat the machine out to the side and went on to demolish a new building at the foot of another ski-lift, destroying the switch-gear inside and causing £13,000 worth of damage. It went on to run out near the bottom of the main access chair. The ski area was closed at the time and there was no danger to the public.

Lodge. Friends, alarmed at their failure to return from the hunting trip, raised a search party. On the site of the cottage they found only a huge mound of snow (Fig. 1.2).

Digging revealed the shattered remnants of the building, its roof gone and its walls almost totally destroyed. Inside they found four bodies, including that of the captain. One or perhaps two bodies lay on a rough wooden bed, the others on the ground. Macpherson was laid to rest in the old St. Columba's kirkyard in Kingussie, where those among the curious who do not frighten easily may still contemplate his tombstone. The body of fifth victim of the Gaick avalanche, Duncan Macfarlane, was only found weeks later, some distance from the cottage, after the melting of the snow, "Lying on his side with his right hand raised, pointing heavenwards". The bodies of the dogs were also found in the ruins of the building. An avalanche claimed another canine victim in 1804, in nearby Glen Tilt. A stalker, Duncan

Fig. 1.3 Blyth Wright at the door of the ruins of the Black Officer's house at Ballachroan, near Kingussie. Further relics of the Black Officer, including his portrait, may be seen at the Clan Macpherson museum in Newtonmore

Blyth Wright

Also in Glen Coe, on January 2, 1991, the private road up Gleann Leac na Muidhe was damaged by an avalanche which also destroyed a number of trees. In the winter prior to this, on the night of 16 to 17 February, 1990, another rare event occurred when an avalanche released from the face of Stob Beinn a' Chrulaiste, crossed the West Highland Way and reached the A82.

In Glen Shee, there is at least one site where avalanches reach the main road: at grid reference 145840. The last occurrence of this avalanche was on February 13, 1997. It is also conceivable that the avalanches which occasionally release on the east face of Carn Aosda might present a similar hazard.

The steep open slopes above the road on the north side of Drumochter Summit on the A9 could present a hazard to traffic, in the exceptional situation of substantial accumulations on west-facing slopes (also a pre-requisite for the Gaick avalanches). The validity of the concern was demonstrated in winter 1996-97. When the road gates, which had been closed for snow clearance, were opened, a colleague of Blyth Wright who had been in the waiting traffic, noted three avalanches which had crossed the road at that point.

On one occasion, when Blyth Wright was driving across Rannoch Moor with the Swiss avalanche scientist, Dr. Othmar Buser of the Federal Institute at Davos, the visitor expressed astonishment at the absence of avalanche protection sheds above the West Highland Railway line as it crosses the face of Beinn Dorain. When it was explained that the return rate of a large avalanche on these slopes might be a hundred years, the logic of the situation was apparent to him. The solution if such a hazard situation arose would, of course, be avalanche blasting either by helicopter bombing or by artillery fire from the A82.

Despite the opinion of some as to the preservative value of instinct, all creatures that walk on the mountains are susceptible to avalanches. Local tradition has it that in the early part of the twentieth century, the spring avalanche on the Great Slab in Coire an Lochain, Cairngorms, discussed in more detail later in this chapter, wiped out a herd of goats which used to live there.

On March 3, 1886, 14 sheep were killed by an avalanche on Lord's Seat in the Cheviots. In February of 1946 an avalanche came down near the stalker's house at Moulzie above Glen Clova, falling about 350m to sweep across the River South Esk on a front of about 150m and piling up at the 300m contour. Huge quantities of stones and turf were carried down and this avalanche is remembered locally for the large number of deer which it killed. Accidents involving deer are quite common, other such events having occurred at Loch Muick, Gaick and else-where. It is to Gaick that we must return for another near miss and also to close the book which that location opened on nineteenth century avalanches.

On Christmas Eve, 1899, 100 years almost to the week after the famous disaster, the keeper and his family sat up late at the present Gaick Lodge, waiting to open their Christmas presents. A great noise was heard and inspection later revealed that a huge avalanche had swept down, crossing the site of the disaster of 1800 and stopping some 30 or 40m short of the new lodge. Another such avalanche is known to have occurred in 1913; one of these destroyed the back wall of the old sheep pen immediately adjacent to the site of the Macpherson disaster.

Despite incidents such as these, no hazard to towns, villages, or communica-tions normally exists in Scotland, although certain main roads are threatened in exceptional conditions. Avalanches are also known to have affected roads in the Lake District and North Wales. However, in much the greater part, the avalanche problem concerns those who use the mountains for recreation, winter hill-walkers, snow and ice climbers and off-piste skiers, who during the present century are the only known avalanche victims in the UK.

Table 1: Total number of avalanche accidents in Scotland

Year	Events	Victims	Buried	Dead	Injured	OK
38-39 to 84-85	-	26	33	177		-
85-86	20	52	10	7	14	31
86-87	7	17	1	2	8	7
87-88	18	43	4	1	10	32
88-89	12	24	2	2	7	15
89-90	17	54	3	0	9	45
90-91	28	52	4	3	12	35
91-92	12	24	5	0	6	18
92-93	8	13	2	1	2	10
93-94	32	65	4	5	11	49
94-95	28	63	9	12	12	33
95-96	15	31	0	2	6	22
96-97	9	18	3	0	6	12
97-98	8	14	0	0	4	10
98-99	10	23	8	5	8	10
Total	224	493	55	40	115	329
Overall	-	-	81	73	232	-

Mountain Avalanches

Time spent in studying the misfortune of others is seldom wasted, which may perhaps explain the popularity of the pursuit. Thus, a study in detail of recorded avalanche accidents in this country may serve to dispel certain cherished illusions.

Until the inception of the pilot Scottish Avalanche Project in 1988, the basic problem facing the student of Scottish avalanche accidents lay in finding information giving an accurate picture of their incidence over the years. The writings of early Scottish climbing and skiing pioneers contain several references to avalanche incidents, some of a spectacular nature. Creag Meagaidh, Ben More, Cruach Ardrain and Ben Lui were known

avalanche sites before official mountain rescue records began, although these incidents produced no serious injuries.

However, the growing use of the hills in the '30s saw the first reports of accidents involving injury. At that time, many avalanche incidents which did not involve injury must have gone unreported. Only in the mid '80s, when a number of individuals had become interested in collating statistics, did sufficient information start to become available for us to be reasonably sure that the majority of incidents were being reported.

The following information is based on official published reports of mountain rescue incidents, the longest-standing reliable source of accident information; allied to these are incidents known to the

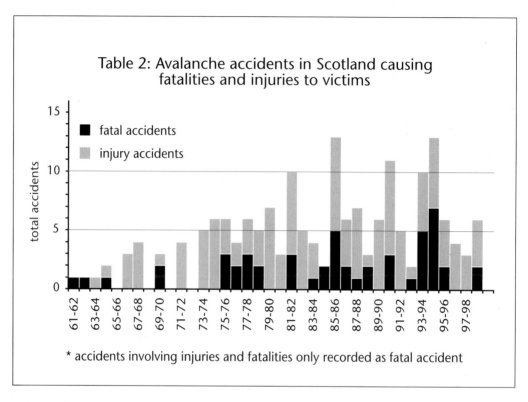

Table 2: Avalanche accidents in Scotland causing fatalities and injuries to victims

* accidents involving injuries and fatalities only recorded as fatal accident

writers through their own observations and those of a wide circle of knowledgeable informants. Since 1988, the daily observations of observers working for the Scottish Avalanche Project and its successor, the Scottish Avalanche Information Service (SAIS), have greatly added to the number of incidents and accidents coming to light. Some self-rescues, sometimes involving quite serious injuries, would not necessarily have been reported to the Mountain Rescue Committee of Scotland. This information has been considerably augmented by the contribution of the general public in providing SAIS with information on observed avalanches as well as accidents.

As can be seen in Table 1, the incidence of deaths and injuries due to avalanches is fairly random over the years, although the general trend is upwards. However, some factors are reasonably constant in injury accidents; an average of two to three persons are involved in each accident, about one accident in three or four involves a fatality and about two in every

three persons involved are injured or killed.

A broader analysis of all avalanche incidents in the UK since winter 1985-86, including those where no injury occurred, produces the figures that, of all those carried down in avalanches, 8.4% are killed and 25.7% are injured. According to available records the total number of fatalities recorded to date in the UK is 99.

Table 2 indicates that since the early '60s, there has been a general trend upward in avalanche accidents, although there is substantial variability from year to year. There is obviously some debate as to what constitutes an injury, while the possibility of an avalanche producing multiple fatalities may give a misleading impression of the situation in a given winter. For this reason, the main index which has been used is fatal accidents.

Table 3 indicates that the high winter months of January, February and March produce the most accidents, although the fact that December has seen twice as much

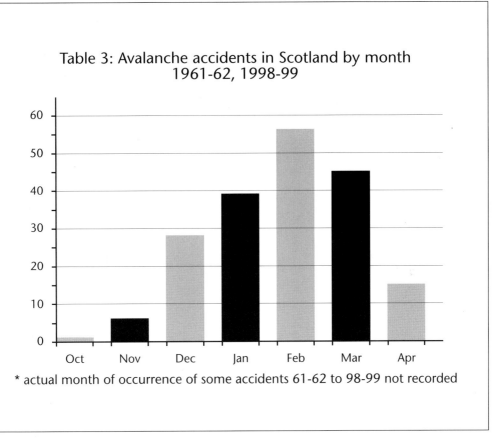

Table 3: Avalanche accidents in Scotland by month 1961-62, 1998-99

* actual month of occurrence of some accidents 61-62 to 98-99 not recorded

trouble as April may be surprising. It may be that a majority of climbers, particularly those from England and Wales, confine their activities to the peak season. Also, the wet snow avalanches which probably predominate in April, although potentially very destructive, are much more predictable than the typical early season windslab avalanche.

The exception to this is the full-depth hard, wet slab avalanche, which is notoriously difficult to forecast. These avalanches are something of a Scottish speciality and in addition to the well-known site in Coire an Lochain, other regular sites have been noted on the Sow of Atholl, Creag Meagaidh, Meall Uaine in Glen Shee and other places. The failure of such hard slabs seems to be much more akin to a sérac collapse than a snow avalanche. As the density of these slabs commonly approaches that of ice, perhaps this is not surprising. Experience both in Scotland and Switzerland indicates that these events may be susceptible to computer forecasting.

It is interesting to note that, according to the records, cornice collapses cause no more accidents in spring than during the rest of the winter. A cornice overloaded due to recent blizzard may be just as much of a hazard as one weakened and overloaded due to thawing. Although only 16 accidents due to cornice collapse are noted, it is sometimes difficult to differentiate them from the common case where the scarp slope underneath the cornice (see Chapter II) avalanches; also, a number of accidents recorded only as due to avalanche must undoubtedly have been due to cornice collapse or to cornice-triggered avalanche.

Popular Mythology

Open Slopes

As long ago as 1961, Malcolm Smith, the then editor of the Scottish Mountaineering Club's *Cairngorms* climbers' guide warned, "...the fact that open-slope avalanches are common in the area, despite the textbooks, ...is not generally appreciated". What is true for the Cairngorms applies equally to other mountain areas; at least 68 of the 190 avalanche accidents recorded in Scotland have been on open slopes rather than gullies. And still, many climbers and skiers seem unaware of the dangers. Even the innocent-looking snow apron below the cliffs in many winter climbing corries, may produce dangerous avalanches. At least 18 such accidents are recorded.

Open-slope avalanches can be of Alpine proportions. For instance, on the night of March 10 to 11, 1995, numerous wet slab avalanches occurred throughout the Northern Cairngorm area, running on two layers of depth hoar. This was the most significant episode of avalanche activity yet seen in Scotland. Several of these avalanches extended the full width of the corries involved, well over a kilometre in

places: some crown walls exceeded five metres. Miraculously, some Scottish parties have survived avalanches of this magnitude, notably a party of eight descending from the Cairngorm plateau towards Coire an Lochain on March 10, 1965.

Another large avalanche seen by the writers of this book, occurred in Coire an t-Sneachda of Cairn Gorm, when the whole corrie east of *Aladdin's Couloir* avalanched in one large slide. The length of the crown wall was about a kilometre, reaching the summit plateau at two points. The avalanche embraced some popular climbs, including the approach to *Jacob's Ladder*, where the crown wall was two metres high and also the shallow corrie at the north-eastern end of the cliffs, a popular off-piste ski run.

The debris was 400 metres wide and had crossed the lateral moraine on the east side of the corrie, spilling over into the main corrie floor. The trigger for this avalanche was a big fall of very heavy, wet snow, falling on a pre-existing windslab layer. A Glenmore Lodge party, sleeping in snowholes 30 metres away from the northerly limit of the avalanche as it came down in the night, were undisturbed by it (Fig. 1.4).

Allen Fyffe

Fig. 1.4 The avalanche in Coire an t-Sneachda, detailed above. The height of the crown wall below the crags was two metres

Fig. 1.5 *Trenches dug during the search for the victims of an avalanche in Coire na Tulaich, Buachaille Etive Mor. In such potent terrain traps, burial depths can be very great*

Malcolm Creasey

Burials

There is widespread belief that complete burials are unusual in Scottish avalanches. In fact, they are quite common; at least 81 more or less complete burials being noted. These burials have resulted in a large number of fatalities due to asphyxia and exposure. At least 21 not resulting in injury are known. Some victims have been recovered from burial depths of more than five metres and when avalanche hazard is known to exist, care should be taken to avoid potential terrain traps such as narrow corries and hollows. Coire na Tulaich (Lagangarbh Corrie) on Buachaille Etive Mor is a perfect example of this (Fig. 1.5).

The 24-hour Rule

It is a fact that in Alpine countries most large avalanches (about 80% to 90%) take place during snowstorms, or in the period up to 24 hours immediately thereafter. The comparable figure for Scotland has not been calculated, but the subjective impression is that the figure is lower. Nevertheless, it is certain that the hazard is higher during and immediately after snowfall; as an example, the two almost simultaneous avalanche accidents in Coire an t-Sneachda of Cairn Gorm on January 21, 1978, occurred during a heavy snowfall. A fatal avalanche accident took place on Lochnagar the same day.

However, many Scottish avalanche accidents happen in cold weather long after the last snowfall, due to wind transportation of snow and consequent build-up of slab. Thus, although the 24-hour rule is valid, one does not have a *carte blanche* to wander unthinkingly on steep slopes after the expiry of that period. The danger of wet snow avalanches during thaw should be obvious. One important fact which does not appear to be emphasised in the literature is that newly-formed slab, especially if created in the past hour or so, is likely to be particularly unstable.

Size of Avalanches

A climber or skier may sometimes feel justified in crossing an unsafe slope when it seems that only a small avalanche could result; but, except in the few Scottish cases where the volume of snow has been so overwhelming as to leave the victim little chance of survival, the size of the avalanche bears little relation to the damage done. Some tiny snow slides have caused death or serious injury by carrying climbers over cliffs or into boulder fields or by sweeping them into gullies and then burying them.

Also, the writers of this book have seen an avalanche which travelled no more than 15 metres bury a man completely in an upright kneeling position. In one North American survey, about half of the fatal back-country accidents noted travelled no more than 100 metres. The avalanche which killed Dougal Haston, whose first ascents included the Eiger Direct and the South Face of Annapurna, travelled no more than 30 metres.

Years of Great Snowfall

Superficially, it would seem that years of great snowfall must produce more avalanche accidents. This is only true, however, in catastrophic avalanche periods in the Alps, when great snowstorms result in disasters to towns and villages. During these periods, on the other hand, access to the high mountains is severely restricted or impossible, resulting in a marked reduction in tourist (i.e. skier and climber) casualties. The notorious avalanche winter of 1950-51 highlighted this point. 'Tourist' casualties in Switzerland fell almost to zero.

In Scotland, nearly all potential avalanche victims are 'tourists'. Admittedly, the problems of access may be less severe, but blocked roads and bad conditions have their effect in keeping people off the hills. A further factor is the effect of heavy snowfall in covering boulder fields. As many Scottish avalanche victims sustain their injuries by hitting rocks during their fall, such heavy snow cover must reduce the level of these injuries.

Thus, even though the total avalanche activity may be greater in a winter of much snowfall, the number of casualties may be lower. Statistical information from the Meteorological Office Snow Survey of Great Britain and from SAIS records, tends to support this view.

Comparison of the winters of 1993-94 and 1994-95, both 'good' snow years, gives an interesting indication of the fairly random results of avalanche involvement. In the former winter, 65 people were carried down by avalanches in Scotland, with five fatalities. In 1994-95, the corresponding figures were 63 and 12.

The Upward Trend

The increase in the number of avalanche accidents since the 1960s is alarming, but it should be seen in relation to the overall increase in winter accidents, which is in itself a reflection of the much increased use of the hills. Since the inception of daily avalanche forecasting in 1988, avalanche fatalities have in fact seen a downturn relative to the overall number of winter fatalities. Obviously there are yearly anomalies, such as the Black Winter of 1994-95 described in Chapter VIII, when avalanche fatalities represented 66% of total winter fatalities. These fluctuations are in part due to the smallness of the sample, in statistical terms. Available evidence appears to indicate not only a reduction in the proportion of avalanche fatalities, but also a reduction in the number of other fatalities in relation to rapidly escalating participation.

There is no room here for complacency among climbers. Some of British mountaineering's best known names appear in the accident reports. In these cases, perhaps familiarity breeds the confidence to stretch luck a little too far. In other instances, only inexperience or the grossest kind of foolhardiness could have led to the accident. In one accident on Ben Nevis, a party which had already been carried 170 metres in one avalanche went on the same day to attempt another climb, where they were again avalanched; the result in this case was terminal.

Some victims have suffered from nothing more than undue bad luck. The four Irish climbers who, on March 26, 1978, were struck by a large, wet-snow avalanche just above the path to the CIC hut on Ben Nevis can hardly be held at fault.

It is worth observing that in about 90% of accidents, the climber or skier's presence upon the slope has triggered the avalanche. This is in accord with experience in other countries. However, with the increasing frequency of climbers in the mountains, the hazard presented by parties higher up a slope triggering an avalanche which affects those lower down is on the increase and precautions should be taken when there is this possibility. Several accidents and near misses are attributable to this cause.

The increased use of helicopters in mountain rescue, however invaluable, may have its down-side. There is a perception among some mountaineers that a low-flying helicopter may trigger an avalanche. Anecdotal evidence tells of some dramatic coincidences, but no research appears to have been done to determine the nature of any hazard. One case is on record in which, during a rescue, the rescuer who had been lowered by winch to the scene of an accident, was avalanched by windslab built up from the down-wash of the helicopter rotor. As the rescuer was still attached to the winch cable, there were no unfortunate consequences.

Avalanche Epidemics

The principle of studying other people's misfortunes has a more direct application; it may warn hill-goers of a potential avalanche epidemic.

These events have been in evidence since the early 1970s, when avalanche accidents in Scotland first began to appear in groups or clusters chronologically. Thus, on January 12-13, 1972, three accidents occurred; on January 19, 1975, four accidents; March 30, 1975, two accidents; March 12-14, 1976, five accidents; January 21, 1978, three accidents; February 19-21, 1978, two accidents; March 16-18, 1980, three accidents; and February 15, 1982, four accidents.

Over the weekend of March 4-5, 1995, the blackest weekend ever for avalanche accidents in the UK, six people died and eight were injured in five separate accidents in the Cairngorms, Glen Coe and the Lake District.

A close attention to avalanche forecasts, press, TV and radio reports may give information as to the location of the accident, slope orientation, type of avalanche and so on. Personal knowledge of recent weather patterns may make it possible to predict whether the hazard is widespread, or likely to be confined to one area; further epidemic incidents may confirm this. For instance, both accidents on March 30, 1975, occurred in the Northern Cairngorms, whereas on January 13, 1991, avalanches occurred on Beinn Eighe, Ben Nevis, Aonach Dubh, Helvellyn and Great End.

An exceptionally hazardous period from 6-8 February, 1988, saw a number of incidents including injuries and a fatality, in locations as widely separated as Beinn Dearg (Ross-shire), Ben Nevis, Glen Coe, Scafell, and Y Garn in North Wales. These incidents led directly to the initiatives which created the pilot avalanche forecasting work of the Scottish Avalanche Project.

Weather forecast information such as temperature and wind direction may enable a prediction to be made as to the location and duration of the high hazard conditions and any change in orientation of hazardous slopes. Attention to accident reports by climbers and skiers should not be regarded as ghoulish but as a vital aid to self-preservation, particularly when activity is planned in areas where no avalanche forecast is provided.

Some Cairngorm Avalanches

The heavily-frequented Cairngorms have been the focus of many of the initiatives in avalanche observation and research since the 1960s. It is natural, therefore, that they have provided the richest record of observed avalanches, certainly in terms of numbers. Because of this density of observation also, the size and type of avalanche observed covers the whole spectrum of avalanche morphology. The following anecdotes explore some of this range of material.

"A Chance in a Million"
Beinn a' Bhuird,
December 28, 1964

The latter half of December 1964 was a period of cold and stormy weather in the Southern Cairngorms. The Snow Survey observer at Derry Lodge recorded a heavy cover of new snow between the 13th and 18th, falling on a previous cover lying everywhere at about 900m, but with large patches down to the 600m level. A heavy frost, with the mercury falling to -8°C, followed on the 19th. After a slight thaw between the 20th and the 23rd, a further heavy snowfall took place on the hills, with a slight fall of 5cm at Derry Lodge, at that time a favourite base for climbers at an altitude of 400m. High winds and severe drifting occurred on Christmas Day and Boxing Day, with a moderation of the weather on the next day. On the 28th, the observer recorded 'Grey cover at (Survey) Station level'.

Alexander MacKenzie and Alasdair Murray were both young men involved in the Scouting movement. MacKenzie wanted to complete a mountain walk in the Cairngorms to qualify for his Rambler's Badge; Murray was to accompany him, and in order to make up a strong party, two university friends of Murray's were invited to come along. The two friends, Robert Burnett and Alexander McLeod, were, like the Scoutmasters, experienced hillwalkers.

The party met on Sunday December 27 at Burnett's home in Cowdenbeath and drove the 80 or so miles to Braemar, setting off for Derry Lodge at about 3.00pm. They passed the night at Luibeg, a bothy adjacent to the lodge, where the stalker, the late Bob Scott, was renowned among the climbing fraternity as a kindred spirit. At about 9.00am the party set out for Beinn a' Bhuird, one of the six highest Cairngorm peaks at 1196m.

Unlike Beinn a' Bhuird's rugged eastern corries and the remote northern Garbh Choire, the south-western aspect of the mountain by which the walkers approached is not very steep, offering superb, long, but fairly easy descents to ski mountaineers. Conditions were deteriorating by the time the walkers approached the top of Beinn a' Bhuird, like nearly all the Cairngorm summits an exposed and featureless plateau. A strong north-west wind with snow and low visibility persuaded them to descend from the south top of the mountain, down a small burn running towards the Alltan na Beinne, a tributary of the Quoich Water. Here a pleasant stand of pines affords a sheltered camp site, where the party intended to spend their second night.

The burn by which they were descending is an innocuous looking feature, set on a slope of no more than 30°. The recent, mainly north-west winds blowing across its length, had caused a heavy build-up of snow on the north, or true right bank; the other side of the burn, strangely enough, was almost completely clear of snow.

As they descended, Alasdair Murray led the way. Between 50cm and one metre of new snow overlay old snow. Robert Burnett tested it and "found it firm". This reflects one of the dangerous properties of hard windslab; it gives good footing and might in certain circumstances be confused with snow ice.

After descending some distance, Murray fell and rolled into the gully; unhurt, he was climbing back to meet his friends on the north side of the burn, when Burnett told him to cross to the other side and meet them at the bottom. The advice probably saved his life.

Alan Hinkes

Fig. 1.6 Mountain rescue teams play an essential part in searching for avalanche victims. However, the best chances or survival are in the first 15 minutes immediately following an avalanche (see p83). Consequently a quick search must be made before going for help

Burnett continued down the north side, the others following. All at once, the snow broke away below his feet into a huge slab avalanche. He remembers falling and waving his arms above his head to attract attention. This action may well have been his salvation, for when he regained consciousness (he passed out for an undetermined length of time), he was lying on his back, completely covered with snow and with both arms extended over his head. Very fortunately, he was able to move his hands and managed to burrow a hole in the snow over his face; his breathing became easier. It is a feature of windslab avalanches that, because of the angularity of the debris, air passages may exist quite deep down; one of these passages saved Robert Burnett's life.

Apart from his arms, Burnett was immovably held, and, panicking momentarily, he began to call for help. "No-one came," he later stated, "and it was some time before I was able to control my feelings," words containing a depth of unwritten horror. While Burnett was undergoing this ordeal, Alasdair Murray, who had observed, unharmed, the disappearance of his friends, was making a desperate search. Whether by instinct or by foreknowledge, he did exactly the right thing. He searched, probing the snow with a stick in the hope of finding his friends alive. This kind of quick search by witnesses forms by far the best chance of survival for avalanche burial victims. After half an hour, with their chances of survival now rapidly declining, he decided to go for help.

Help in the Cairngorms is seldom near at hand, except in the crowded northern corries of Cairngorm, and Murray ran for 5 miles to the nearest human aid, at Mar Lodge, which at that time was being developed as Scotland's latest ski resort. Police were informed and a rescue party quickly raised, consisting of four police mountain rescue team members from Braemar and Ballater, climbers, skiers, youth hostellers, gamekeepers and the local Nature Conservancy officer.

As they made their way over the long distance to the scene of the accident, few could have entertained much hope for the survival of any of the buried men. Their experience and common sense must have told them that hope bordered on self-deception. This feeling must have been reinforced by the discovery of Alexander McLeod's body that night. About 4.00am, as their torch batteries were failing, the rescuers gave up for the night.

Reinforcements arrived next morning, when 30 soldiers from Aberdeen joined the rescue. After some hours of fruitless searching, one of the police rescuers noticed a small hole in the debris, yellowed around the edges. Peering down this, he saw Burnett, alive and calling for help. The feelings of all concerned can be imagined. He was buried between 30 to 60cm deep, but was soon dug out suffering from frostbite, and evacuated to Braemar. This was at 12.30pm on Tuesday, December 29, after a burial of some 22 hours. This is remarkable not only as the longest recorded survival time in a Scottish avalanche burial, but as one of the longest survivals in full contact with the snow on record anywhere.

Hope must have revived for a live rescue of Alexander MacKenzie, but in truth such a large measure of good fortune was unlikely to be granted twice and MacKenzie was found dead some hours later.

The Beinn a' Bhuird avalanche was of a kind which has unfortunately become typical of Scottish avalanche accidents. It was a large avalanche (some reports say that it was nearly 1km wide) of hard slab, following high winds and drifting onto a thawed and refrozen base. With hindsight it is easy to see the classic pattern in the Snow Survey records. It was on an open slope. Did Robert Burnett and the others realise they were on windslab? Were they reassured by the shallow angle of the

slope? Looking at the site of the accident, it is easy to see why they imagined themselves to be in no danger.

Burnett stated that he thought the avalanche was "a chance in a million". In fact, this phrase occurs with astonishing frequency in survivor accounts of avalanches over the years. Given the level of snow and avalanche knowledge at the time, that might have seemed a valid judgement. Of course, we might say, today we would know better; and yet similar accidents continue to occur.

A small slab avalanche Coire an Lochain, March 12, 1976

Mountaineers and off-piste skiers operate in a twilight zone of snow safety knowledge. Even trained avalanche forecasters, with access to specialised weather information and other aids such as computer-assisted forecasting, still find occasional difficulty in making judgements. In mountaineering situations, the practitioner is often trying to make judgements on snow stability of a level of sophistication which the specialist would not attempt.

Forecasting services, where they exist, score a high success rate, achieving overall accuracy rates of around 80% in differentiating 'avalanche days' from 'non-avalanche days', the failures lying almost invariably in an excess of forecasted 'avalanche days'. The avalanche days not successfully differentiated mainly feature dry slab avalanches. What is difficult for the 'experts' with their specialised information, knowledge and equipment must be more so for the average mountain-goer, armed only with eyes, experience and common sense.

In practice, there is no infallible method for assessing the stability of a given slope and the mountaineer or skier can scarcely stop every 50 metres to make detailed observations and calculations: at times in serious mountaineering situations, there is no choice but to proceed. There are, of course, certain criteria to which most avalanches will adhere; they are unlikely to start on a slope under 22°; boulders protruding through the snow will tend to anchor the snow cover; and

Fig. 1.7 Climbers on the Goat Track, a popular line of ascent and descent at the far right-hand end of Coire an t-Sneachda

Tom Prentice

a concave slope will generally be less prone to avalanche than a convex one. At times, however, avalanches do not observe even these conventions.

On the morning of March 12, 1976, several mountaineering groups set out as usual from Glenmore Lodge. The weather forecast gave no cause for special concern, with a 40 mph, south-west wind forecast, backing southerly during the day. Some light snow was predicted and snow conditions were generally good, with a thawed and refrozen layer of hard snow above about 800m.

As the day progressed and the weather behaved as forecast, groups on the hill noted a certain amount of soft windslab accumulation. Even although this was falling on to a hard base which would provide a good sliding surface, the build-up was not as yet sufficient to warrant anxiety in normal circumstances; only a few centimetres.

It is worth saying something about the experience and qualifications of the two Lodge instructors about to be embroiled in tragedy, both of whom have now sadly been taken from us by fatal illness. Roger O'Donovan had made a particular study of the technical aspects of the avalanche problem and had written several articles on the subject. He was later to become Deputy Principal at Glenmore Lodge. Jack Thomson, with 28 years service at the Lodge, was the complete outdoor pursuits professional and probably possessed an unrivalled practical experience of Scottish snow conditions.

About 11.15am, Thomson had arrived in Coire an t-Sneachda with his group of eight students. He spent some time demonstrating to them the basics of crampon technique, which they practised on a boss of easy angled ice in the floor of the corrie. The party was then split into four groups of two, so that the students could practice pitched climbing to the plateau, via the steepish slopes of the Goat Track, a normal winter descent route.

The party had already practised snow belaying and set off by parallel routes, fairly close together so that the instructor could check each belay quickly. While Thomson's party was climbing up the Goat Track, other parties were pursuing a similar programme at different locations in the Northern Corries.

As is normal during winter courses at the Lodge, the mountain rescue base radio in the main office was on standby. At 2.24pm a call came in from Jack Thomson. His party had been avalanched. One person was injured and help was required. Other Lodge groups were alerted by radio and several parties were diverted to the scene.

At 3.07pm Roger O'Donovan and his party of eight students were contacted in Coire an Lochain next door. When O'Donovan asked the students whether they were fit and willing to participate in the rescue, all had answered in the affirmative. Some were doubly motivated, as they had friends in Thomson's party, but in any case it is still one of the better traditions of British climbing that help is freely given when other climbers are in trouble.

All in all, this party should have had little to fear on their rescue mission, by normal standards. But then, as we have mentioned above, avalanches sometimes do not abide by normal standards. Twenty minutes later, O'Donovan radioed in; on their way from Coire an Lochain over the Fiacaill a' Coire an t-Sneachda to the accident site, his party had also been avalanched; six were hurt, some seriously.

The terrain which O'Donovan's party had to cross was not difficult in mountaineering terms. It was an area of boulder fields interspersed with patches of hard snow and with a slope angle of no more than 20°. They had already passed that way in the morning and noted that there was some slab build-up. Since then, probably only a few centimetres had been added. Certainly, the weather was not favourable, with a wind of about 40mph and 25 metres visibility, but again it was by no means bad for the Cairngorms in winter.

The climbers had been crossing a zone of snow patches interspersed with boulders, the students following in single file behind the instructor. As the slab deposits had thickened slightly, to about 10cm, O'Donovan decided to stop at some boulders a few metres up-slope to consider the best route. The present situation did not appear dangerous, but to wander in the limited visibility on to a steeper slope with a bigger build-up might have been unwise.

Then, without warning, the slope was moving beneath them. O'Donovan felt himself hit at knee level by blocks of slab, and with an instinctive quick step up the slope, found himself on safe snow. He turned round, expecting to see his companions laughing and joking about the mini avalanche. No one was to be seen.

The potential seriousness of what had happened was obvious; below and all round were fields of jagged boulders. If the members of the party had been carried far, they might be seriously injured. Following the track of the avalanche down, O'Donovan immediately found two students unhurt. They lined out across the slope, and sweeping downhill soon found the others among the boulders between 60 and 100m below. All six were injured. O'Donovan made his radio call and a major rescue operation was launched.

In addition to the ground parties and RAF Rescue helicopter already deployed for the first accident, a second helicopter was summoned to the second accident, as well as other rescuers on foot. Over the next three hours all the casualties were evacuated to Glenmore Lodge where, after examination by a doctor, they were taken by a waiting fleet of ambulances to Raigmore Hospital, Inverness.

In due course all were discharged, after treatment for various injuries including broken arms and legs, with the exception of Philip Hadfield. At first, he had not appeared seriously injured, but had in fact sustained serious head injuries, despite

Mountainsportphoto.com

Fig. 1.8 Even a small avalanche can have disastrous consequences

wearing a safety helmet. Tragically, his condition deteriorated and he died one month after the accident. So the name of Philip Hadfield was added to the list of those who have lost their lives going to the aid of others on the Scottish hills; the first to perish by avalanche.

Several things may be learned by examining this avalanche, which caused injury out of all proportion to its size. Technically, it was not even large enough to be classed as an avalanche, the slab which broke away being approximately 5m wide and 6 to 8m high; it was less than 15cm thick.

The mass of snow was very small and injuries were not due to burial but to the victims hitting rocks. This is typical of Scottish avalanche accidents and illustrates the danger which results from even a tiny avalanche if the runout is dangerous. Injuries sustained in uncontrolled falls into boulders are usually much more serious

than would seem possible.

Secondly, this slope was studded with boulders which might have been expected to provide effective peripheral anchorages for the slab. They did not. Again, this slide took place on an unusually shallow slope, implying a very weak bond between the slab and underlying hard layer. The authors know of only two other incidents on slopes of a similar angle; both took place one day on Stuc a' Chroin and Ben Vorlich, when two parties were avalanched by soft slab, luckily without injury.

Lastly, we have mentioned that Roger O'Donovan escaped to safe ground by making a couple of rapid steps upward. He was probably fortunate in being near the fracture line, but his instinct was the correct one. There is often a fraction of a second available for action before the avalanche takes one's feet away; it may be possible to jump up-slope to safe terrain above the fracture line or elsewhere.

"A great white billowing mass... with DEATH written on it"
Beinn a' Bhuird,
January 4, 1990

It may be embarrassing to recall the words of a former icon of Scottish mountain-eering, that "Scottish snow is... not much prone to avalanche". However, in the context of the time, when mountaineers were few and days upon the mountains probably rarer than now, the judgement was not widely disputed. There was a paucity of opportunity to observe avalanche activity.

Equally, in the mid 1980s, we were able to assert without much fear of successful contradiction, that airborne-powder, or 'aerosol' avalanches were unknown in Scotland. These were assumed to be creatures of the Greater Ranges only, with their massive speeds of up to 250mph and devastating destructive air blast. Their technical aspects are discussed in Chapter II.

There had been a report of a very large example in Observatory Gully on Ben Nevis in 1978, which was said to have thrown blocks of debris as high as the top of the Douglas Boulder (200 metres!) and to have filled Coire Leis with snow dust. Because of the snow conditions at the time, it was felt a leg-pulling exercise might be taking place and the report was mentally filed for future corroboration. We felt that the length of slopes available in Scotland would not, in general, be sufficient for avalanches to attain the critical speed necessary for airborne development.

In the winter of 1988-89, the Scottish Avalanche Project was launched. Its observers were on the mountains daily in Glen Coe and the Northern Cairngorms, with a weekend presence on Lochnagar beginning the following winter. The existence of the project was attended with a fair amount of publicity and the public were invited to notify any avalanche activity they might observe. Thus, in a short space of time, the observational potential increased enormously.

Beinn a' Bhuird in the southern Cairngorms lay outside the area covered by the project's observers. It has already been described above as the scene of Robert Burnett's remarkable survival. It was now to be the stage for a drama which divested us of yet another cherished misconception.

In the early days of 1990, on January 4, two climbers approached the cliffs of Beinn a' Bhuird. Residents of the North-East of Scotland, they had extensive winter hill-walking and climbing experience. On that day, their objective was *Twisting Gully*, in the remote Coire na Ciche. However, although the weather was favourable, with blue skies and wind speed of 20 to 30mph on the summits, snow conditions seemed much less propitious.

An examination of the snowpack on the 25° apron at the foot of the cliffs, showed that the dry, slabby snow was very unstable. Climbing on steeper slopes or gullies was deemed to be out of the question and retreat was decided upon. It is ironic, that having made the safe decision, the party was then to be involved in an accident.

Just after 1.00pm, as they traversed the slopes below *Twisting Gully* on the way down, one of the pair was turning round to have a last look at the cliffs, when he was alarmed to see a huge cloud of snow dust towering over the plateau rim above *Twisting Gully*. Even more frighteningly, hurtling down the gully towards them was something later described as "a great billowing mass of whiteness with DEATH written on it".

There was little time for any defensive action, but one of the climbers spotted a one-metre high boulder just nearby and succeeded in diving behind it. His companion, less fortunate, found no shelter and bore the full force of the avalanche which now burst upon them. The climber behind the boulder could hear the roaring of the powder as it passed over, along with "the draught tugging at my rucksack," the first evidence we had at that time of air blast accompanying an avalanche in Scotland.

In 10 to 12 seconds it was all over, but the victim exposed to the avalanche had gone. He was quickly found, however, some 50 metres lower down, on the surface of the debris. Although not buried, he had

SCOTTISH MOUNTAIN SAFETY GROUP

Avalanche Recording Form

AP

DESCRIPTION OF AVALANCHE

DATE 4 Jan. 90 THURS.   TIME OF DAY 1310

NAME OF HILL/MOUNTAIN BEINN A' BHUIRD , COIRE NA CICHE, TWISTING GULLY

GRID REF. OF STARTING ZONE

DIMENSIONS OF SLIDE PATH 20-30 FT, MAINLY DOWN THE PATH OF 'TWISTING GULLY' AND NEIGHBOURING TOPOGRAPHY

SLOPE ASPECT AT STARTING ZONE (N/S ETC) EAST minimum

DIMENSIONS OF DEBRIS SPILLED DOWN c. 300-400 FT FROM BASE OF CLIFFS

AVERAGE ANGLE [struck out] 60°

SLOPE ASPECT OF DEBRIS (N/S ETC) DUE EAST

↓60° FOR 400 FT, THEN 25° FOR 300 FT WEATHER

MET CONDITIONS AT TIME OF AVALANCHE   TEMPERATURE (ESTIMATE) 0-1 °C   WIND DIRECTION E   WIND SPEED 10-20 kts

PRECIPITATION NIL RAIN ☐ SNOW ☐ IF SNOW RATE OF BUILD UP CM PER HOUR

MET CONDITIONS IN DAYS PRECEDING AVALANCHE HARD FROST THE NIGHT BEFORE - ALL MOORLAND BURNS & POOLS - THICK ICE. CLEAR CLOUDLESS SKIES IN THE BRAEMAR AREA, TEMP & WIND AS ABOVE

INFORMATION ON VICTIMS–IF ANY
IF MORE THAN ONE PLEASE COPY FORM

AGE ① 37 ② 30   SEX ① M ② M

NATIONALITY (SCOTTISH/ENGLISH ETC) ① SCOTTISH ② SCOTTISH

EXPERIENCE (YEARS/HILLWALK/CLIMB) ① (HW) 20 (C) 7 ② (HW) 20 (C) 10+

EXPERIENCE (YEARS/WINTER HILLWALK/CLIMB) ① 7 ② 10+

ACTIVITY (PLEASE TICK)   WALK ☐ CLIMB ☐ SKI TOUR ALPINE ☐ SKI TOUR NORDIC ☐ EXTREME SKI ☐

OTHER (PLEASE SPECIFY) TRAVERSING/ THE BASE OF 'TWISTING GULLY' AREA - PREPARING TO (WALKING) WITHDRAW & LEAVE CORRIE

WAS THE VICTIM AWARE OF AVALANCHE HAZARD YES - ON OBSERVING CONDITIONS IN CORRIE (YES) NO

NATURE OF INJURIES
① ESCAPED UNINJURED
② FRACTURED SHAFT (R) FEMUR

IF YES, WAS THE SOURCE OF THE KNOWLEDGE
OWN OBSERVATIONS ☑ OTHER (PLEASE SPECIFY)
PUBLISHED FORECAST ☐

FATAL YES (NO)   BURIAL YES/NO (IF SO, TO WHAT DEPTH) ① NO ② NO   DURATION OF BURIAL N/A.

HOW LOCATED – PROBE/DOG/TRANSCEIVER ETC   N/A.

BRIEF VERBAL DESCRIPTION OF INCIDENT
1310 hrs, 4/1/90; - WE WERE ABOUT TO LEAVE THE CORRIE (ON EXAMINING THE DRY, POWDERY & SLABBING NATURE OF THE SNOW AT THE BASE OF TWISTING GULLY) I (①) LOOKED UP AT THE RIM OF THE CORRIE, (& AT THE 'AMPHITHEATRE' & NEIGHBOURING MINOR GULLIES ETC AT THE TOP) - SAW A LARGE BILLOWING MASS OF WHITENESS TUMBLING DOWN TOWARDS THE START OF 'TWISTING GULLY' PROPER. I DIVED BEHIND A 3 FT HIGH ROCK AND CLUNG DOWN ON MY AXE. WITHIN 2-3 SECONDS I WAS AWARE OF THE POWDER ROARING DOWN OVER THE BOULDER, WITH THE DRAUGHT TUGGING AT MY RUCSAC (NO CHANCE TO REMOVE). 10-12 SECONDS LATER IT WAS OVER.

Fig. 1.9 The Avalanche Recording Form (front) submitted by the victims of the 1990 Beinn a' Bhuird accident, to the Scottish Avalanche Project

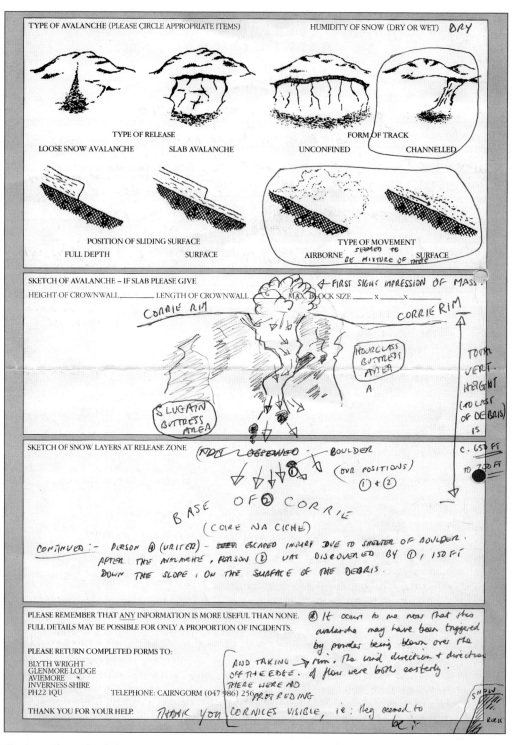

Fig. 1.10 The Avalanche Recording Form (back) submitted by the victims of the 1990 Beinn a' Bhuird accident, to the Scottish Avalanche Project

a broken femur, a serious situation in such a remote location. Despite the injury, his companion considered it wise to drag him further down the slope, to a place which seemed beyond the reach of any further avalanche activity.

As in the case of the 1964 accident, a long trek was now necessary to summon help. By the time the police had been alerted, the fine weather had deteriorated to the extent that poor visibility prevented the RAF helicopter from flying to the scene. Thus, a long wait for the victim and a long carry by the members of Grampian Police and Braemar Mountain Rescue Teams resulted (Figs. 1.9 & 1.10).

Since this, the first recorded airborne-powder avalanche, many others have been observed both by SAIS workers and members of the mountaineering public. However, probably the first witnessed, although not seen, was by Andy Nisbet on February 5, 1977 during the first ascent of *Grovel Wall* on Lochnagar. The gully on the left of this route, *Raeburn's Gully*, is one of the classic winter climbs of a former era. It still features, however, at the top of the list of accident black spots in Appendix IV. Visibility was poor, but as the climbers reached the first belay, about 40 metres up the cliff, they heard a noise like an approaching express train. They did not see the avalanche as it passed below them, but they felt the air blast and light powder was deposited around them.

From an analysis of many accounts of such avalanches in Scotland, it seems that a very common feature of the snowpack when they occur, is a high graupel content. This may provide a very mobile layer which may help the avalanche accelerate to the required speed on a relatively short slope. This was noted by John Mackenzie, in a very close encounter with a large airborne avalanche on Ben Wyvis on February 3, 1994. Mackenzie also noted a complete lack of debris after the avalanche had settled. This is also a typical experience and it is likely that much of the airborne snow dust sublimes away into the atmosphere.

As the final word for the moment on Scottish airborne-powder avalanches, it has been reported that prior to all the above events, the gamekeeper who used to reside at Altnafeadh in Glen Coe, witnessed an airborne avalanche which started near the Lagangarbh Buttress area on Buachaille Etive Mor. As it developed, the dust cloud completely obscured the view of the Buachaille as seen from the keeper's house and looked at one stage as though it would cross the river to the main road. To those who know the topography of the Buachaille, that may give food for thought.

Inside the Avalanche Coire an Lochain, January 11 1997

Coire an Lochain of Cairn Lochan, that distinctive outlier of Cairn Gorm, is the classic avalanche site of the massif. The full-depth spring-time avalanche on the Great Slab is a well-known feature of the Scottish mountain calendar. Its date is always a subject of conjecture in Strathspey and money may well have changed hands on the result. It has occurred as early as April 11, but on at least one occasion, has been delayed until the third week of June.

The lochans which give the corrie its name nestle in a bowl at the foot of the Great Slab, but avalanches from all round the back of the corrie run out on to the surface of the lochans, which usually consists of ice up to half a metre thick. Occasionally, the huge impact of a large avalanche may smash this ice and drive it forwards out of the lochans into a pile of blocks metres deep.

Saturday, January 11 1997, was not particularly inviting from the point of view of hill-walking. However, on that day, three mountaineers, accompanied by a pet dog, approached Coire an Lochain, bound for Ben Macdui. Two of the walkers were about to be involved in one of the most remarkable avalanche survivals ever known. Their names do not appear in this account, as there still exists among some mountaineers a belief that to get into trouble on the mountains is something of which to be ashamed. We are obliged to respect such a responsible if austere point of view.

Visibility was poor and the winds were about 30mph from the south-west. There had been some fresh snow and SAIS observers on the headwall of Coire Cas that day noted a weak layer of facetted crystals in the snow cover 30cm down.

At the bottom of the slope which would lead them up out of Coire an Lochain to the broad spur on its west side and thence to Lochan Buidhe, the party stopped to review the situation. One member of the party decided that he did not wish to continue and turned back. Although this decision was to spare him a great deal of anguish, it should be noted that the decision was made on the basis of the inclement weather and not of perceived avalanche hazard. The remaining two carried on, along with the dog.

Generally, an avalanche-safe route exists close to the path ascending the west side of the corrie. However, it requires to be followed closely and may not be easy to follow in poor visibility. Both to the right and particularly, to the left, just beyond the Twin Burns, steeper slopes exist which are frequent avalanche paths. It appears that the party wandered in the poor visibility too far left, on to that part of the slope where the maximum accumulation of new windslab lay. The result was not long delayed and without warning, both were carried off in a large slab avalanche.

The immediate aftermath is unclear in the minds of both victims, but what is certain is that they were carried from near the plateau, down through a vertical interval of about 150 metres, on to the lochan and buried. It seems that both were unconscious for a time and that initially they were completely buried at a depth of about 2.5m. At that stage, their survival for more than a few minutes would have been most unlikely.

Then came the event which transformed their no-hope situation into one which, almost incredibly, gave them a chance of survival. It seems that, as the full force of the avalanche came to bear upon the surface of the lochan, the ice fractured and allowed a substantial mass of the debris to pour into the lochan itself. As this happened, cracks or crevasses opened up in the debris. One of the victims regained consciousness. He was aware of being buried, trapped. However, he was also aware of being able to breathe. Astonishingly, he could hear the dog barking. It had evidently survived the avalanche. He shouted and was immensely relieved to receive a reply from his companion, but from what position or direction, he was unable to determine.

He gradually became aware of his position, which was bizarre in the extreme. He was buried, still at a depth of about 2.5m, with his body held immobile in the snow. However, his face was exposed in the wall of one of the crevasses which had opened up and he had a clear air passage through to the surface. He could hear his companion, but still not identify his position. The dog stood guard at the top of the crevasse, barking furiously. The will to survive took charge. The only part of his body which he could move was his head and that only in a restricted, nodding fashion. Using this ability, over a period of time which must have amounted to hours, he succeeded in burrowing down to his right hand, which as fate would have it, was held in the debris just above the left breast pocket of his jacket. Having freed his hand, he then was able to open the pocket, which contained his compass. Using this implement as a shovel, he then proceeded to dig himself out of the snow.

Darkness was falling and relief at his own extrication was tempered by concern for his companion. He was alive, but where was he? Then the first survivor made the amazing discovery that the two of them had actually been buried beside each other, with the second man's arm touching the first man's leg. The second victim was much further from the wall of the crevasse, but eventually, with the aid of his ice axe which he had held onto, he also was liberated.

Bob Barton

Fig. 1.11 Coire an Lochain showing the runout from the central Great Slab to the lochan below

It would have been understandable if, exhausted by their efforts, the pair had stayed put and awaited rescue. After all, their friend who had turned back would be concerned at their failure to arrive back before dark and might already have alerted the rescue services. This is in fact what had happened and the Cairngorm Mountain Rescue Team was gathering to search for them. However, the two survivors showed further evidence of their self-reliance by setting off back in the dark, to reach the car park at the ski area just as the rescue team was setting out. An ironic final footnote to this remarkable story is that, even without

their own heroic efforts, the two men might well have survived. When, a couple of days later, they came to relate their tale in the SAIS office at Glenmore Lodge, they revealed that at no time during their burial had they felt cold. They would probably have survived until the rescue team's arrival and in addition, the faithful dog would still have been barking to indicate their position.

In coping with the avalanche problem, experience, common sense and observation all have their part to play. Allied to these should be a basic knowledge of the theory of snow structure and avalanche release.

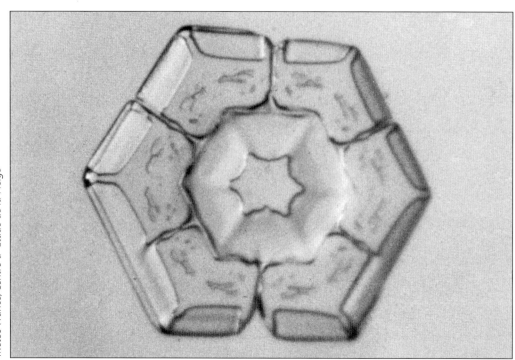

Fig. 2.1   A plate crystal

Fig. 2.2   A stellar crystal

II Avalanche Anatomy

Water in its solid form – snow and ice – is one of the most variable substances known. Some manifestations such as water-ice are very strong, others such as stellar crystals are very fragile indeed. To complicate things further, the situation is dynamic with individual crystals, under the influence of variations of temperature and humidity, constantly growing, transforming, changing shape or bonding to their neighbours.

Many of the factors influencing avalanche release arise from these varying properties of snow crystals; as they are formed in clouds, as they travel through the air and when they are on the ground as part of the snowpack.

If we understand what is happening at the level of individual crystals, we are in a stronger position to predict the behaviour of threateningly large masses of snow – potential avalanches. In this chapter we will look at the formation, deposition and modification of different types of snow crystals, and relate these changes to the large–scale properties of snow masses.

- **Snow in the Air** examines the **formation** and initial properties of the main types of snow crystal.
- **Snow on the Ground** considers how the main types of snow crystals are deposited in a snowpack, and how they are subsequently modified by **metamorphism**. The formation of loose snow avalanches is examined (Fig. 2.1 & 2.2).
- **Snowpack Structure** considers the **layering** of the snowpack and examines the factors relating to the release of slab avalanches and the formation and behaviour of cornices.

It should be understood that the boundary between snow surface and air can often be an ill-defined maelstrom of whirling snow. A snow crystal may be deposited, re-transported, re-deposited and so on. The changes affecting the snow crystal are continuous and snow in the air and snow on the ground are convenient labels rather than necessarily separate parts of the process.

Snow in the Air

The size and shape of a snow crystal is largely determined by the conditions of temperature and humidity that it experiences, both at its point of formation and during its journey to the ground. The different forms include a wide variety of shapes such as needles, stellar crystals, columns and plates.

This variety of shape occurs because growth in the initial plane (a-axis) has an hexagonal symmetry, while the lengthwise growth (c-axis), which is at right angles to the initial plane, has not. Thus, a column will be hexagonal in section (a-axis) but linear along the c-axis.

Different conditions of temperature and humidity will lead to preferential growth along one axis or the other and so will tend to favour the formation of a particular crystal type. From the moment of its formation a crystal may pass through a number of different regimes of temperature and humidity, each promoting different kinds of growth. This mechanism of formation helps to explain the tremendous variability in the detailed structure of snow crystals. The Snow Crystal Research website contains some breathtaking electron microscope

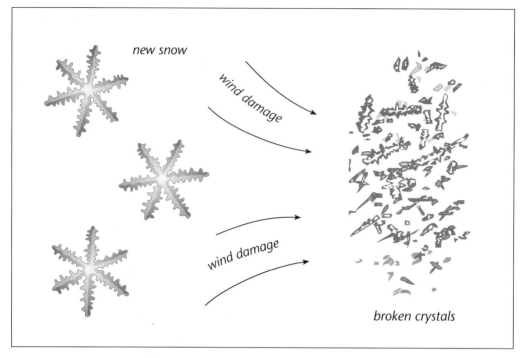

Fig. 2.3 Broken crystals

photographs of crystals (see Appendix V).

Forms such as needles, stellar crystals, columns and plates are typical of crystals at their point of formation in a cloud. In fairly calm conditions they can fall to the ground more or less intact, either individually, or as clusters of several crystals (snowflakes). All these forms are included in the single term **new snow**.

While falling to the ground these 'new' snow crystals can be modified in various ways: If the snow is falling in winds above, say, 20mph, the crystals will be damaged to some degree, and all extensively wind damaged crystals can be called **broken crystals** (Fig. 2.3). Partially broken forms will contain identifiable fragments of the original form – the arm of a stellar crystal or a broken needle – but soon the crystals are pulverised to a near dust-like constituency. This is the raw material of windslab which will be described below.

The more delicate stellar crystals are particularly prone to wind damage. Meteorological records for Cairn Gorm summit (1245m) indicate that for the period October 25, 1978, to May 31, 1979, only one day in six had a mean daily windspeed below 22mph. This suggests that broken crystals are likely to be the predominant form in the Scottish hills. Wind transport of snow is extremely prevalent in Scotland – it has been described as the "wind transport capital of the world" – and so wind damage can continue to occur even after the snow has reached the surface, as the crystals bounce and rattle across endless wind-scoured snowfields.

In winter a thick, white crust of rime-ice often forms on the windward side of boulders, ski-lift pylons, and other exposed objects, sometimes growing fantastic feathers out into the teeth of a gale. This riming occurs through tiny, super-cooled water-droplets in the air freezing onto the surface of the object concerned. To climb crags transformed to fairy-tale castles by ubiquitous riming is one of the peculiar joys of winter climbing in the damp Scottish climate (Figs. 2.4 & 2.5).

Snow crystals can be involved in a

similar process both in the cloud and while falling to the ground, so that they in turn become encrusted in a coating of rime. Riming is particularly likely with the turbulence associated with mountain barriers or the passage of cold weather fronts, and the original form of the crystal may be completely obscured by the encrustation of rime. These heavily rimed pellets are called **graupel** and are a common and uncomfortable component of Scottish winter storms. All extensively rimed forms can be termed **rimed crystals** (Figs. 2.6 & 2.7).

If the air temperature near the ground is above 0°C, some melting will affect all the previous types of new snow to produce **wet snow**. We will not look closely at the fate of falling wet snow, since the thaw with which it is associated is likely to have its greatest effect on the already existing snowpack. In the field, it is worth noting that a storm which starts with wet snow and then gradually turns to drier, colder snow is likely to deposit snow which is more firmly anchored to its base, than one which starts cold and dry and becomes wet.

Any snowfall is likely to include

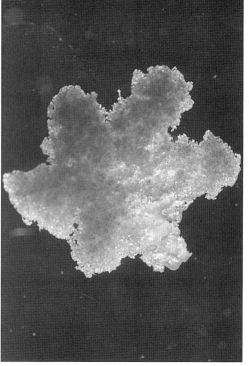

Météo France/Centre d' Etude de la Neige

Fig. 2.4 A heavily rimed snow crystal. Such riming will ultimately produce a graupel pellet

Nigel Shepherd

Fig. 2.5 Atmospheric riming on the summit shelter of Ben Nevis

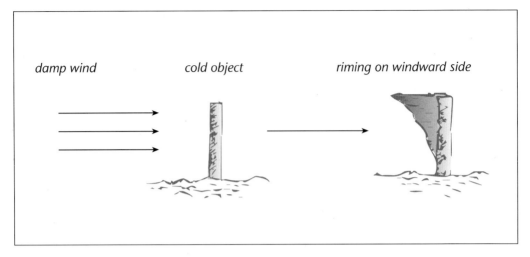

Fig. 2.6 Riming on a post

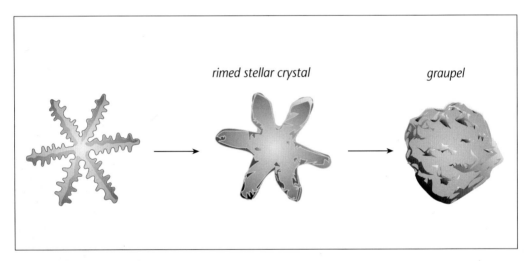

Fig. 2.7 Riming on a crystal

several of these different snow types simultaneously, (though usually a single form is dominant) and a hand lens will reveal this variety among the crystals caught during a storm on a dark jacket sleeve, or a cold metal plate.

Snow on the Ground

New Snow

New snow will remain unbroken during its journey to the ground only in relatively still, cold air. In these conditions it will tend to be deposited as a fairly uniform blanket of light, fluffy powder snow which, volume for volume, contains much more air than snow. This type of snowfall is more commonly seen in Scottish valleys than on exposed mountains, but when it does occur on the tops, the snow will often adhere to the faces of crags and other steep slopes. This is possible because the more feathery crystals can intermesh and provide enough cohesion to support the very low density snow.

If we ignore wet snow, we are left with three main categories of newly fallen snow: **new snow**, **broken crystals** and **rimed crystals**.

The International Commission on Snow and Ice (ICSI) has developed a more detailed classification system of the main crystal types: columns, needles, plates, stellar crystals, irregular particles, graupel, hail and ice pellets. This full schedule of classification can be found in *The International Mountain Rescue Handbook* by Hamish MacInnes, 1998 and *The Avalanche Handbook* by McClung and Schaerer, 1993, listed in Appendix V.

The size of crystals is generally between 0.2mm and 5mm with 1 to 2mm being common. Each of these can be deposited and subsequently modified in different ways.

Rounding (Dry Snow Metamorphism)

If you could put a number of stellar crystals in your freezer – a condition of constant temperature and humidity – they would not remain unchanged like a pack of frozen peas. Instead, they would lose their feathery form, and over a few days, change into rounded ice-grains. These grains would attach themselves to neighbouring grains to form a relatively strong structure where each crystal is joined to several neighbours (Fig. 2.8).

It is a basic property of snow crystals that there is a higher vapour pressure at their points than at their hollows. This promotes a migration of molecules from regions of high vapour pressure to those of low vapour pressure. The practical effect of this is that a net transfer of material occurs, ice being moved from the points to the hollows. This leads to a conversion of complex, branched crystals to more simple, rounded ones. An alternative way of considering this change is that the snow crystal 'wants' to change to the form with the lowest thermodynamic entropy – the rounded grain.

It should be noted that the transfer of material is by **sublimation**, which involves a direct transition from ice to water vapour or back again. Melting or the presence

of liquid water does not play a significant part in the process.

This process, converting complex branched crystals to more simple rounded ones, is called **rounding**, or **dry snow metamorphism**, the latter word meaning change of shape, and will affect all snow crystals in non-thawing snowpacks. In the past, dry snow metamorphism was known as destructive metamorphism. The crystals that develop in the absence of a significant gradient of temperature are called **equilibrium forms** and include: (a) rounded grains or rounds, (b) firn snow and (c) wet grains.

Although in a laboratory it is possible to keep snow in an environment of uniform temperature and humidity, this is unlikely to occur in the field and the influence of temperature gradients within the snowpack and the heat flow that these promote, tends to eclipse the effects of crystal shape as the main driver of metamorphism. This is generally good news for skiers and climbers, because

Météo France/Centre d' Etude de la Neige

Fig. 2.8 A stellar crystal in the early stages of rounding and still showing much of its original shape

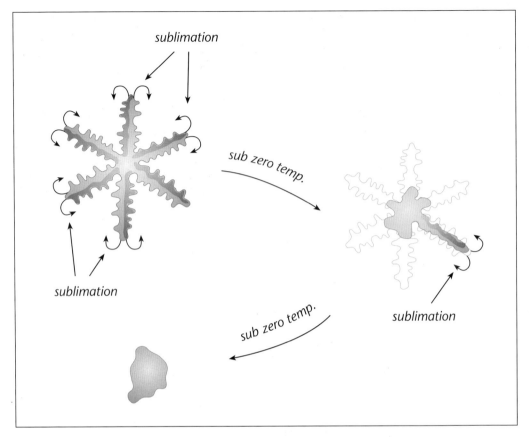

Fig. 2.9 Rounding (dry snow metamorphism)

the rate of change and, ultimately, of stabilisation is speeded up.

The crystals in our uniform blanket of new snow will be affected by rounding (dry snow metamorphism) and will undergo the change of shape shown in Fig. 2.9. This means that some of the cohesion provided by the intermeshing crystals is lost and the snow becomes more free-flowing. This phenomenon might explain the observation that the best powder for skiing often occurs some time after the snow has fallen. The delay allows metamorphism to act on the snow. Some workers now believe that this process is driven by a strong temperature gradient at the surface.

If the blanket of new snow is poised on a relatively steep slope, this loss of cohesion – like converting a pile of cornflakes to rice grains – can cause a dry,

loose snow avalanche (Fig. 2.11). Such loose snow avalanches start with the movement of a few crystals, but a chain reaction ensues, which can ultimately lead to a huge avalanche. More commonly, **sluffs**, small loose snow slides, will be seen on steeper slopes. The distinctive feature of loose snow avalanches is their fan-like shape with a more or less single point of origin – a **point release**.

In Scotland, small powder snow sluffs – spindrift slides – are common and the main danger is that they dislodge a climber or skier in their wake (Fig. 2.10). On larger slopes, powder snow avalanches can be large, and if their speed reaches about 40mph, they can become airborne – a near explosive process which 'feeds' on the uptake of increasing quantities of snow to produce a destructive shock wave and a suffocating cloud of snow dust. Although much more common in the greater ranges, airborne powder avalanches have been observed in Scotland at various locations including Coire na Ciste on Ben Nevis, *Easy Gully* on Creag Meagaidh, *The Flypaper* ski-run in Glen Coe, *Raeburn's Gully* on Lochnagar and *Castlegates Gully* on Shelterstone Crag.

One incident below *Twisting Gully*, in Coire na Ciche, Beinn a' Bhuird, described in detail in Chapter I, hit a climber with enough force to knock him down and fracture a femur. Because a dust cloud will accompany any dry snow avalanche to some degree, it is difficult for observers to be certain that what is seen is a true airborne powder snow avalanche, with most of the snow carried in turbulent suspension. Also, airborne powder avalanches leave little or no detectable debris and so, unless directly observed, they may escape detection.

If the mass of 'new' snow survives the initial loss of cohesion without avalanching, metamorphism will continue, but will begin to have a stabilising effect, because the transfer of material from convexities will tend to build up a network of bonds – necks – between adjacent snow grains. This process is called **sintering** (Fig. 2.12).

If the snow is subjected to extensive metamorphism, the end product will be a strong structure of **firn** snow where all the grains are interlocked or sintered. Firn snow is the normal stable snow of Alpine regions, but is less common in Britain because of the greater degree of melting and re-freezing that is likely to occur as the dominant process. The speed with which metamorphism proceeds depends on temperature; near 0°C it is rapid; at -40°C it ceases altogether. This means that falls of 'new' snow may constitute a threat of loose snow avalanches for long periods when the temperature is very low. This is a more common problem in the greater ranges.

Fig. 2.10 A powder snow avalanche from the steep cliffs of Beinn Bhan, Applecross

Chris Forrest

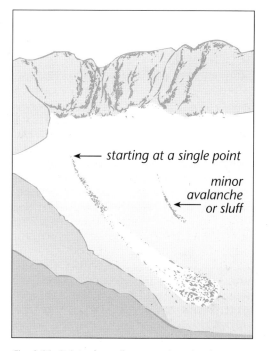

Fig. 2.11 Point release (loose snow) avalanches

← *starting at a single point*

minor avalanche or sluff ←

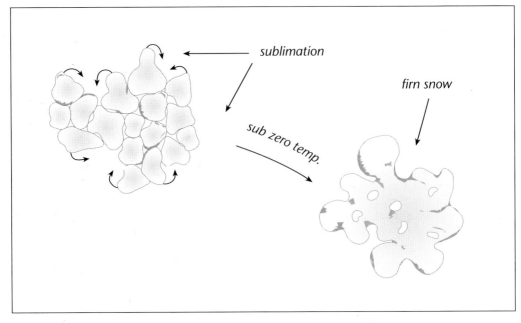

Fig. 2.12 Sintering

Faceting (Kinetic Growth)

This process of metamorphism affects all snowpacks not subject to melting and one of the driving forces behind the process is the presence of a temperature gradient in the snowpack.

In any snowpack in temperate regions, the insulating effect of snow retains ground heat to keep the ground surface at, or very near, 0°C, allowing many plants to survive the winter. The snow temperature at surface may be much lower, and so a temperature gradient will exist through the snowpack. Investigating temperatures at different heights in a snowpit will allow the temperature gradient to be plotted. If the gradient were uniform (it rarely is) a snowpack 50cm in depth with a surface temperature of -10°C would have a gradient of 20°C per metre – a strong gradient (Fig. 2.14).

If the temperature gradient is a strong one, greater than 10°C per metre, a second metamorphic process called **kinetic growth** will become dominant. Kinetic growth is synonymous with the older terms temperature gradient metamorphism, or constructive metamorphism,

and can lead to the development of some very poorly bonded or fragile crystals such as **facets** and **depth hoar** (Fig. 2.13).

The strongest gradients (i.e. the maximum rate of temperature change with depth) occur when low air temperatures are in conjunction with shallow snowpacks. When these conditions prevail for a time, especially if the snowpack is unconsolidated, there is a vertical migration of water vapour through the snowpack – vapour flux – and a particular stepped and faceted kind of crystal begins to be built up. This process is at a maximum close to 0°C.

These crystals are called kinetic growth forms or facets and under the hand lens they have a distinctive faceted appearance reminiscent of imitation glass 'gemstones'. If deciding whether you are looking at facets or rounds – look for the angles. Rounds, as might be expected, do not have any.

If the strong temperature gradient persists, large, fragile crystals marked with ladder like striations can develop. The most developed forms of these crystals are hollow, fragile cup-crystals. When facets begin to show striations they are usually described as depth hoar. The gradient of 10°C/m or 1°C/10cm only has to be established at a particular level in the snowpack for kinetic growth to occur – it is not necessary for the gradient to be established across the entire depth.

When technical examinations of snowpits are made, temperature gradients can be plotted by measuring temperatures every 10cm through the snowpack. Considerable variations in gradient with depth can be seen in many snowpacks, together with a diurnal variation which extends down to a level in the snowpack where it is no longer affected by the daily variation of daytime and night-time surface temperatures.

Kinetic growth forms include: **facets** or **'sugar snow'**, **ladders**, **cup crystals**, **crevasse hoar** and **surface hoar**. In the past, facets or kinetic growth forms have also been called temperature gradient grains. All the forms commonly display

Météo France/Centre d' Etude de la Neige

Fig. 2.13 A laboratory photograph of depth hoar showing the distinctive striations or 'steps'

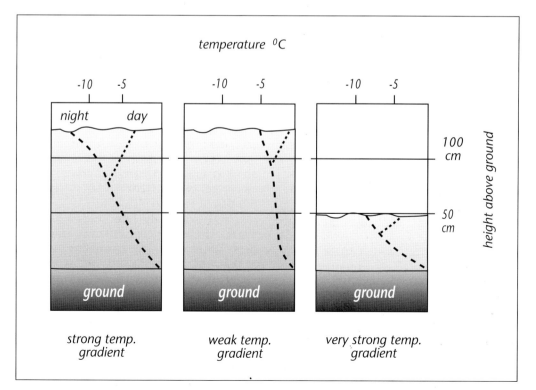

Fig. 2.14 Temperature gradients

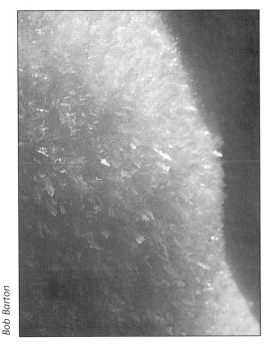

Bob Barton

Fig. 2.15 A deposit of fragile surface hoar. Such deposits usually only persist on shaded slopes or in the snowpack

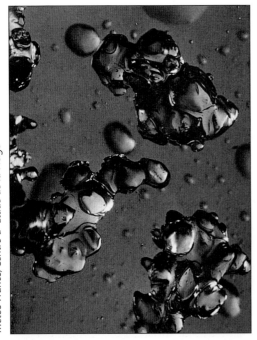

Météo France/Centre d' Etude de la Neige

Fig. 2.16 When a thaw ensues, all snow crystals will eventually become ice grains surrounded by a film of liquid water

some or all of the following features:

- Angular or faceted form.
- Striated or stepped surfaces.
- Fragility.
- Poor bonding to each other and adjoining layers.
- Development in the snowpack, or in the case of surface hoar, on the snowpack, rather than being a direct result of precipitation – they never fall straight out of the sky.

The combination of fragility, poor bonding and hidden formation within the snowpack can build a dangerous layer that forms the critical weakness that will ultimately release a slab avalanche. Typically the formation of this layer occurs in shallow early season snowpacks during sustained cold spells. In North America and the Alps the formation of such a layer has often produced lethal avalanche conditions, particularly when ever increasing loading from repeated snowfall triggers a **climax avalanche** by catastrophic failure of the dangerous layer. Until recently, it was thought that with the exception of surface hoar, kinetic growth forms did not play a significant part in Scottish avalanches. However, systematic observation, particularly of shallow snowpacks, has shown facets to be widespread and other forms not infrequent. Several Scottish avalanches, including one on Bidean nam Bian involving a large party and a fatal one in the Red Burn on Ben Nevis, have released on layers of facets developed within the snowpack.

However these forms are less frequent than in more continental climates, probably because: a) the typical Scottish winter involves too many rapid fluctuations of temperature to allow a stable gradient to be established, b) we rarely experience the prolonged, hard frosts which would lead to a very strong temperature gradient, c) most snowfalls in the Scottish mountains are windpacked and such compact slabs may not allow the easy migration of water vapour that encourages kinetic growth forms.

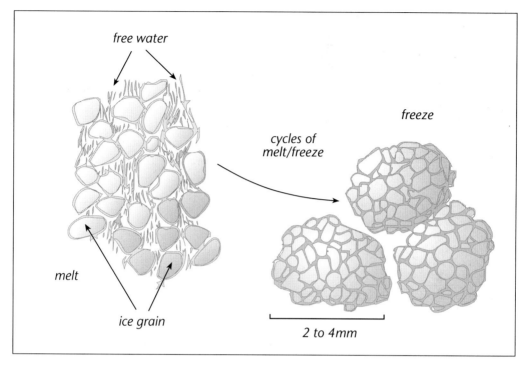

Fig. 2.17 Melt freeze cycles

However, it is also sometimes observed that a barrier to vapour migration can promote their formation!

Surface hoar – this forms from moist air on still, cold nights and is the solid equivalent of dew. It is deposited on the snow surface as brittle, erect plates, sometimes several centimetres across. These provide delightful skiing, but if a subsequent snowfall buries them, the fragile plates form a very weak foundation, which can be very hard to detect in the snowpack. They quickly perish in the sun and so northerly aspects and shaded forest glades are the places where surface hoar endures and correspondingly, the most likely places for the hazard of buried surface hoar to occur (Fig. 2.15).

The striations that can be seen on the plates of surface hoar give away their family connection to depth hoar and their shared history of being formed in a strong temperature gradient. On clear nights, radiation to outer space can cool the snow surface so strongly that a temperature gradient of 20°C/cm (equivalent to 200°C/m) can be established, 200 times stronger than the 'critical' gradient within the snowpack of 10°C/m. It is therefore not surprising that different crystal forms result.

Digging regular snowpits enables you to spot the presence of buried depth hoar or the formation of facets in the snowpack.

Melt-Freeze (Melt-Freeze Metamorphism)

Both rounding and faceting (dry snow metamorphism and kinetic growth) are processes which occur in the absence of any melting in the snowpack. If a cycle of melting and re–freezing affects the snow, then the dominant process is called **melt-freeze metamorphism**.

In thaw conditions practically all snow crystals are reduced to rounded ice grains surrounded by a film of liquid water (Fig. 2.16). A subsequent freeze will cement these grains together into a very strong structure, and a cycle of melting and

Bob Barton

Fig. 2.18 A small spontaneous slab avalanche released from the scarp slope of an actively forming cornice

freezing will produce large, coarse melt-freeze grains (Fig. 2.17).

During the melting phase each grain becomes lubricated by a film of water and in heavy thaws the snow forms a slurry which can lead to wet, dense, loose snow avalanches. Because of the density of the snow these avalanches are very destructive particularly if channelled, but their likelihood is often clearly indicated by the very wet nature of the snow underfoot. Such an avalanche, where a heavy thaw acted on a recent new snowfall, led to the serious avalanche in *Great Gully*, Buachaille Etive Mor, during February 1970. In March 1976, a climber sustained multiple injuries when a wet snow avalanche carried him 230 metres out of *Central Gully*, Bidean nam Bian, also in Glen Coe.

The greatest melting is produced by warm, wet winds and by rainfall percolating the snow. Solar heating becomes progressively more important as winter changes into spring and the sun moves higher in the sky.

When freezing affects a wet snowpack

a strong, rigid material ideal for crampons and ice axes is formed. Most British climbers would call this **névé**, although properly speaking that term is synonymous with firn snow. The mechanism of melting and re-freezing is a most important one for stabilising the snowpack in Scotland during winter and the 'freeze' phase of the cycle gives our best winter climbing conditions. In high Alpine regions, which lack our variable climate, dry snow metamorphism is the major stabilising influence leading to the formation of firn snow and, ultimately, glacier ice.

Broken Crystals

Wind transport of snow is probably the most important factor influencing avalanches in Scotland.

Winds in excess of about 20mph will cause appreciable damage to the new snow crystals, both by turbulence in the air and by trundling them along the ground – **saltation**. It is instructive to observe the variability of wind direction and speed that occurs across mountain terrain, even in steady winds and to relate this to the deposition of drifting snow. The carrying capacity of a wind is largely dependent on its speed, possibly by a third power relationship, so that a doubling of wind speed could result in a eightfold increase in the amount of snow carried in a given volume of air. As a result, broken crystals tend to be dumped in areas where the wind is decelerating. These areas become **accumulation zones** and are the sort of places where a person might try to seek shelter from the full force of the wind. They include lee slopes, corries and minor hollows. When a snow bearing wind blows across a slope the process is called **cross-loading** with deposition occurring in streambeds or on the leeward side of ridges (Fig. 2.19).

The corresponding areas exposed to the full power of the wind, particularly where it is accelerating, are **erosion zones** where snow can be stripped away and re-transported. A slope could be an accumulation zone with north-east winds, but an erosion zone with south-west winds. These wind shifts may occur within a couple of hours and cause a dramatic re-distribution of snow cover.

When deposited in an accumulation zone, the pulverised nature of broken crystals allows them to weld into a compact, cohesive slab of **windslab**. Simpler snow crystals such as needles can pack in a similar way without being extensively broken.

Windslab is much denser than new snow and fractures into blocks when broken. Its chalky, unreflective surface comes from the wind pulverising the reflective surfaces of the new snow crystals. The surface is sometimes gently rippled and the snow can squeak when walked on, as the crystals rub together, and there is little internal structure. Windslab has a rather homogenous, felt-like appearance.

Windslab exists in a wide range of hardnesses which are related to the wind speed. In light winds a very soft slab forms, while higher winds will usually produce a more rigid and denser slab. The continuous spectrum of hardnesses is arbitrarily divided into **soft slab** and **hard slab**, determined by whether or not the surface can support a person on foot. It would be quite possible to sink thigh deep into a very soft slab and to require crampons for hard slab.

A deposition rate of 3cm of new snow per hour is considered dangerously high, but it is common for drifting to deposit windslab at an even greater rate. This can lead to highly dangerous conditions in an accumulation zone, not just because of the sheer quantity of slab formed, but also because *newly and rapidly deposited windslabs seem to be particularly unstable.*

There is some evidence that winds over 65mph create such widespread turbulence that windslab is dissipated as fast as it is formed, except in sheltered pockets. However, it would be unwise to rely upon this to indicate 'safe' conditions.

It is now thought that when snow is in turbulent suspension in the atmosphere, it actually 'disappears' by the process of

Bob Barton

Fig. 2.19 Snowfall on a moraine ridge showing erosion on the windward (right-hand) side and deposition of windslab on the leeward (left-hand) side

Malcolm Creasey

Fig. 2.20 Raised footprints – evidence of substantial erosion and re-deposition

sublimation and becomes atmospheric water vapour. The consequence of this is that most of the snow that drifts to form windslab travels close to the surface, perhaps mainly up to waist height.

Windslab is subject to the processes of **metamorphism** in a similar way to new snow. Dry snow metamorphism will tend to increase the strength and rigidity of soft slabs, and may increase their adhesion to the layers of snow beneath. The progress of kinetic growth will be accompanied by settling, but to a lesser degree than occurs with new snow, since the initial soft slab has a much greater density than new snow. Hard slab is similarly affected, but with an even less pronounced settling. The relatively dense snowpack of windslab restricts the free movement of water vapour and can therefore inhibit the development of facets.

The release of free water in the snowpack by a thaw will reduce the strength of the windslab and may loosen its adhesion to lower layers of snow. This will be looked at in more detail in the section

on slab avalanches later in this chapter.

A freeze following a thaw will strengthen the slab and improve its adhesion to any lower layers, and this is probably the main factor limiting the danger from slab avalanches in Scotland.

Wind Erosion

In non-thawing conditions, existing snowpacks in exposed locations can be eroded by the wind. The broken crystals produced will be carried and re-deposited as windslab in an accumulation zone. Evidence of this erosion includes blowing spindrift, wind carved ridges in the erosion zone called **sastrugi** and raised footprints and ski-tracks, where the compacted snow in a track has been able to resist the eroding wind, but the surrounding snow has not (Fig. 2.20). When any of these signs are visible it is safe to assume that the eroded snow has been deposited as windslab in nearby accumulation zones.

As long as the temperature remains below zero, a particular snowfall may be deposited, eroded and re-deposited elsewhere a number of times. This means that windslab may be built up on a site *in the complete absence of a fresh snowfall.*

After a period of melt-freeze, the coarse, icy melt-freeze grains are much more resistant to erosion and widespread wind transport is then unlikely. Thus, 45mph winds at 900m would normally cause dramatic drifting if acting on an existing cold snowpack of new snow or partially broken crystals, but would have a negligible effect on an icy pack.

Metamorphism of Rimed Crystals

Graupel pellets will often collect at the foot of gullies or hollows, but they can also be incorporated in the snowpack as a layer. Because of their near spherical form, they are thermodynamically stable and very resistant to all types of metamorphism. Graupel pellets can exist in the snowpack for weeks without any major change, and only a major melt-freeze episode will bind them firmly. These layers of unconsolidated, rimed crystals are common in promoting the release of Scottish slab avalanches.

Snowpack Structure

If a mountain, heavily loaded with wind-slab on its southerly slopes, is subjected to a period when the freezing level rises to 2000m with rain and strong south-westerly winds, then considerable thawing will produce a wet snowpack, and with it a danger of wet snow avalanches. If, however, very cold easterly winds had prevailed instead, then the windslab hazard could be expected to have shifted from the southerly to the more western slopes.

But these scenarios only look at the behaviour of a more or less uniform mass of snow. Windslab is not a threatening phenomenon in itself. So before it or any other type of snow becomes a slab avalanche, several other contributory factors must be present simultaneously.

Broadly speaking these will relate to:

- The accumulation of snow.
- The terrain.
- Weak layers in the snow.
- The avalanche trigger.

Slab Avalanches

A slab avalanche occurs when an entire plate of snow detaches from the surrounding snowpack. This slab can vary from a few metres to hundreds of metres across and from 10cm to 10m in depth. It will almost always rapidly break up into a jigsaw of smaller blocks, even though at the moment of release it breaks away as a single piece (Fig. 2.21). Slab avalanches are the number one killer in UK avalanches, and in most cases they are triggered by the victims themselves.

For slab avalanches, one of the most important features is the layering of the snowpack. In a continental climate, this stratification may reflect a whole season's weather history, with an identifiable layer for each snowfall, but in Scotland it is fairly common for a major thaw to merge together all but the most distinctive layers into a more or less uniform mass. The influence of layering and other contributory factors is best examined in

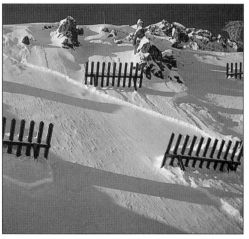

Bob Barton

Fig. 2.21 A shallow slab triggered by a skier at an Alpine resort. Note the clean fracture lines of the crown wall and the bed surface

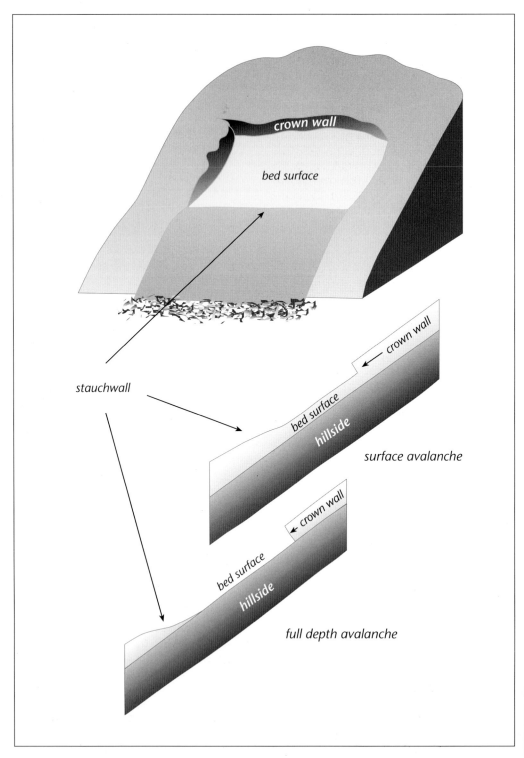

Fig. 2.22 Slab avalanches

the context of the basic mechanics of slab avalanche release.

In simple terms a slab will release when the forces pulling it down the slope, mainly gravity, exceed the strength of the anchors keeping it in place. When gravity finally overcomes the anchors, the slab will fracture underneath, across its top and along its sides. Of these fracture locations, the most useful to consider are those at the **bed surface** and the **crown wall** (Fig. 2.22).

When a slab releases, the component of the weight (W) acting down the slope exceeds the resistance (R), anchoring the slab to its surroundings. R is the sum of various components but, because it has much the greatest area, the most important factor is usually the adhesion between a slab and the snow or ground beneath it; the bed surface. For release to occur the crystalline bonds that join the slab to its foundation must be broken and the frictional resistance against sliding on the bed surface must be overcome (Fig. 2.23). On occasions the weak layer will fail, but the frictional resistance is not overcome. Someone on the slope is likely to be aware of a 'collapse' or 'whumpf' and a narrow escape!

The **bed surface** is most commonly found between the slab and a lower layer of snow (surface avalanche), but it can occur at the ground surface (full depth avalanche). The bed surface makes the greatest contribution (95% or more) to the strength of the anchors holding the slab in place, and so failure at the bed surface is very likely to result in a slab avalanche release. Indeed, it is usually the immediate precursor of any such avalanche.

The **crown wall** is almost always perpendicular to the bed surface, and is usually arched across the slope. The presence of such a break-off wall is the definitive feature of slab avalanches, since the debris may be so broken as to contain no recognisable blocks. The fracture across the lower edge of the slab usually leaves an indefinite, ledge-like wall. This is sometimes called the **stauchwall**.

The crown wall fracture is a result of tension failure of the snow. The bed surface

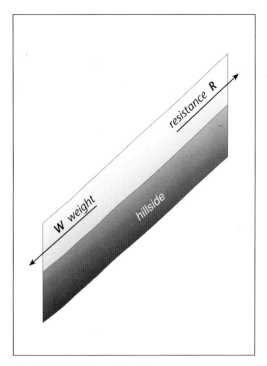

Fig. 2.23 Equilibrium of a slab

fracture is a result of shear failure in the snow, or at its point of attachment to the ground. Compression failure is also seen, under the feet in footprints, but also when a fragile under-layer collapses through being overloaded by additional weight. Field tests such as the shovel shear and the rutschblock, (see Chapter III), examine shear failure of the snow. It is a peculiarity of slab avalanches that immediately after a slab has released, the tension in the slope is relieved and the slope above the crown wall is usually stable.

Accumulation

The likelihood of an avalanche occurring is closely related to the rate of snow accumulation and the thickness to which slabs are built up. If all other things could be kept equal, a deep layer of windslab would be much more likely to avalanche than a shallow one, since the increased weight would put a much greater strain on the anchors of the slab.

Fig. 2.24 represents two points on

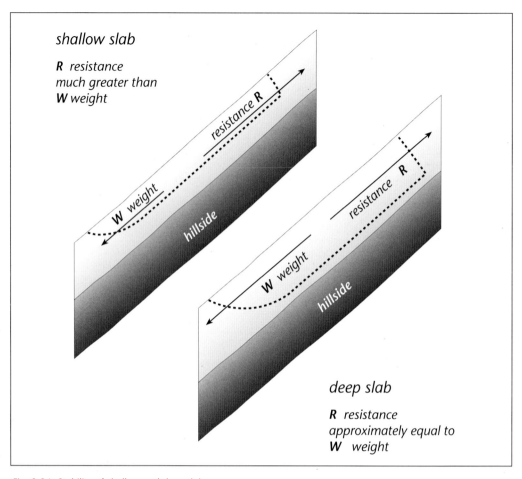

Fig. 2.24 Stability of shallow and deep slabs

a slope, differing only in snow depth. In (a) the weight (W) of the shallow slab is much less than the possible resistance (R). The slab is stable unless a large additional load is introduced.

In (b) the weight of the deep slab is now greater and W is approximately equal to R. The slab is unstable, and is poised on a hair-trigger. Any increase in W by a further build-up of snow, or a decrease in R by a weakening of the slab's anchors, will release an avalanche.

This is, of course, an over-simplification of a complex state of affairs, but it leads to a conclusion that is borne out by the available statistics. *Almost all large, dry slab-avalanches follow a period of heavy snowfall or considerable drifting*, when thick windslabs have been built up.

When a number of parties are in the mountains at the same time as a high hazard exists in the snowpack, then the four main contributory factors necessary for avalanches can easily come together at different sites. This is particularly well seen in the records of avalanche 'epidemics', such as the one of January 21, 1978, where three separate avalanche accidents followed a period of heavy snowfall and drifting (see Appendix III), or the incidents of March 1995 described in Chapter VIII.

The thickness of a slab also influences the severity of any resulting avalanche. Slabs shallower than 15cm might not be considered to present a great hazard, but the funnelling effect of gullies and the local variations in slab thickness can make this judgement very unreliable. *High rates of deposition of windslab seem to produce slabs which are particularly unstable, especially when newly formed.* Furthermore, it requires very little moving snow to knock over a climber or a skier.

Terrain

Slab avalanches most commonly start on slopes of an inclination between 30° and 45°, with the maximum occurrence at about 37°. This is much steeper than most commonly skied slopes, but is just the type of terrain that a winter mountaineer will often frequent. On slopes steeper than 45°, there is insufficient snow accumulation for very large avalanches, but even a small

avalanche on such terrain can knock down a climber or skier and cause a very serious fall. It is instructive to use a clinometer to measure the angle of slopes that have previously been estimated, as it is common for people to overestimate the angle of a snowslope by 10° or 15°. It should be noted that a person on relatively easy-angled terrain can trigger a dangerous avalanche on steeper terrain above – you must see the whole picture.

A mass of snow is not absolutely rigid, but will deform slightly under its own weight. On a uniform slope the tension tends to increase with height, while on an undulating slope regions of tension and compression occur at convexities and concavities respectively (Fig. 2.25).

Regions where the snow surface is

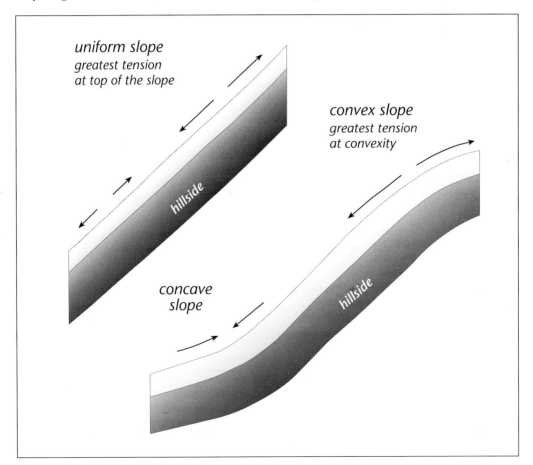

Fig. 2.25 Stability of concave and convex slopes

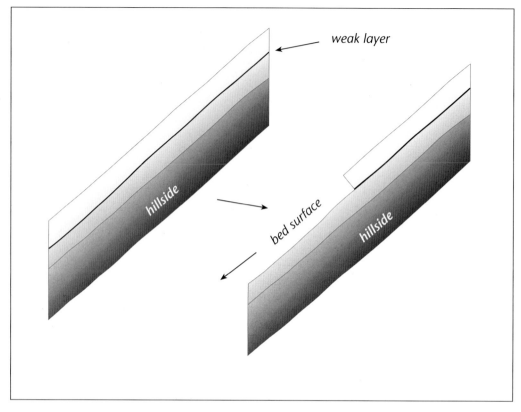

Fig. 2.26 Action of a weak layer

under tension are more likely to develop the transverse fractures that can lead to the crown wall fracture of a slab avalanche. It is common for such fractures to occur in or just below the tension zone associated with a convexity. These are often called 'zipper' fractures and commonly follow the tracks of a skier or someone on foot.

A hard, smooth layer forms an ideal bed surface for a slab avalanche. Full depth avalanches often run on smooth rock slabs, or flattened long grass; partial depth ones on layers of hard icy snow. The first snowfall of a season will often be firmly anchored to an angular boulder-field, but there are isolated reports of avalanches in these circumstances, possibly due to a layer of ice concealing the irregularity of the boulders beneath. In any case, once the first snowfall has masked the boulders they offer little further anchorage to the snowpack above.

Weak Layers

When a slab avalanche has occurred, one of the remarkable features is often the flatness and regularity of the bed surface. This suggests that the fracture, a shear failure, has taken place at a definite level in the snowpack. In fact, the bed surface can often be shown to correspond to a definite weak layer in the snowpack, or a distinct lack of adhesion between adjacent layers (Fig. 2.26).

Sometimes the weak layer is a stratum of fragile or unconsolidated crystals in the snowpack. A layer of ball-bearing like graupel or fragile cup crystals are clear examples and a similar problem is caused when crystals of surface hoar are buried. A spate of avalanches in the Cairngorms in December 1977 ran on a base of buried surface hoar.

Much of the practical defence of the mountaineer against avalanches rests on attempts to *identify the weakest layer in the snowpack.*

If a rigid hard slab is laid down over much softer snow, the snow will settle under the influence of dry snow metamorphism, and leave the hard slab poised over a hollow empty layer (Fig. 2.28). This is a very dangerous state of affairs. Any major difference of hardness, wetness or crystal size between adjacent layers often indicates a poor adhesion between these layers, for example, a new slab laid over a hard, icy base, will rarely adhere satisfactorily (Fig. 2.27). In thaw conditions, ice layers collect the melt-water and lubricate the release of the slab above.

This is most common in full depth wet snow avalanches, where melt-water lubricates the bed surface on a rock slab.

Such is the mechanism of the full depth wet slab that often occurs on the Great Slab of Coire an Lochain in the Cairngorms during the spring thaw (Figs. 2.29, 2.30 & 2.31).

Tom Prentice

Fig. 2.27 Surface snow breaking away from an icy underlayer at the top of Point Five Gully, Ben Nevis. A larger release threatens!

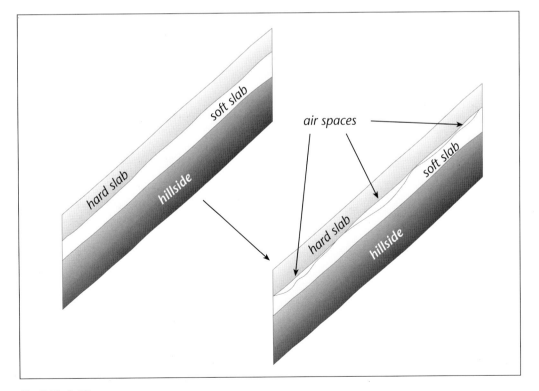

Fig. 2.28 Settling

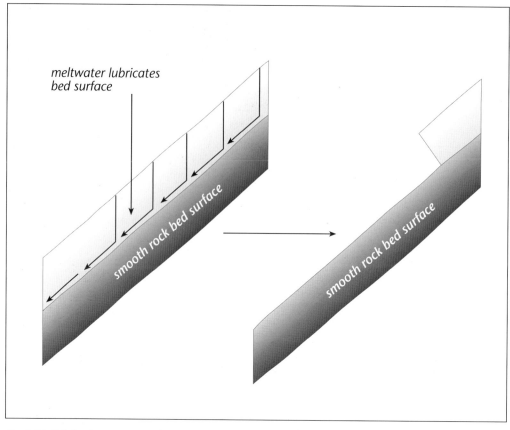

Fig. 2.29 Full depth wet snow avalanche

Often no clear discontinuity is seen in the snowpack, but blocks will fracture on a definite line. This probably corresponds to

Bob Barton

Fig. 2.30 The debris of the Great Slab avalanche can run out across bare ground and into the lochan itself

a change in snowfall intensity, wind direction or temperature. Storms that start warm and become colder are likely to produce more stable slabs than those that start cold and become warmer, since in the latter case, cold brittle crystals, which do not readily adhere to the lower snow layers, are overloaded by more compact, denser snow. The identification of the weakest layers in the snow is examined in more detail in Chapter III.

Trigger

The factor which can be identified as the trigger of a slab avalanche is the increase in load, or decrease in resistance, that breaks the bonds between the slab and the main slope (Fig. 2.32).

Internal triggering through the reduction of resistance (R), can be caused

Fig. 2.31 The regular full depth wet snow avalanche in Coire an Lochain, Cairngorms. Note the smooth bed surface of the Great Slab. Snow depth high on the slab can be four metres or more

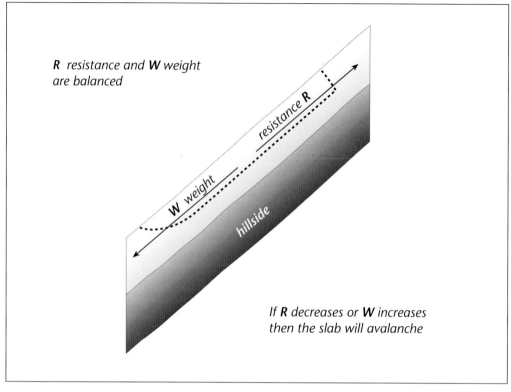

R resistance and *W* weight are balanced

resistance *R*

W weight

hillside

If *R* decreases or *W* increases then the slab will avalanche

Fig. 2.32 Triggering

by the collapse of a layer of fragile crystals, or the destruction of the cohesion of the lowest layers of a slab by melt-water. Any rise in temperature will normally weaken the anchors of a slab, even if melting does not occur. Occasionally in alpine regions the release of avalanches can be seen to coincide with the sun leaving a slope in the evening. This is probably a result of contraction due to sudden cooling, leading to an increase in the tension in the snowpack.

External triggers usually involve an increase in the loading through increased weight (W) on the slab. Possible triggers include the weight of extra snow or rain, a cornice collapse, or the weight of a climber or skier.

The European Avalanche Hazard Scale recognises 'high additional load' as a strongly negative influence on snow stability and there is no doubt that *large parties apply a very considerable additional load to the anchors of a slab.* Ten people plus

equipment can easily weigh a tonne, and a number of the incidents recorded in Appendix III have involved large parties.

The shock waves associated with explosives or sonic booms can initiate fractures, but stories of the similar effect of a loud shout are likely to be apocryphal. Most slab avalanches that cause injury are triggered by their victims' disturbance of the slope.

A Case History

The four critical factors contributing to a slab avalanche and the main questions they raise are:

- Accumulation – is there sufficient snow on the slope?
- Terrain – is the slope steep enough? Is there a convexity?
- Weak layer – is a weak layer present in the snowpack?
- Trigger – are you going to go on to the slope?

It is worthwhile to consider these factors and the questions they raise in the context of an actual incident in the Cairngorms in 1975.

Towards the end of March that year an Arctic airstream influenced Scotland, with widespread snowfall. March 30 was a weekend and a Bank Holiday and two climbers were in Coire an Lochain. As they crossed the upper part of the Great Slab, aiming for a climb in the vicinity of *The Vent*, they were caught in a large slab avalanche perhaps 200m wide and to a maximum height of 1.5m at the crown wall. They were carried about 180m to just above the lochan and were lucky to escape with relatively minor leg injuries (Figs. 2.33 & 2.34).

The most notable features of the weather in the five days leading up to the avalanche were: (a) consistent sub-zero temperatures above an altitude of 1000m, (b) considerable precipitation (as snow) and winds 17 to 30 mph (excluding gusts) at 1000m, varying between the north-east and north-west quadrants.

Bob Barton

Fig. 2.33 At the crown wall of the 30 March 1975 avalanche

Bob Barton

Fig. 2.34 The site of the windslab avalanche of 30 March 1975 on the Great Slab, taken the following day. When an avalanche has occurred the remaining slope above the crown wall is usually secure

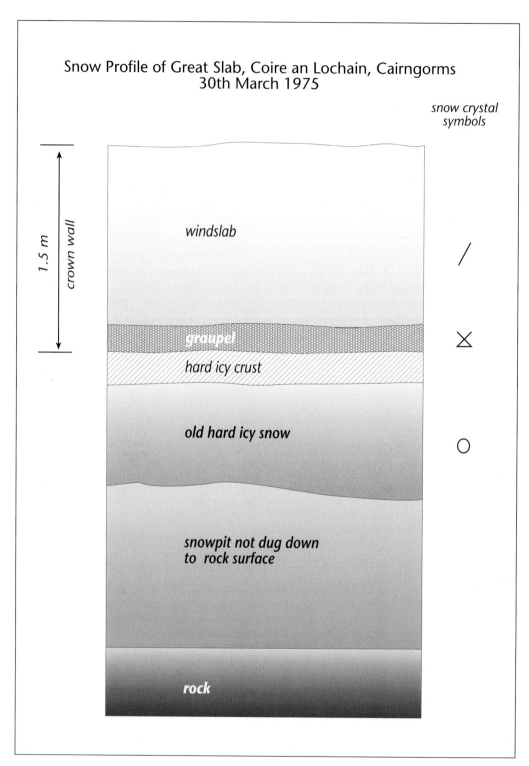

Snow Profile of Great Slab, Coire an Lochain, Cairngorms
30th March 1975

*snow crystal
symbols*

1.5 m   *crown wall*

windslab

/

graupel

×

hard icy crust

old hard icy snow

○

snowpit not dug down
to rock surface

rock

Fig. 2.35

The incident can be analysed by considering the four factors listed above: accumulation, terrain, weak layer and trigger.

Accumulation – Coire an Lochain is situated on the edge of the Cairngorm plateau – an ideal collecting area for snow which can then drift into the corrie to produce the very deep slabs observed in this case.

There had been considerable snowfall in the preceding week and the combination of consistently low temperatures and generally northerly winds of 17 to 30mph indicated considerable drifting and a widespread build up of windslab. One would expect this to be most widespread on south-west and south-east slopes, but this prediction ignores local variations in wind direction. Evidently, many slopes were being loaded with windslab, as the avalanche was on a north-west facing slope (GR 984027), and indeed, observers had reported widespread avalanche hazard during the preceding days. Cold fronts had resulted in the deposition of quantities of graupel.

Terrain – The Great Slab is a large, uniform rock slab set at 30° to 35°, within the range where large avalanches commonly occur.

Weak layers – The cold weather in the last week of March had been preceded by a warmer, wetter spell. On March 21 the freezing level was above 1700m, with rain and high winds, so all existing snowpacks would be subject to a thaw. The subsequent freeze would produce a hard, icy snowpack. This would provide a perfect bed surface for a slab avalanche to slide on.

An examination of the crown wall surface and the layers beneath on the day after the avalanche revealed the section shown in Figs. 2.35 & 2.36. The icy bed surface was covered in a 1cm thick layer of very fragile snow pellets (probably graupel). The entire slab was supported on this fragile underlayer. The very deep windslab above was almost uniform, with a slight change of texture at half

Bob Barton

Fig. 2.36 A profile of the snow at the crown wall. This is summarised in Fig. 2.35

height. This suggests that just one or two snowfalls or bouts of drifting laid down the windslab.

Trigger – The continued build-up of windslab would be overloading the weak layers beneath. Over the preceding days the slab would have been subjected to increasing tension as the entire mass tended to creep downhill under the force of gravity. The climbers traversing onto the slope provided the final trigger. The fracture at the crown wall surface crossed their tracks.

This was an unusually clear-cut case, where all the contributory factors seemed to point toward a high avalanche hazard. This was underlined by the fact that later on the same day, a party of skiers was avalanched near the top of the March Burn above the Pools of Dee in the Lairig Ghru, on a west-facing slope. It would be reasonable to assume that the features of the snowpack were similar in the two

Fig. 2.37 A mature cornice on the East Face of Aonach Mor. This would have been very insecure until stabilised by a cycle of melt and re-freeze. Cornice collapse has frequently troubled climbers here

Graham Moss

instances. The second party also noted a sudden increase in temperature, shortly before the avalanche occurred. This could reduce the strength of the anchors of the slab, and provide further encouragement for it to avalanche. This latter incident is described in more detail in Chapter V.

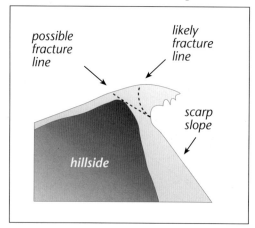

possible fracture line

likely fracture line

scarp slope

hillside

Fig. 2.38 Cornice fracture

Cornices

Wind speeds of 10 to 55 mph, blowing over a ridge or a crag edge, generate a kind of cylindrical eddy on the lee slope. If the wind is carrying broken crystals, the circular motion of the air in the eddy will deposit the crystals as windslab. However, this windslab will not take the form of a plane surface, but that of an exquisite, shell-like cornice (Fig. 2.37).

Just below the eddy, snow which we would recognise as windslab will be deposited as a plane surface, to form what is called the **scarp slope**. This scarp slope is often soft slab and is usually deposited at an angle of about 52° (Fig. 2.39). It is almost always found in association with a freshly formed cornice.

Cornices can overhang as much as 10m and are intrinsically unstable. The larger the overhang and the steeper the slope beneath, the greater the hazard. They are most dangerous when freshly formed or when subject to heavy thaw conditions. In these conditions it can be very risky to venture into a gully with a cornice above.

Avoiding a cornice to one side is always advisable, but if a frontal assault is necessary, the narrowest point should be crossed, and a sound belay taken with the belayer protected from the potential debris fall line, should the cornice collapse. One of the authors witnessed a dramatic example of cornice instability when a well intentioned climber on the plateau above the cliffs of Coire an Lochan, attempted to assist a leader approaching the top of *Right Branch Y Gully* by stamping a breach in the narrowest part of the large cornice.

Unfortunately, the entire cornice immediately collapsed, sweeping away the leader in a flurry of snow blocks. That he was held successfully by his second and unharmed, was a tribute to good belaying and the effectiveness of a Deadman snow anchor. That he dusted himself off and climbed up again to surmount the now innocuous cornice is a tribute to a certain *sangfroid*. Tunnelling is aesthetic but rarely advisable. In February 1979, five climbers were carried down *Number Five Gully* on Ben Nevis, when the cornice collapsed while being tunnelled.

Cornice collapse, or falls from the rotten snow of a cornice, cause many mountain accidents. One of the most insidious cases can be when drifting snow rapidly builds up a dangerous cornice and scarp slope on the last 30m of an otherwise unaffected slope.

Another hidden hazard is caused when a cornice begins to sag under its own weight. This builds tensions within the snow and may cause the fracture line to be further back from the edge than would be expected from the configuration of the underlying ground (Fig. 2.38). It is wise to give a cornice a wide berth on the wind-ward (eroded) side to avoid this possibility.

It is worth mentioning that due to drifting snow, visibility in the vicinity of an actively forming cornice is often poor. This makes it easy inadvertently to wander into the danger zone on the upper surface of the cornice. If terrain close to cornices cannot be avoided in poor visibility, then very careful navigation and orientation are necessary. It may be wise to have the navigator operating 20m ahead of the rest of the party with the protection of a rope. Everyone else must be briefed to avoid moving from the navigator's tracks and certainly not in the direction of the cornice. Although uncommon, double cornices spectacularly formed on either side of a narrow ridge, present challenging choices to the route finder.

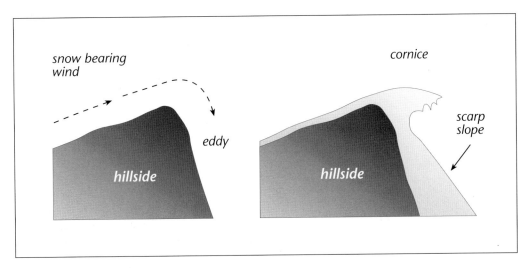

Fig. 2.39 Cornice formation

Nigel Shepherd

Fig. 3.1 Sticking to ridges is one way of reducing exposure to avalanche hazard

III Improving the Odds

"Remember, the avalanche does not know you are an expert"

André Roch

Avalanche Awareness

Just as it is likely to prove ineffective to examine the map only when lost, it is too late to start thinking about avalanches only when confronted by a threatening slope. Sound decision making can only spring from a careful consideration of many factors. These include:

- Weather history
- Current weather
- Avalanche forecasts and observations
- Recent avalanche activity
- Slope angle
- Slope aspect
- Ground surface
- Runout
- Local observations of snow cover
- Existence of terrain traps
- Snowpit analysis
- Nature and state of party
- Time of day
- 'Sixth sense'

This final factor recognises that the skilled mountaineer can build up an intuitive awareness of avalanche hazard. This integrates many of the above factors into a personal 'expert system'. Ignore its messages at your peril! Every time you go on the hill in winter you should look closely at the snowpack. Pick up a sample and crumble it in your hand. Note how it varies with altitude and aspect, how it behaves underfoot, whether it is cold or warm (dry or wet), if any recent avalanche activity is to be seen, whether any weak layers are present, whether conditions are stabilising or deteriorating. This way you are educating your skills of judgement to apply to future snowpacks. However, this process of judgement should start before you leave home.

By the time you set foot on the snow you should have made a pretty good prediction of what conditions will be like, what level of hazard exists and where it is likely to be located. Your field observations modify and update this prediction and apply it to the specific case.

It is easier than it has ever been to make a reasonable prediction of snow conditions on the hill. Not only can this alert you to the possibility of avalanches, but it can also allow you to guess where the best climbing or skiing conditions will be found. It has always been possible to make this prediction from day to day observation of the patterns of snowfall coupled with wind and temperature over the previous days or weeks, but today, modern communications technology and the establishment of SAIS (Scottish Avalanche Information Service), have opened up valuable sources of data. SAIS's history and work are described in more detail in Chapter VII.

Primary Prediction

If planning a trip to the mountains, the starting point is the current SAIS report and forecast for your intended area. Combine these with regional weather forecasts and observations and you should have a good understanding of the current snowpack and how it might change.

The SAIS website (see Appendix V) is useful for accessing SAIS forecasts and various standard sources of weather information. Other sites provide real time weather observations from Cairn Gorm summit and reports on current climbing conditions. More traditional sources of data such as climbing guidebooks may give some information about avalanches (the Scottish Mountaineering Club's *Ben Nevis*

Bob Barton

Fig. 3.2   Prime avalanche conditions on Ben Nevis as indicated by the large quantity of snow, evident windslab and extensive cornice development. The climb here, Number Two Gully Buttress, is a reasonable choice, but avalanche hazard is widespread

guide, for instance warns about the Castle gullies) and an examination of the map, especially a 1:25000 or 1:10000 sheet, gives the aspect and inclination of slopes.

At 1:25000 scale and with contours at 10 metre intervals (as on Ordnance Survey maps) a contour spacing of 0.5mm. represents an inclination of about 37°, the prime angle for large slab avalanches.

Having collected data, the next task is one of interpretation.

Snowfall

Heavy snowfall is a likely hazard, both in itself and by overloading existing weak layers in the snowpack. Snowfall at 1000m is likely to be about twice that recorded at sea level because of orographic lifting of the airstream by the mountain mass, a process which induces precipitation. Of course, snow precipitated high on the mountain may be drifted to lower levels.

A typical pattern associated with heavy snowfall in the Scottish mountains is a cold, northerly airstream of Arctic maritime air, but any moisture-laden wind may bring snow. In the Cairngorms heavy snowfalls are often associated with occluded fronts. The effect of a fall of snow must be interpreted in the light of information available on wind and temperature (Fig. 3.2).

Depth of Snow

Thick, heavy layers of windslab produce a much greater shearing force on any weak layer than would a shallow windslab. On an open slope, a slab 5 to 10cm in depth is not normally considered a serious hazard, but any funnelling of the snow, or any local increase in thickness, could make it so. These local variations of slab depth are easily missed in conditions of bad visibility. Some workers hypothesise 'hot spots' on a suspect slope. These are unusually sensitive points where a shear fracture can be readily initiated before being propagated to the rest of the slope.

Wind

Snow falling in cold, still air would be expected to produce a uniform blanket of powder over the hills. This is a comparatively rare treat in Scotland and it is usual for winds of 20mph and above to accompany a snowfall.

In these conditions snow is deposited as windslab on lee slopes and in sheltered depressions. This allows one to make a reasonable prediction of the most likely accumulation zones for a particular direction of snow bearing wind. Thus a north-east wind would be expected to load slopes in the south-west quadrant with cornices and windslab. It should be understood that this is only a first approximation, and that the ever changing airflow over complex mountain terrain can deposit isolated pockets of windslab even on windward slopes (Fig. 3.3).

Temperature

A major thaw occurs when the freezing level is above the mountain tops. Warm winds and rainfall aggravate this. The sun becomes progressively more important as a melting influence as spring advances, but anyone who has tried to climb on the south facing cliffs of Hell's Lum in the Cairngorms on a sunny day in February will be well aware of how much the snow is being warmed. Snow next to areas of bare rock is especially vulnerable. During a thaw, free water is released by melting of snow and this can destroy the cohesion of the snowpack and erode the strength of the anchors that hold the slab in place.

A heavy thaw indicates a danger both of wet, loose snow (point release) avalanches and of wet slab avalanches, together with a potential risk of cornice collapse. On occasions all three might occur, but usually the extant snowpack will lead to one effect being dominant. One of the authors visited Coire an Lochain in the Cairngorms on a very mild February day when dozens of wet, point release sluffs and avalanches could be seen, along with several collapsed cornices. One large recent avalanche had gone full depth and bulldozed boulders and metre thick

Grahame Nicoll

Fig. 3.3 An actively developing cornice and scarp slope both present hazards. The problems for an incautious walker in poor visibility are evident

Bob Barton

Fig. 3.4 The destructive energy of a large wet, point release avalanche in Coire an Lochain, Cairngorms, has bulldozed ice blocks from the lochan

slabs of ice out of the lochan. It was half term holidays so, of course, dozens of people were climbing (Fig. 3.4).

In heavy thaw conditions, climbing and off-piste skiing are likely to be unpleasant in wet, heavy 'porridge'. However, a freeze following the thaw produces a very hard, strong snowpack. It will take some hours for the freeze to penetrate well into the wet snowpack but when it does, any avalanche activity is very unlikely, and this hard snow is ideal for climbing. Few people enjoy the effect of such a freeze-thaw on skiing conditions, but sharp edges and a positive attitude should do the trick.

In normal, windy, conditions with below zero temperatures, fresh snowfall will be deposited as windslab. Any existing snowpack that has not been stabilised by freeze-thaw could be eroded, transported and re-deposited elsewhere as windslab. This is a serious source of unstable windslab in Scotland and one that shows the limitations of the rule not to venture

onto new snow for 24 hours, since this type of deposition has little direct connection with the timing of the initial snowfall.

At sub-zero temperatures, rounding (dry snow metamorphism) is the main stabilising influence on the snowpack, but at temperatures below -10°C the metamorphism proceeds slowly and windslab or powder snow can remain unstable for long periods. A combination of shallow snowpacks and sustained low temperatures produce the strong temperature gradients that promote the development of facets.

Many of the most destructive avalanches in Scotland have followed a week or more of consistently cold weather with snow showers or drifting. *These conditions should be regarded as powerful indicators of potential avalanche danger.*

In winter the air temperature usually drops about 1°C for every 200 metres ascended, and so Ben Nevis summit at 1344m is likely to be 7 to 8° colder than Fort William at sea level.

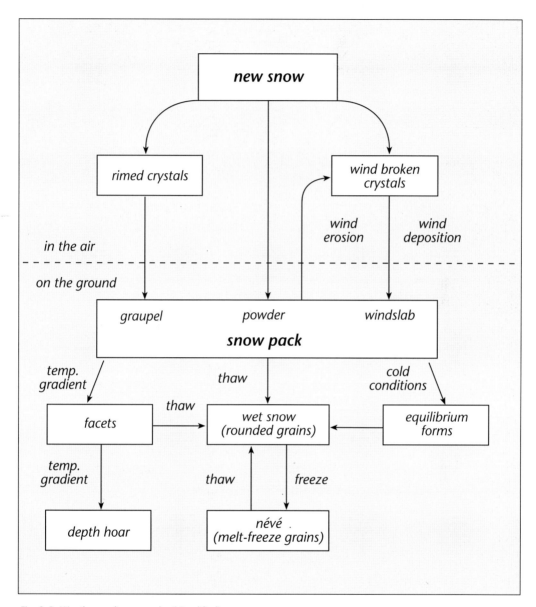

Fig. 3.5 Weather and snow cycles (simplified)

General Observations in the Field

An awareness of changing snow-types and weather during a journey in the hills provides, in combination with the Primary Prediction described above, a basis for the evaluation of avalanche hazard (Fig. 3.5).

Temperature

This term is used imprecisely in skiing and mountaineering, because we rarely recognise that there may be a difference of 20°C between the temperature of the ground surface below the snow and the air at head height.

Subjective judgements of temperature can be even more misleading. A winter

Keith Geddes

Fig. 3.6 Snow accumulation on the Great Slab, Glacier du Coire an Lochain!

anticyclone can give sunny weather with very hard frosts, but this can *feel* much warmer than a strong rain or sleet-bearing wind that is actually melting snow. The most important decision to make is whether or not the snowpack is melting.

In thawing conditions – rocks near to snow are black and usually wet, surface snow crystals are of a simple rounded shape and surrounded by a film of water, snow has a greyish white colour, ropes and gloves in contact with snow quickly become damp, rime falls off the rocks on which it is encrusted and in heavy thaws, water can be squeezed from snowballs

In freezing conditions – rocks are covered in rime or a sprinkling of snow,

bare rock is dry and lighter coloured and gear stays relatively dry.

A thermometer is useful in allowing you to predict where the freezing level will be. Thus, if it is 6°C in Fort William it is likely that the freezing level will be at about 1200m, so the higher routes on Ben Nevis, such as *Good Friday Climb*, should have freezing conditions. Whether this equates to good conditions depends on the recent history of the snowpack. When a significant change of temperature occurs it takes some time for the change to penetrate the whole snowpack so, for instance, the upper 20cm can be hard frozen above a base of wet snow.

In thaw conditions, wet snow avalanches and collapsing cornices are possible and it is wise to avoid steep slopes and corniced gullies. The heavier the thaw, the more dangerous the snow conditions are likely to be.

Fortunately, these conditions are not too difficult to recognise and wet snow avalanches often give some degree of warning. Thus, wet loose snow avalanches can be preceded by smaller sluffs and the very large wet slab avalanches, such as the regular spring slide in Coire an Lochain, are usually heralded over several weeks by the appearance of impressive crevasses and bergschrunds in the corrie (Fig. 3.6).

A thaw is particularly dangerous when any kind of snow slab lies on smooth rock slabs or long grass. These can become excellent sliding surfaces when lubricated by melt-water. Melt-water creeping under blocks of old snow poised on a band of granite slabs often threatens parties making a spring descent from Cairn Gorm

to the Saddle and Loch Avon.

In very cold, still conditions, atmospheric water vapour can freeze onto the snow surface as brittle, striated plates of surface hoar. Hoar forms from water vapour, rime from tiny liquid water droplets. These crystals are very beautiful, but can constitute a hazard if they survive for long enough to provide a fragile foundation for a subsequent snowfall. This is most likely on shady northerly slopes, where the heat of the sun cannot destroy the surface hoar (Fig. 3.7).

Blyth Wright has done an analysis of about 800 snowpack temperature readings made by SAIS observers at observation sites in Glen Coe and on Cairn Gorm, and taken at a depth of 10cm below the surface. The average reading for Glen Coe was –1.3°C, on Cairn Gorm it was – 2°C. Since the Cairn Gorm observation sites are on average higher by about 140 metres, this

Blyth Wright

Fig. 3.7 Surface hoar

Bob Barton

Fig. 3.8 Sastrugi: elegant wind carved ridges indicating an erosion zone

suggests that the common assumption that East Coast mountains are much colder than those on the West Coast may be erroneous. More wet snow avalanches are recorded for Glen Coe but this may be due to the fact that there is a great deal of steep terrain low down on these mountains and therefore these avalanches occur at much lower (and warmer) altitudes.

Wind and Snowfall

In cold conditions, windslab is usually the main hazard. It is important to observe local wind speed and direction and to note any new or continuing build-up of windslab. Erosion features such as sastrugi or raised footprints and deposition features such as cornices or drifts behind boulders are all pointers to the development of windslab on lee slopes (Fig. 3.8).

Any blowing spindrift is direct evidence of drifting, but it is easy to underestimate its degree. If the actual rate of build-up of a windslab can be observed, this can quantify the intensity of precipitation. An increase of slab depth of 5cm per hour is considered dangerously high and this is easily exceeded in accumulation zones. A clue to recent wind direction can be gained from fresh deposits of rime ice on rocks, which always form on the windward side.

Any cracks appearing across a slope of windslab are likely to be danger signs and hollow sounding hard snow-slopes are likely to be hard slab over an air gap. Sometimes a section of the upper slab will collapse to provide a timely warning.

If a heavy snowfall occurs with light winds, powder snow avalanches are a possibility. These are usually small and relatively harmless, but certain gullies and depressions can concentrate them with great effect. *Zero Gully* on Ben Nevis is notorious for this funnelling effect, and several struggling leaders have been plucked from the narrow bottom section of the climb when routine spindrift has inexorably built up into an intense stream of powder snow.

The component parts of a storm should be noted. A preponderance of needles can lead to compact, unstable slabs, or a shower of graupel from the passage of a cold front may become the weak layer on which an avalanche runs days or weeks later.

Completing the Picture

Discovering the conditions in the snow-pack is an important part of forming a complete picture of the current hazard and how it might develop. Digging some form of snowpit is one of the best ways of doing this and every time you dig one you mentally file away your findings and add to your own 'expert system'.

Above all, the exercise is concerned with the detection and assessment of potential weak layers in the snowpack. We recommend that the 'full' snowpit described below should be dug whenever you have not been on the mountain for a few days or if you believe that important changes might have occurred. What you find will give the context for your overall decisions about stability and hazard.

The Snowpit

The snowpit is dug using a shovel, ice axe or the heel of a ski, to leave a vertical

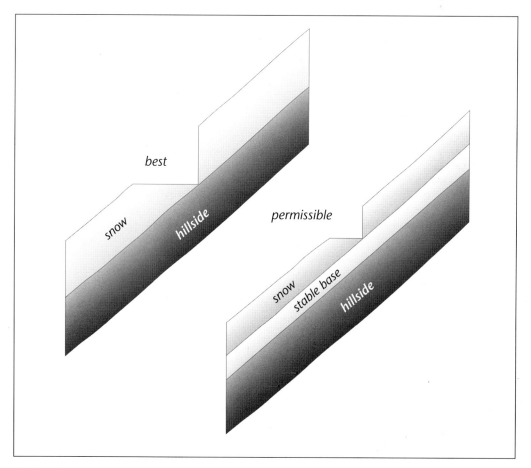

Fig. 3.9 Snowpit profiles

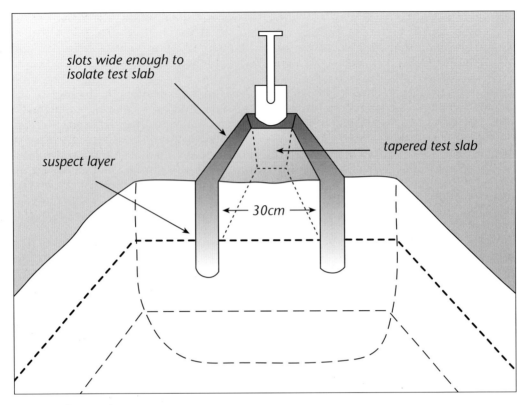

*slots wide enough to
isolate test slab*

tapered test slab

suspect layer

30cm

Fig. 3.10 The snowpit

Fig. 3.11 Preparing to perform a shovel shear test

back wall exposing the stratification of the snowpack. Ideally it should be dug down to the ground surface, but this can be both strenuous and time consuming. Sometimes an investigation will be limited to the upper layers above a known stable layer. This is much better than nothing, but be aware that you are trading accuracy for speed and convenience (Fig. 3.9).

For maximum information, the pit should be dug at the suspected starting zone of an avalanche, although it is rarely wise to do this on a potentially dangerous slope. Instead, the pit is dug at a protected location to the edge of the main avalanche path or one sheltered by, for instance, a rock outcrop. Much digging will be saved if a relatively shallow part of the snowpack is chosen – a probe helps you to judge the depth. About 60 to 100cm is ideal (Fig. 3.10).

The assumption made is that the stratification seen in the pit will show the same major features as those that would be found at the avalanche starting zone. The closer the two sites are, then the more valid this assumption will be. It is also assumed that there are likely to be considerable similarities between different slopes of the same aspect and altitude so that all east-facing slopes at 1000m would normally display similar snow profiles.

The pit will indicate the likely sequence of layers at the starting zone, but will give no information about the relative depths of these layers, nor indeed the total snow depth at other locations. However, if a cornice and scarp slope are present near the top of a slope then a snowpit below this level will give no indication of their existence (Fig. 3.12). Consequently, digging a snowpit in poor visibility before setting off

on a climb does run the risk of discovering an unstable and unseen scarp slope higher up, when retreat may be difficult or dangerous.

Examination of the Snowpit

Before examination of the pit, it is useful to measure **foot penetration** by standing on one foot on undisturbed snow. Repeat two or three times. The average depth of your footprints gives a crude indication of the amount of snow available for surface avalanches.

Aim to leave the back wall of the pit smooth-cut and perpendicular and investigate for different layers by: direct inspection, gentle probing and scraping with a pencil or the edge of a compass and cutting through the layers with a credit card – one of the few inexpensive uses of this item.

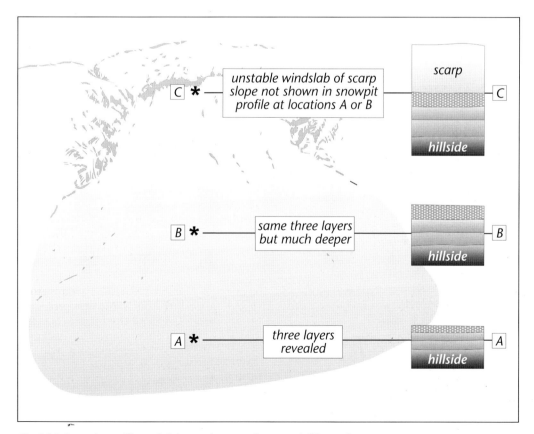

Fig. 3.12 Snowpits at different heights on the same slope reveal different data

TABLE 1

Assessment and grading of physical properties of snowpit layers

testing hardness

(i) Hardness: Hand Test
   (apply a consistent force)

1. Gloved fist	F	SOFT
2. Gloved fingers	4F	
3. Single finger	1F	
4. Pencil/axe spike/pick	P	
5. Knife blade or harder	K	HARD

F = fist, 4F = 4 fingers, 1F = 1 finger,
P = pencil, K = knife

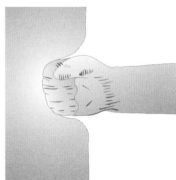

testing wetness

(ii) Wetness: Snowball Test

1. Snow will not make a snowball	dry	DRY
2. Forms dry snowball	moist	
3. Snowball and a few drops of water	wet	
4. Much water can be squeezed out	very wet	
5. Slush	slush	WET

(iii) Crystal size

1. Homogenous or less than 1mm	SMALL
2. Less than 2mm	
3. Less than 3mm	
4. Less than 4mm	
5. More than 4mm	LARGE

Note variation of crystal types and adhesion to each other

The latter is useful for revealing thin icy layers, especially when cutting up through the snowpack. The magnifying lens on a compass can be used to examine snow grains more closely. Taking a small sample and breaking it up on a hard surface will help you to do this. A photographer's/printer's lupe glass with a transparent shield used on a black metal plate gives by far the best results as it prevents crystals blowing away.

If adjacent layers are very different in physical properties, there is often a poor adhesion between them. Thus, any abrupt change in any of the above criteria indicates a potential weak layer (Fig. 3.13).

In examining the snow profile, particular note should be taken of:

- Spaces between layers.
- Layers of loose, uncohesive crystals such as depth hoar or facets.
- Icy crusts which often occur at the bed surface of a slab avalanche.
- Any shears that occur while digging or handling the snow.

Shovel Shear Test

After careful examination of the profile, use a snow saw to isolate a section of the slab above a supposed weak layer so that only the questionable layer supports it (Fig. 3.14). The standard size for the test slab is 30cm by 30cm, roughly shovel width. The shovel or your flat gloved hands are inserted behind the test slab and a gentle but increasing force is applied.

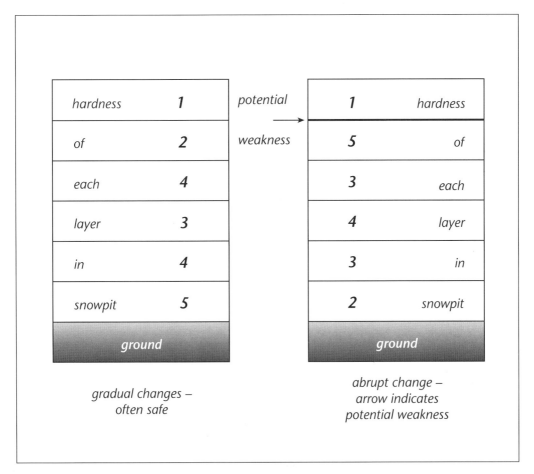

Fig, 3.13 Interpretation of the snowpit

Fig. 3.14 A snow saw can be used when cutting the block prior to a shovel shear test

It is important to avoid levering with the shovel – ideally the force is applied parallel to the snow surface, along the shear plane.

The force necessary to break this test slab from its anchors gives an idea of the strength of any weak layers. In some situations the test slab may break away under its own weight; on other occasions, it is necessary to jump on the slab to dislodge it. A very easy shear certainly raises great concerns about the overall stability of the snowpack but it should be realised that *the main value of the Shovel Shear Test is to identify and examine weak layers at which shear failure can occur.*

Technically, the test looks at too small an area to reliably predict the overall stability of the slope. For this, a rutschblock test (see below) is considered better, but multiple shovel shear tests at different locations are thought to give comparable reliability. Some statistical analyses have suggested that at least two rutschblock tests 15 metres apart should be used.

If you get an easy shear at a particular layer you should repeat the test at a different location. If you then get the same result, it is prudent to assume that there is a significant slab avalanche hazard. The limitations of the test become apparent if no easy shear is detected. Unfortunately, in that case you cannot assume that the slope is stable.

There is a theory, espoused by the Swiss Werner Munter, but not universally accepted, that a map of stability across an apparently uniform snowslope would show great variation from point to point. Within a few metres there will be points where R is locally much greater than W and others where W and R are almost equal and thus delicately balanced. A shear test at each of these locations would give a different indication of stability. The point where a delicate balance exists can be regarded as a 'hot spot' where a small additional load (such as a climber or skier) can trigger a shear. The theory suggests that once a local shear has occurred it can propagate and overwhelm the strength of the slab anchors at the points of apparent stability. The accumulation of snow cushions of greater depth may be one of the means by which hot spots are created.

After a shovel shear test has confirmed a weak layer, a quick test of the suspect layer can be repeated at intervals by cutting a small triangular slab with the axe. These only take seconds, but allow you to monitor changes in the upper layers of the snowpack. Seeing how the depth of a releasing slab can increase to a hazardous degree as you move into a zone of greater accumulation is particularly valuable.

Sometimes a slab will consistently fracture at a particular level in an apparently homogenous section of the snowpack.

These weaknesses may correspond to a change in the pattern of the storm that deposited the snow. In any case, if a shear occurs you should examine the surface at which it occurred in order to spot any clues to the cause of the shear, such as the presence of buried surface hoar crystals.

If the upper layers of the snowpack are found to be loose, uncohesive snow either as powder snow, or very wet snow, then loose snow avalanches are more likely than slab avalanches.

Rutschblock Test

This translates as 'sliding block test' and was developed by Alpine researchers as an avalanche stability test. In its original form for use by ski mountaineers, the test examines a block about 2 metres by 1.5 metres (Fig. 3.15).

a) Select a section of slope with un-disturbed snow at an inclination of 30°
b) Isolate a block 2 metres wide (the length of a ski) and 1.5 metres high (the length of a ski pole) by cutting vertical slots on either side with a shovel or a ski
c) Take the excavation down to ground level and do not disturb the isolated block
d) Cut the back wall down to ground surface with a knotted rope or a ski
e) Progressively load the block and note the load that produces failure.

The block is tested for stability and scores:

1 – if it fails while digging
2 – if it fails when person wearing skis steps carefully onto it from above
3 – if it fails when person on skis makes rapid knee bend
4 – if it fails when person jumps
5 – if it fails on a second jump
6 – if fails when person jumps onto block without skis
7 – if there is no failure

This stability score determines the overall avalanche hazard:

1 = stability poor. Avalanches can start with small triggers
2 = as above
3 = as above
4 = stability fair. Avalanches can be triggered on steeper slopes
5 = as above
6 = stability good. Skiers or climbers may trigger small avalanches on the steepest slopes
7 = as above

The correlation between the rutschblock test score and the level of avalanche hazard is a far from proven relationship. *The authors would avoid making important decisions about a slope solely on the evidence of this or any other single test.*

However, it is generally considered that the area of slope examined by the test is sufficiently large for the results to be reliable as a stability test, being of comparable magnitude to the area of the snowpack loaded by a skier.

It should be noted that this test can take up to 40 minutes and is hard work in anything except low density snow. It is important to realise that the rutschblock test should be done on a slope of 30° inclination or more. For layers deeper than about a metre the test becomes unreliable due to the levering effect of the test column of snow. Time can be saved by digging only to a known stable foundation in the snowpack. The test is aimed at producing a clean, regular shear. When failure of the test block produces an irregular, broken shear the results are inconclusive.

A modified form of this test called the **walking rutschblock** has been developed for people on foot (Fig. 3.16).

a) Isolate a block 1 metre by 1 metre down to a known stable layer or the ground
b) Approach carefully from above and load the block with feet toe to heel
c) Progressively load the block and note the load that produces failure

The block is tested for stability and scores:

1 – if it fails while digging
2 – if it fails while tester approaches from above
3 – if it fails while loading the block and standing upright
4 – if it fails when crouching down
5 – if it fails with a soft jump
6 – if it fails with a hard jump
7 – if there is no failure

This stability score determines the overall avalanche hazard:

1 = stability poor. Avalanches can start with small triggers
2 = as above
3 = as above
4 = stability fair. Climbers can trigger avalanches on steeper slopes
5 = as above
6 = stability good. Climbers may trigger small avalanches on the steepest slopes
7 = as above

This is a more convenient test in that a somewhat smaller block is used. However, loading the block evenly and consistently

Andy Sallabank

Fig. 3.15 A skier performing a Rutschblock test – a single jump

Andy Sallabank

Fig. 3.16 A walking Rutschblock – the climber has just stepped carefully on to the block

is more difficult on foot than on ski, as in the original test, and the walking rutschblock has not been subjected to the extensive statistical analysis of the original test. It is, however, a valuable technique and probably gives a level of reliability part way between the shovel shear and the rutschblock tests.

Burp Test

This is of limited application, but is useful for looking at the newly deposited, low density, upper layers of a snowpack that are too fragile to respond to a shovel shear (Fig. 3.17).

A 30cm by 30cm section of the upper layers is isolated and lifted on the shovel which is then tilted back so that the layer sits at an inclination of about 30°. The underside of the shovel is then struck firmly with a flat gloved hand. Any shear that occurs should be noted and examined. Although such a shear may not constitute a current avalanche hazard it may be buried and contribute to future instability.

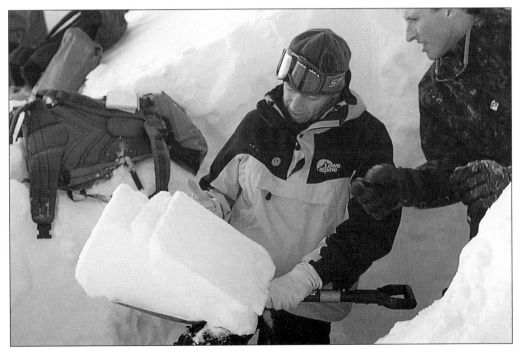

Bob Barton

Fig. 3.17 The result of a Burp test showing the shearing of several surface layers

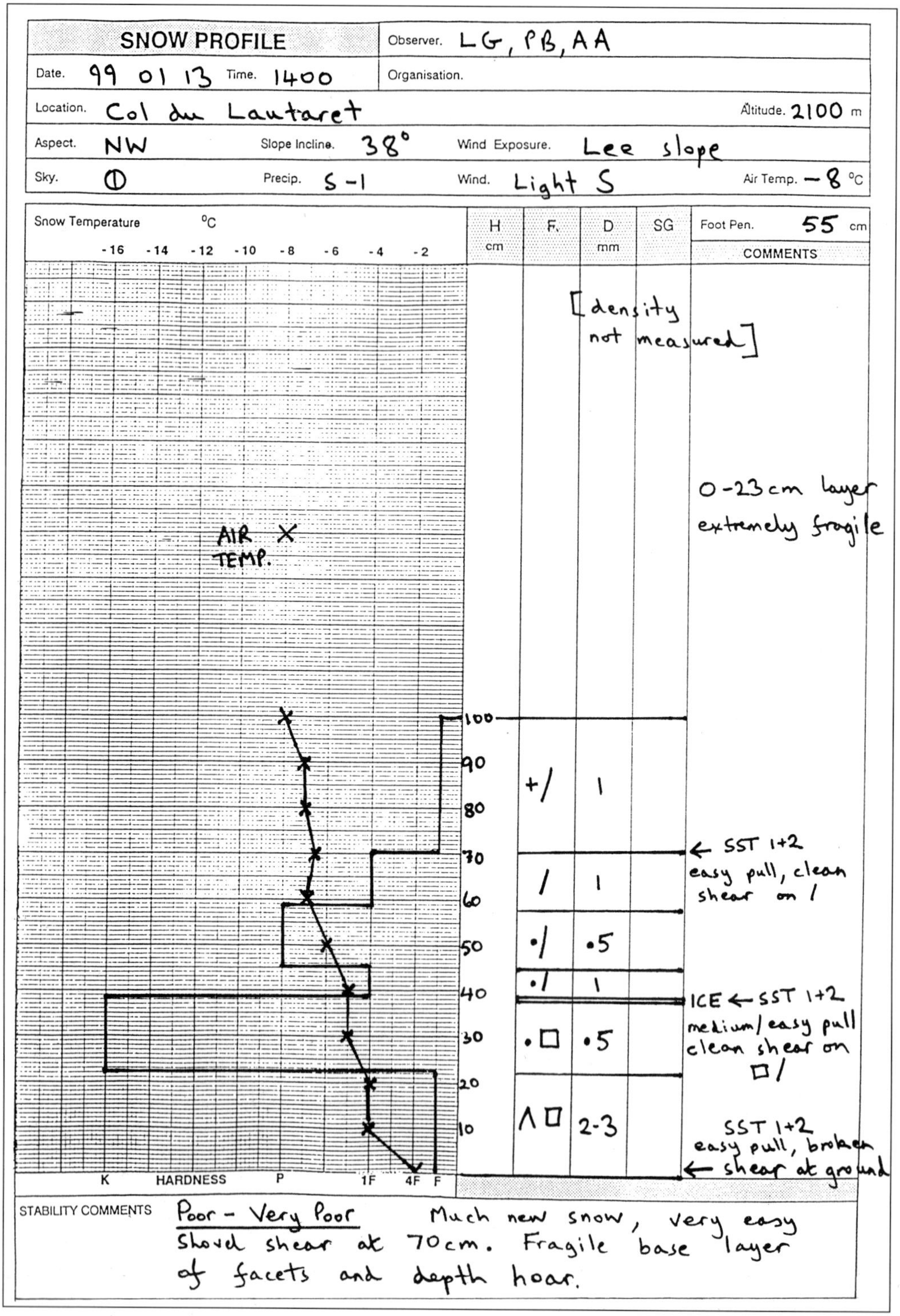

Fig. 3.18 Col du Lautaret snow profile

Test Release

Forecasters and field observers sometimes test ski or jump on a small slope to see if it is possible to trigger an avalanche. This can be informative, but is not to be recommended without companions, nor if there is any risk of triggering the big one.

Technical Investigations, Snow Profiles

Regular observation by skilled observers followed by analysis forms the basis for all avalanche forecasting services. This is described in more detail in Chapter VII on the work of the SAIS. Such observation will often employ a system similar to the snowpit described, but with the addition of temperature measurements and usually, some form of data recording.

Penetration resistance or hardness may be determined by the hand test in Table 1 (p66) and accompanying figures, or by the use of a ram penetrometer and these characteristics are the primary methods of defining different layers in the snowpack. The data is usually presented graphically as a 'snow profile'.

The detailed technical investigation of the snowpack is outside the scope of this book. Excellent accounts are to be found in *The Avalanche Handbook*. It is worthwhile learning how to read snow profiles since they are commonly published in the literature. Some of the main features commonly recorded include:

- Identity of observer and date.
- Location and terrain.
- Local weather observations.
- A histogram which defines the main layers showing how penetration resistance (fist, knife, etc) varies with depth.
- The crystal types and sizes observed for each layer, the density of each layer, the variation of temperature with depth – the gradient.
- The results of shear tests.
- An overall stability comment (Fig. 3.18).

Typical symbols used by field observers to record crystal types	
New snow	+
New snow rimed	+r
Broken crystals or partially settled	/
Graupel	✕
Rounds	•
Facets	□
Depth hoar	∧
Melt freeze grains	O
Surface hoar	V

The snow profile shown is from an Alpine rather than a Scottish location – an accumulation zone near the Col du Lautaret – but similar principles apply. It is of interest because:

- It shows clear instability with easy shear tests at several levels.
- Within minutes of the completion of the profile a large group triggered the release of a slab avalanche on the same slope.
- The slab was about 50 metres wide with a crown wall up to 1.5 metres in height and appeared to release on the 40cm layer before stepping down to the base layer of depth hoar.
- On the same day a small party of ski patrollers released a much larger avalanche on a slope of similar altitude and aspect a few miles away. Conditions were judged to be so hazardous as to result in the entire ski area being closed for several days.

Hazard Evaluation and Forecasting

Hazard evaluation (sometimes called stability evaluation) estimates the likelihood of current and future avalanche activity in a particular area. Risk assessment is concerned with the interaction between avalanches and people or property and estimates what danger of loss or injury exists.

Hazard evaluation brings together all

of the factors described above. A checklist is a helpful approach, with each factor scored as a positive or negative influence. The overall decision considers all the unstable influences together. Treat the notes with caution – the comments do not apply to all situations.

- Depth of snow – the more snow the less stable.
- Current avalanche activity – a strong indicator of instability.
- Past avalanche activity – recent or historical?
- Slope tests – rutschblock, shovel shear or test release?
- Slope use – a heavily used slope tends to be more stable.

- Snowpack structure – easy shears, weak layers indicate instability.
- Snow temperature – if very cold instability persists. Melting?
- Foot penetration – deep penetration is an indicator of instability.
- Old snow surface – good sliding surfaces are an indicator of instability.
- Precipitation – precipitation tends to promote instability.
- Wind – drifting and accumulation promote instability, erosion stability.
- Air temperature – thawing or freezing?
- Solar heating – snowpack likely to thaw – instability.
- Settlement – active settlement a sign of stability.

Hazard Evaluation Checklist

Date

Location

Observer

	Comment	Stable	Unstable
Depth of snow			
Current avalanche activity			
Past avalanche activity			
Slope tests			
Slope use			
Snowpack structure			
Snow temperature			
Melting			
Foot penetration			
Old snow surface			
Precipitation			
Wind			
Air temperature			
Solar heating			
Settlement			

Current stability evaluation

Expected trend

Risk assessment and forecasting

Risk Assessment and Forecasting

What you are trying to decide is:

- Could the slope produce avalanches?
- Is the snow stable or not?
- What could happen if it did avalanche?
- Are conditions getting better or worse? (Fig. 3.19).

The second and last of these important questions are largely answered by a local application of the hazard evaluation, the first and third by a consideration of the local terrain and the local features of the snowpack.

Terrain

Steeper slopes are more likely to fracture than gentler ones of the same structure. The range of 30 to 45° are the common slope angles for large slab avalanches with a peak at 37°. There seem to be no upper limits of angles for avalanches in Scottish gullies. The channelling or funnelling effect in a gully will also greatly amplify the force

Nigel Shepherd

Fig. 3.19 Raised footprints in Number Four Gully, Ben Nevis. These are most likely to be the result of erosion by an up-gully wind. Since material is being removed from loaded slopes they are usually a favourable sign for that slope

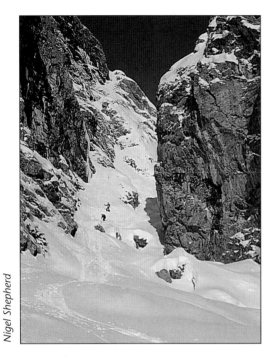

Nigel Shepherd

Fig. 3.20 A dramatic terrain trap. Any avalanche activity above will be channelled and amplified by the gully

of an avalanche. All other things being equal, bigger slopes and deeper snowpacks will produce bigger, more destructive avalanches.

Terrain Traps

The danger posed by an avalanche to those in its path is strongly influenced by the nature of the runout zone and the terrain beneath the point of release (Fig. 3.20). If an avalanche sweeps a person over a cliff or onto the thin ice of a frozen lake the results of even a small slide can be lethal.

Skiers often ski along the sidewalls of innocuous, gently angled streambeds. A small release from the sidewall will accumulate in the stream bed and can bury the victim at a depth out of all proportion to the size of the avalanche. Solo travellers are especially vulnerable.

The canyon leading into Coire na Ciste on Ben Nevis would be a terrifying place to be when avalanches release from the slopes below the Douglas Boulder Gap.

Type of Snow

A small avalanche of fluffy powder snow will be much less destructive than one of concrete-like wet snow. The intact blocks of a hard slab avalanche can be much more damaging than those of a soft slab, whose blocks soon break up as they slide (Fig. 3.21). The nature of the debris also has a strong influence on the possibility of survival when buried, as blocky debris is more likely to allow the free passage of air to anyone buried.

The very largest slab avalanches are usually of hard slab, since only a hard, rigid material is able to propagate fractures over long distances.

Nature of Party

Even a partial burial can have fatal consequences for the solo traveller. A strong party practised in rescue might be expected to have an improved chance of survival but, in the event of a complete burial, one person in five does not survive long enough for even the most rapid rescue. The weight of a large party is very much more likely to trigger an avalanche.

Local Hazard Forecasting

A rapid local accumulation of snow is a strong danger signal. Current or recent avalanche activity is an indicator not to be ignored. What you see may be the precursor of something much larger.

Route Choice

Route choice is the practical expression of your decisions about stability and hazard.

Initial Choice

Your initial choice of venue and overall route should be made in the light of the current SAIS forecast and your primary prediction. You should aim to avoid accumulation zones particularly if they are indicated as a hazard in the forecast. Walkers not too set on a particular objective should normally be able to plan a

Fig. 3.21 *Large blocks of debris from a cornice collapse avalanche*

Tom Prentice

route that avoids such areas, generally by following ridge lines and areas exposed to wind erosion.

Analysis of the aspect and inclination of the planned route will allow you to spot where the tricky sections might be and to take a view on whether the obstacle to progress might be serious. The problem is likely to lie on the slopes leading to and from the ridges (Fig. 3.22).

Winter climbers are in a much more difficult position. Their sport tends to take them to north-east facing cliffs that are natural accumulation zones in prevailing south-westerlies. Although buttress routes and ridge lines can give reasonably safe conditions, the approach to the foot of the route and the often corniced exit can both be hazardous.

It will sometimes be the case that

no routes on a particular cliff can be approached and climbed safely. Looking elsewhere to regions of lesser accumulation or crags of a more windward aspect is the best bet. The south facing delights of Hell's Lum might offer safer and better climbing when the Northern Corries are besieged with snow, or refrozen snow in Torridon when Ben Nevis is waist deep in powder.

Route Finding and Defensive Travel

If your planning has been sound and you have chosen a basically safe route, much heartache can be avoided. The next priority is to focus your attention on a finer level of detail as the route unrolls. In conditions where unstable snow exists you

Bob Barton

Fig. 3.22 Attempting to minimise exposure to windslab by sticking close to outcrops. Such strategies can improve the odds but rarely eliminate the hazard completely

should be engaged in a constant process of hazard evaluation that directs your footsteps towards the least threatening areas. Sometimes just a few metres make the difference between safety and disaster and the following are good general guidelines for avoiding avalanche hazards.

- Travel between islands of safety.
- Avoid having the whole party on a suspect slope.
- Watch out for local cushions of accumulated snow.
- Give cornices a wide berth when on a ridge or beneath them in thaw.
- Avoid ploughing furrows through deep, steep snow.
- Be alert for the few metres of hazard on an otherwise safe route.
- Have a constant sense of whether things are getting better or worse.

- Make sure others follow exactly if you are choosing a careful defensive route.
- Avoid triggering something onto parties below.
- Be cautious not to wander into terrain traps.
- Always be ready to stop to re-assess and re-plan.

High Risk Situations – The Suspect Slope

At the end of a long day, when the only alternatives seem more risky, or in serious mountaineering situations, such as in the greater ranges or on rescues, one can be faced unavoidably with the prospect of crossing a slope judged as 'unsafe'. This is a decision of enormous gravity. If there is really no alternative, the following might improve the odds a little.

Slope profile – Generally speaking, it is better to cross a suspect slope high up, so as to be near the top of any potential avalanche. This leaves the possibility of escape upwards and also means that burial may be shallower. Against this, it is wise to avoid the zones of tension which exist on convexities. In areas such as the Cairngorms where convex slopes abound, the decision where to cross can be a fine one. If the choice exists, direct descent is always preferable to traversing, as the horizontal weaknesses produced by traversing may more easily propagate a crown wall fracture.

One at a time – There is no point in exposing the whole party to avalanche hazard simultaneously. The members who are awaiting their turn, or who have already crossed or descended should stand in a safe place observing the progress of the person currently negotiating the slope. It is worth remembering that an avalanche may occur even after several persons have already crossed the slope. Even if moving simul-taneously, a spacing of 10 or 15 metres between individuals may be desirable. A wide spacing also minimises the additional loading on the slope.

In blizzard conditions with zero visibility, the necessity for keeping the party together may overrule this advice.

Belaying – If the dangerous slope is a small one, for example a narrow gully which must be crossed, it may be possible to belay party members individually with a rope. There is a possibility that a person held by a rope in this way may be injured by the crushing action of large masses of avalanche snow, or that the belayer is also pulled into the maelstrom. These disadvantages should be weighed against the possibility of an unroped person being swept over cliffs or into other hazardous situations. Belaying will be impracticable on a long open slope, but it may then be possible to link up islands of safety, such as groups of large boulders.

Clothing – Many avalanche casualties die of asphyxia. To prevent blocking of the mouth and nasal passages with snow, cover the face with a scarf or tightly fastened anorak hood. Also, a warmly clothed victim has a better chance of surviving a long, cold burial.

Skis – In some snow conditions a ski will have a much greater cutting effect than would a traverse on foot, while in others the skis will prevent the mountaineer from cutting a dangerously deep trough (Fig. 3.23). In general, it is probably wise to remove skis, since they are a serious encumbrance if an avalanche does occur. The feeling of security in speed that skis offer is largely an illusion and while accomplished skiers have skied out of avalanches, many more cases exist where skis and sticks have dragged the wearer further down into the debris.

Finally, it must be stressed that all these 'precautions' are a very poor substitute for avoiding a dangerous slope altogether.

Nigel Shepherd

Fig. 3.23 An impressive point release avalanche that travelled across the line of an Alpine ski tour

John Greener

Fig. 4.1 *This walker was carried down by a small sluff avalanche on steep ground. Neither he nor his companion who took the photograph was injured. The consequences of a bigger slide, or a similar event from above, are clear*

IV   Survival and Rescue

"Whereas from the second the avalanche commences it is a case of every man for himself, once it has fallen all 'sauve qui peut' tactics are at an end and the most disciplined teamwork is necessary."

G Seligman 1936

Survival Action if Caught

The fate of a person caught in an avalanche will largely be a matter of luck, but there may be the possibility of some defensive action. Improvisation on the following themes has sometimes been of help. Act with determination and concentration – your life may depend on it.

Delaying departure – Driving an ice axe or other implement into the sub-strata, or hanging on to rocks, may prevent the climber being swept away if the avalanche is a small one. Even if these actions only delay departure for a few seconds, this will have the beneficial effect of helping to ensure that the victim is deposited nearer the top of the avalanche where a shallower burial is likely. If near the fracture line of a slab avalanche, a convulsive leap up-slope may land you on safe ground above the wall.

Getting rid of gear – It is normally advised to loosen rucksack waist straps and remove ski safety straps to lessen the possibility of being impeded or injured by these items. Removing the rucksack does not seem to be a realistic action when the avalanche strikes – there are more urgent priorities and you may need its contents later. The rucksack may also provide a degree of flotation in the flowing debris. Ski brakes are much to be preferred on touring skis and bindings should not be set too tight. Taking your hands from the straps of ski sticks is certainly worthwhile.

A quick look round – Before departure and while falling, it is often possible to take a look round to see where you are in relation to safe ground. This may enable you to run, ski or roll off to the side of the moving debris.

Shouting – This may attract the attention of your companions or other observers. Your chances are enhanced if they are able to follow your progress down the slope.

The ice axe – The question is whether to retain or attempt to throw away the axe. Some climbers have been badly injured in avalanches by ice axes, perhaps whirling uncontrolled on the end of a wrist loop. In practice, if a sling is in use, it is unlikely that the climber will be able to remove it in an avalanche. If no sling is used and the climber has not dropped the axe in the initial confusion, it is probably worth trying to retain it. At least one climber has succeeded in ice axe braking on the hard substratum, allowing the avalanche to pass over him. However, co-ordinated movement underneath a moving avalanche is difficult, even in powder.

Escaping – Rolling like a log on a downward diagonal to the side of the avalanche track is quite an effective technique as it maximises the chance of staying on the surface. Skilled skiers have often skied out of an avalanche, but this can hardly be relied on.

Riding it down – If a victim is fortunate enough to be on the surface, strenuous efforts should be made to remain there. Swimming motions may help; the writers can recommend backstroke (Fig. 4.1). In a hard slab avalanche, try to remain on top of a block, thus sledging down. Several amazing escapes are attributable to this

Tom Prentice

*Fig. 4.2 Snow density, snow block size and
temperature can all influence the chances of survival*

method. Whatever method you use, try very hard to keep your head up-slope.

Terminal stages – As the avalanche comes to a halt make a huge effort to get to the surface, or at least to thrust a hand out of the snow. Many people have been rapidly rescued due to a protruding hand or foot. The other hand is probably best employed in covering the mouth and nose and in trying to preserve an airspace round the face. Many people have perished in avalanches by asphyxiation as a result of snow blocking their airway. Try to get a final deep breath before becoming submerged and if not overwhelmed by snow, as the debris comes to a halt.

If possible fend off blocks of snow in the final seconds of the avalanche so as to leave a space for air or manoeuvring. When the avalanche has stopped, if you are able to move a hand or arm you may be able to start to dig yourself free (see p21, Chapter I).

Most authorities advise the buried victim not to panic. This is terribly difficult, but unproductive shouting or struggling will only use up more air and

more of your vital reserves. It is unlikely that all the members of the party will have been buried and help will probably be at hand. If someone may be close at hand energetic shouting can sometimes be heard on the surface and has saved many lives.

A positive mental attitude is of great value in survival situations of this kind. A Canadian heli-ski guide recently survived burial in one avalanche only to be re-buried in a second (and much larger one) whilst being dug out of the first. He survived a very long and very deep burial and this appears to have been greatly assisted by excellent warm clothing and the fact that he was able to hear radio traffic on his ear-piece and so knew that another rescue team was searching. Some people have survived burials of several days.

In summary, these methods may not ensure survival, but many of them have been of value to parties in the past. Some of them are mutually exclusive, but circumstances will dictate which are feasible.

The Odds of Survival

The Avalanche Handbook quotes the following results from the analysis of a large number of cases of people being caught in avalanches in North America and the Alps:

- **80%** of people caught will survive if they remain on the surface of the debris.
- **40%** to **45%** survive if partially or completely buried.

The most common causes of death are:

- **65%** asphyxiation.
- **25%** collisions with obstacles.
- **10%** hypothermia and shock.

The collection and interpretation of data concerning the survival of completely buried casualties is difficult. Fig. 4.3 summarises the results of an extensive survey, the key results of which were:

- If a person survives the initial avalanche uninjured and is dug out within 15 minutes, they have better than a 90% chance of survival.
- Survival chances of buried victims fall dramatically up to about 45 minutes and then decline more gradually.
- Although survival chances decline as the time of burial increases, your chances are never completely extinguished.

Shallow burials carry the greatest survival chances because recovery from deep burials is slow and chances of injury or asphyxiation are increased.

This is a terrifying lottery in which to find oneself but some lessons are clear;

- Avoid being avalanched.
- Avoid at all costs being buried.
- Avoid having the entire party buried.
- Locating and digging out a victim within 15 to 30 minutes maximises their survival chances.
- Wear a transceiver and make sure your companions also wear and can use them.

Avalanche Rescue

Carrying the Correct Gear

As we keep emphasising, prevention is both better and more reliable than cure. However, should an avalanche occur (either affecting your own party or others close by) carrying appropriate equipment in the party can considerably increase the chances of successfully recovering any buried victims. About one Scottish avalanche incident in five involves burial of one or more people, but not surprisingly, burials follow many of the larger avalanches and proportionately more fatalities occur.

Multiple burials involving two or more people are relatively common and on occasions the entire party has been buried. It is noted elsewhere that axes and the heels of skis are far less effective for excavating a buried victim than even the most rudimentary shovel, yet how many British winter climbers carry such a lightweight shovel? Similarly, probing with

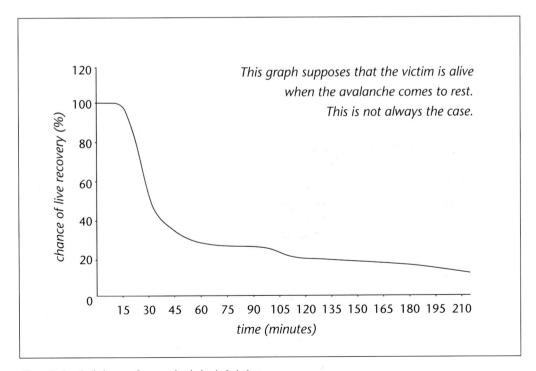

This graph supposes that the victim is alive when the avalanche comes to rest. This is not always the case.

Fig. 4.3 Survival chances for completely buried victims

Snow + Rock

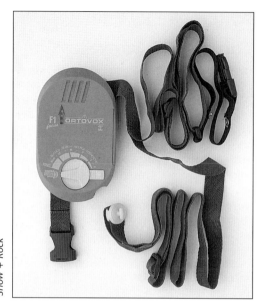

Fig. 4.4 *Ortovox F1 Focus. A widely used model of avalanche transceiver that uses both audible and visible indicator signals for the searcher*

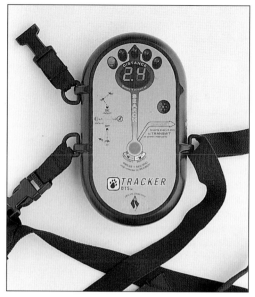

Fig. 4.5 *Tracker DTS. A digital form of avalanche transceiver that can indicate both direction and distance to the buried set*

Snow + Rock

axes and normal ski sticks is far less effective than the use of purpose-built collapsible probes.

Ski mountaineers are particularly at risk, because their sport takes them into snow accumulation areas and they can arrive rapidly in a dangerous situation. Much of the recognised best field practice of avalanche avoidance and recovery has grown out of Alpine ski touring and research in Alpine countries. A well equipped Alpine ski-touring party of six engaged with a tour such as the Chamonix – Zermatt Haute Route would probably carry most of the following items of equipment for avalanche rescue and observation: one transceiver per person, one shovel per person, two or more collapsible probes per party, group bivouac sack, first aid kit, rope (Figs. 4.4 to 4.7). The following items are not essential, but would also be considered: radio receiver for weather forecasts, two way radio or mobile phone, thermometer, clinometer for measuring slope angle, lupe eyeglass for examining snow crystals.

In addition, people will carry ski-poles that can be converted to probes by removal

of the baskets. Some specially designed poles can be joined to make a very effective 2.5 metre probe. Each member of the party would be expected during a practice session in an area of about 10,000 square metres, to locate two buried transceivers within five minutes.

Transceivers are invaluable aids to avalanche rescue and their use is detailed below. It is worth noting that a lightweight shovel, a collapsible probe and a transceiver weigh only 1200gm and with a little ingenuity one can construct a shovel that attaches to the shaft of an axe, or to its adze in the manner of an entrenching tool. It would be wise for those involved in serious ski-tours in Scotland to emulate this level of preparedness.

Parties on foot in Scotland also gravitate towards accumulation zones, otherwise known as Grade I gullies, and they frequently venture forth in bad weather. Although parties on foot have a much wider choice of route (and therefore a better chance of avoiding high hazard areas) it seems quite likely that the level of exposure to avalanche hazard is at least equal to that experienced on alpine ski-tours. However, there is as yet no tradition of carrying comparable protective equipment. At an absolute minimum, we would recommend that when a significant avalanche hazard exists parties should carry lightweight shovels. These have an additional use in that they facilitate the digging of snow profiles and the construction of emergency shelters.

Although there is something of a minimalist or even a Luddite tradition in Scottish mountaineering, the main reason for transceivers and probes not being in wide use would seem to be the considerable cost of such equipment. Given the high occurrence of fatalities following avalanche burial already detailed in Table 1, Chapter I, the investment in avalanche rescue gear of a sum similar to the cost of a pair of specialist ice tools should be seriously considered. The authors believe that the arguments for the use of transceivers by Scottish mountaineers are very persuasive.

But it must be said again, if you are in doubt about the security of a slope then avoidance is the only sure remedy. One should beware of any illusion of invulnerability that a transceiver bestows and remember that many people wearing transceivers have been avalanched and rapidly recovered – but not alive.

Solo mountaineers and skiers are most vulnerable to avalanches, as even a partial burial can have dire consequences. Some years ago, a lone, cross-country skier was avalanched above the Chalamain Gap in the Cairngorms and although only buried up to the knees, his escape was a long, arduous struggle.

Self-rescue

Sometimes people are able to dig themselves out after burial by an avalanche. They are more likely to succeed in this if they manage to avoid panic and are unhampered by rucksacks, skis and ski sticks. The accounts of many survivors emphasise the tremendous difficulties that an unaided person faces in escaping even a partial burial. The incident already described in Coire an Lochain in January 1997 is a remarkable example both of good fortune and of the possibility of self-rescue.

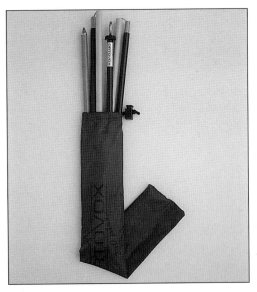

Snow + Rock

Fig. 4.6 If you ever have to dig anyone out of an avalanche you will be grateful for a strong shovel with a large blade and a strong handle. This model is made by Life Link

Snow + Rock

Fig. 4.7 Collapsible probes save time in the final stages of a transceiver search and can also be used for conventional probe searches. They are also useful for detecting significant layering in the snowpack

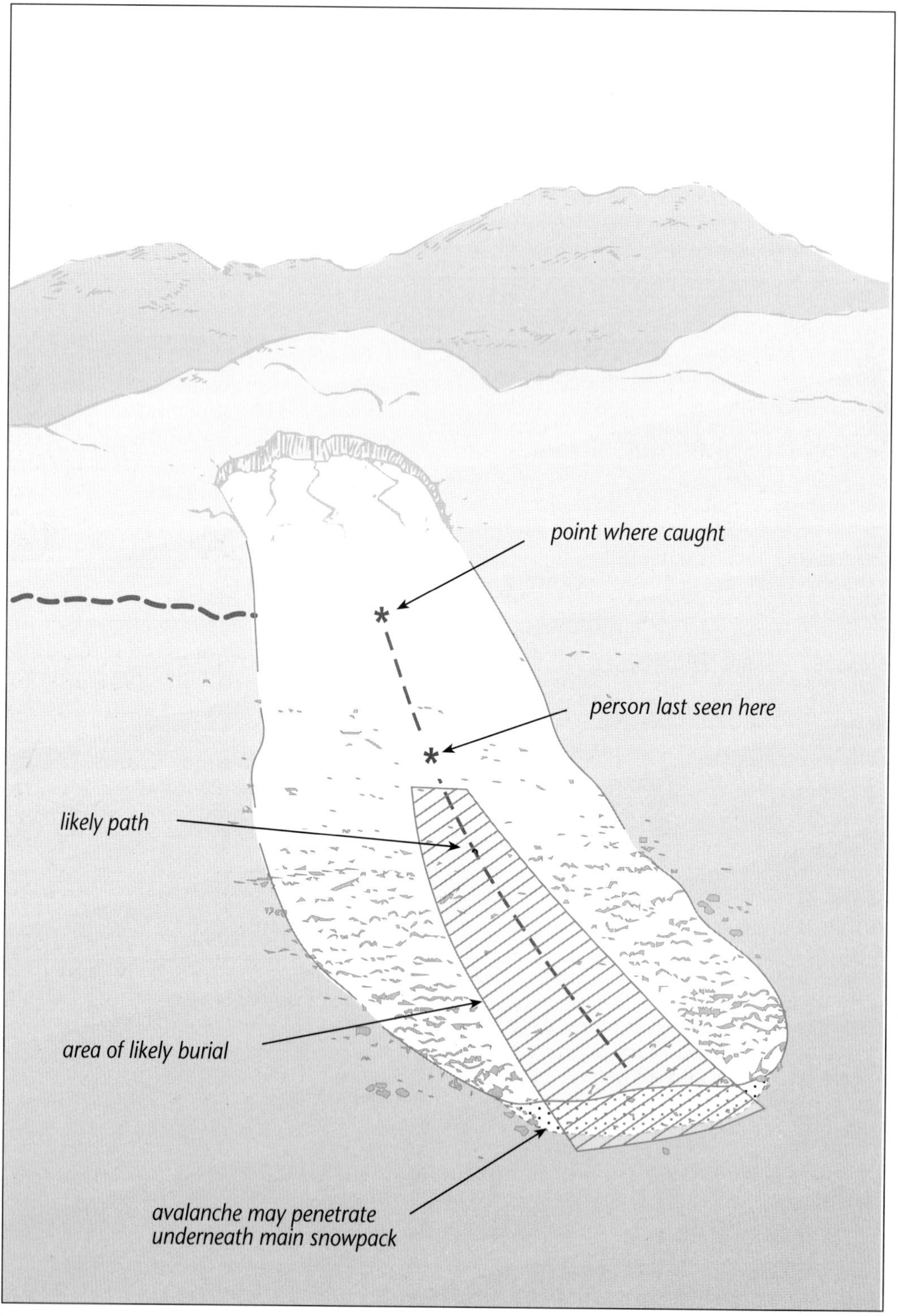

point where caught

person last seen here

likely path

area of likely burial

avalanche may penetrate
underneath main snowpack

Fig. 4.8 Path of victim and likely burial area

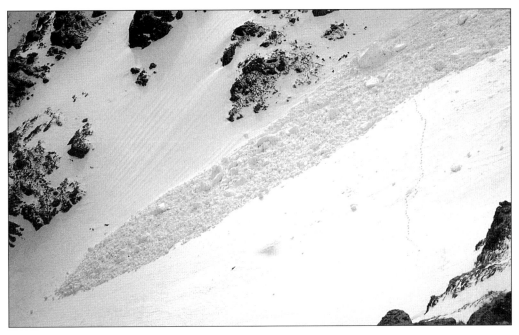

Tom Prentice

Fig. 4.9 Fix the last point where the victim was seen. This large avalanche on the North Face of Beinn Ime, Arrochar, was caused by a cornice collapsing

Rescue by Companions

The witness or survivor of an avalanche that carries other people away has undergone a shocking and disorientating experience, yet it is his or her capacity for clear thought and speedy, efficient action that will maximise the chances of survival of anyone still in the avalanche.

The graph in Fig. 4.7 shows that after two hours only 20% of completely buried victims are recovered alive. This makes it clear that the companions of the buried members of the party, working immediately with limited resources, have a greater chance of making a successful rescue than a well equipped rescue team arriving some hours later. It should be noted however, that a small chance of live recovery remains even after several days' burial.

In the light of these and other statistics it is possible to suggest the strategy that is likely to give maximum success (Fig. 4.8).

Check for further danger – Sometimes, particularly in branched gully systems, one avalanche may trigger off another. A brief check that another avalanche is not imminent is worthwhile but this should

not distract you from the vital next steps.

Mark last point seen – Marking the point at which a victim was struck by the avalanche and the point where they were last seen moving with the debris, will help to define the path down the slope (Fig. 4.9). A line through these points and continuing down the flow-line of the avalanche can be estimated and marked and there is a good chance that the victim will lie close to this line.

The points should be physically marked with ski sticks or rucksacks, as merely fixing the position by eye is unreliable. This can be difficult and it may be best for one person to keep an eye on, and a finger pointing to, the spot to be marked while directing another where to place the marker. Although valuable, this should not use vital time that can be employed for the essential next steps:

Count the survivors – Be sure how many people are in the avalanche.

Quick search – The party must make a *quick search of the debris looking for obvious signs of a buried person* and listening carefully for calls or whistles. This search is of vital importance – lives have often been lost when shocked survivors have gone for help, leaving an easily located victim partially buried but unable to breathe. Even two or three minutes lost can cost a life. Bloodstains, articles of equipment or clothing can all be valuable pointers to the track followed.

Transceiver search – A party equipped with transceivers and practised in their use has a much better chance of locating a buried companion than one without these aids (Fig. 4.10). It is wise to follow the instructions of the manufacturer in using these instruments, but normally the search consists of three phases:

1) long range search – when the party sweep the slope in order to detect the signal from the victim
2) short range search – when the position of the victim can be narrowed down to a few metres
3) pinpoint search – when position is pinpointed to an accuracy of about one third of the depth of burial.

Location times of just a few minutes are perfectly feasible (digging out can take much longer). These techniques are detailed below.

Thorough search – If the quick search fails to recover all the victims, the party without transceivers must make a more thorough search, paying particular attention to the avalanche tip and to any points where debris can pile up against ledges, boulders, or other obstacles. Probing with axes, ski sticks or collapsible probes, should be systematic and well organised. A coarse probe on a grid of about 70cm is probably best. Alpine statistics indicate that the average buried depth is about 1.4m, so improvised probing with axes is of much less value than that with longer probes. However, most live rescues occur from a depth of 1m or less. When searching, occasionally stop everyone and everything to listen for voices.

Send for help – If the party is fairly large one or two people can be sent for help by a safe route, while the rest of the party continue the search. The previously

mentioned survival times indicate that, unless unusually close to help, a solitary witness is probably best advised to search for at least one or two hours before leaving the scene to enlist assistance. Mobile phones, radios or attracting the aid of passers by can allow the alarm to be raised without diluting the search efforts on site.

SUMMARY
Check Further Danger
Mark Last Seen Point
QUICK SEARCH
Transceiver Search
Through Search
Send for Help

First Aid

When the victim is located they should be dug out at once. Try to dig rapidly but with care and avoid standing on the casualty. A portable shovel is about five times as effective as an ice axe or the heel of a ski. As soon as the victim's head is exposed, resuscitation or the supply of warm drinks should be commenced. The person who has been buried may be severely hypothermic and may have no apparent signs of life. Research has shown that the moment of recovery is extremely hazardous for victims (due to sudden movement and sudden removal of the protective blanket of snow) and every effort should be made to minimise any trauma. Remember that the casualty may have sustained major injury such as a spinal fracture and handle accordingly. Unconscious casualties will need protection of their airway.

Fig. 4.10 A transceiver search. Having shovel and probe readily available in the final stages of the search can save vital minutes

Above all, guard against the feeling that, once location has been made, the problems are over. The next few minutes can be crucial for survival of the casualty.

Avalanche Transceivers

Transceivers (transmitter/receivers) undoubtedly offer the best chance of rescue by one's companions. Many different types are now available, some models use audible signals, others flashing lights, some use analogue technology, some digital. Common features tend to be a frequency of 457kHz (some older models on 2.275kHz or dual frequency may still be in use), a normal maximum detection range of 30 to 50 m, power from AA cells, a battery check function, an approx. weight of 300g and an internal aerial.

Tests commissioned by the International Commission on Alpine Research show the digital sets seem to allow a more intuitive approach to searching, and as a consequence new users may have better success in searches.

When using transceivers make sure:
- That the batteries are new and of the correct specification.
- Battery life and the transmit and receive functions of each set are checked before each day of use.
- Each member of the party must wear a transceiver and be practised in its use.
- The transceiver must be worn under the clothing (not carried in the rucksack) and close to the head.
- When travelling in the mountains the set must be in transmit mode and shovels (and if possible, probes) must also be carried.

Adverse weather and wind noise make searching by transceiver considerably more difficult. In these conditions, the use of a supplementary ear-piece protected from wind noise under a hat can help. Sets with a visual display are much less affected.

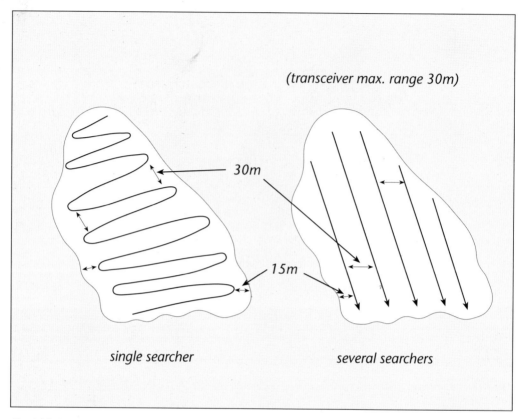

(transceiver max. range 30m)

30m

15m

single searcher

several searchers

Fig. 4.11 Long range search

Daily Function Check

Battery life should be checked according to the manufacturer's recommendations. Check function as follows:

1) Leader's set on transmit, group's sets on receive, maximum range
2) Leader approaches group from 50m distance and checks for distance at which signal is first detected (normally about 30m)
3) Group's sets on receive, minimum range
4) Leader goes to each person in turn and checks for a clear signal
5) Leader switches to receive, maximum range and goes to stand 50m from group
6) Group switch to transmit and in turn approach leader
7) Leader checks range for each person (normally about 30m)

8) Leader switches back to transmit

With a little practise this method is less laborious than it sounds.

Practice

In avalanche rescue, lost minutes can cost lives. Frequent practice of a transceiver search is invaluable, some practice is essential. The normal method of practice is to bury a set (it must be on transmit!) inside a plastic bag in an area of simulated debris. A search is then undertaken.

When people have reached a reasonable proficiency two or three sets can be hidden at different points in the debris. Locating two sets in an area of about one hectare in less than five minutes would be considered a good performance. It is often straight-forward to discriminate between two or three separate signals when searching.

A full-depth avalanche on the Great Slab of Coire an Lochain, Cairngorms

Allen Fyffe

SAIS avalanche observer taking temperature readings following new snow fall in the Creag Meagaidh area
Tom Prentice

Small powder snow sluffs – spindrift slides – on the flanks of Aonach Mor. Such slides are a common feature of Scottish snow conditions
                                                                        Blyth Wright

Surface cracking is a clear indicator of a weak layer in the snowpack and high avalanche danger on loaded slopes
                                                                        Bob Barton

The main danger of spindrift slides is that their force can easily dislodge a climber or skier in their wake

Allen Fyffe

Performing a Rutschblock Test. The skier steps carefully on to the excavated block and with a rapid knee bend makes a single jump

The single jump has caused the excavated block to separate from the snow layers below, indicating a dangerous weak layer in the snow pack. The Rutschblock Test score is 4

Bob Barton

A laboratory photograph of depth hoar showing the distinctive striations or 'steps'
Météo-France/Centre d'études de la neige

Asphyxiation isn't the only threat posed by an avalanche. Head and internal injuries and broken bones frequently result in fatalities. Thankfully this young climber was not seriously injured
Grahame Nicoll

If a blanket of new snow is poised on a relatively steep slope, loss of cohesion can cause a dry, loose snow avalanche
Allen Fyffe

The slanting rock bands in the vicinity of the Castle Gullies on Ben Nevis make the area a notorious avalanche blackspot

Dave Cuthbertson

Search Patterns

The manufacturer's guidance should be followed, but the following is a method in wide use (Figs. 4.11 & 4.12).

Long range search –

The searcher or searchers sweep the slope systematically in order to pick up an initial signal from the victim.

1) After checking for further danger, marking last seen point and quick search (as above), searchers switch their sets to receive, maximum range. If a signal is immediately heard then go direct to step (3).

2) Search the debris so that a searcher passes within 20m of every point on its surface. The exact pattern will depend upon the size of the debris and the number of searchers available.

3) When a signal is detected start the close range search.

4) If more than one person is buried, two searchers undertake the close range search on the signal detected, the rest continue the long range search.

Close Range Search –

1) Orientate the set for maximum signal (this is normally when the aerials of

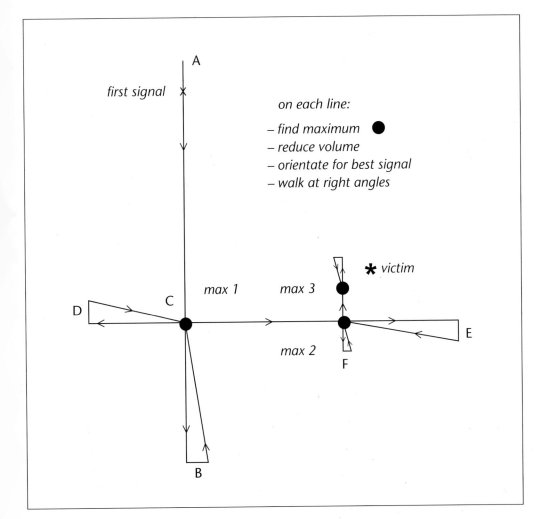

on each line:
– find maximum ●
– reduce volume
– orientate for best signal
– walk at right angles

Fig. 4.12 Close range search for audible signals

Fig. 4.13 Dogs from the Search and Rescue Dog Association play a significant role in locating avalanche victims

the transmitting and receiving sets are parallel). Maintain this orientation.
2) Continue walking in a straight line until the signal reaches a maximum and then begins to reduce.
3) Return to the point of maximum signal.
4) Reduce the volume (range) until this signal is just clearly audible.
5) Walk at right angles to the initial line.
6) If the signal reduces, retrace your steps and walk in the opposite direction.
7) If the signal increases, identify the maximum as in (3) and repeat the process as (4) to (7).
8) When a clear signal can be detected with the search set on minimum range you are close to the casualty (two or three metres). Start the pinpoint search.

Pinpoint Search –

1) Maintain orientation for maximum volume (strength of the signal).
2) Scan the surface of the snow moving the set over an area of about 3m by 3m.
3) The position is pinpointed when moving the set in any direction reduces the volume.
4) The victim's position is normally located to an accuracy of about one third of the depth of burial.

5) Use a probe to confirm the victim's position and to keep the shovelling on track.
6) When the victim is recovered it may be necessary to switch off their set in order to prevent distracting signals confusing other searchers.

Organised Avalanche Rescue

Avalanche Dogs

Trained avalanche dogs are highly effective in locating buried persons and in good conditions they can search an area in perhaps one tenth the time taken by a team of 20 people equipped with probes (Fig. 4.13).

Compact, non-porous, icy snow will limit the passage of the buried person's scent and make the use of dogs less effective, as will the presence of distracting scents and severe weather.

Trained dogs will always be used with their handler and usually work from down-wind. If a dog is immediately available it is wise to keep other rescuers off the avalanche debris and to discourage them from urination near the site, so as not to confuse the dog. 'Resting' the slope for 10 minutes after searchers have operated will allow many of the false scents to dissipate. In any case, the vital search by people on the spot must not be delayed by the expectation of the appearance of a dog.

Typical times for the through search of a 100m wide square (one hectare) by a well trained dog would be about 30 minutes for a coarse search and one to two hours for a fine one, but it may be much faster.

In Britain, the Search and Rescue Dog Association (SARDA) undertake the provision and training of such dogs and their handlers. Even an untrained dog may be able to give an indication of where a casualty is buried, especially if the victim is the dog's owner (see *Inside the Avalanche* p21).

Bob Barton

Fig. 4.14 A probe line in action. Note the controller, the use of flags to define the area and the use of a shovel party behind the probe line

Probing

This is the traditional method of searching for buried persons and involves the systematic probing of the debris with rigid metal probes of about 3m in length (Fig. 4.14). It is worth noting that the avalanche tip may drive under the main

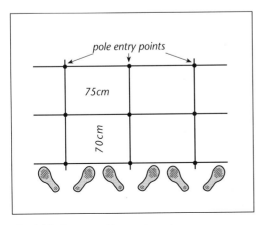

Fig. 4.15 Coarse probing

snowpack. This is most likely with dense, wet snow avalanches and allowance for this should be made in the area searched. Working in a probe line is difficult, demoralising work and it is vital to keep up morale and a belief in the possibility of a live recovery.

Ideally, each probing team consists of 20 searchers under the direction of a controller (much larger teams are very unwieldy). A shovel party backs them up and if necessary a lookout is posted in a safe place to warn of a further avalanche. The searchers should be briefed on an escape route in such an event.

The area to be searched should be marked with coloured flags and clear marking of the area that has been covered is essential. If sufficient resources are available, two searchers holding a cord along the line of probes at snow level is useful to keep the line straight. The controller's job is to ensure that probing follows a systematic pattern. Several types

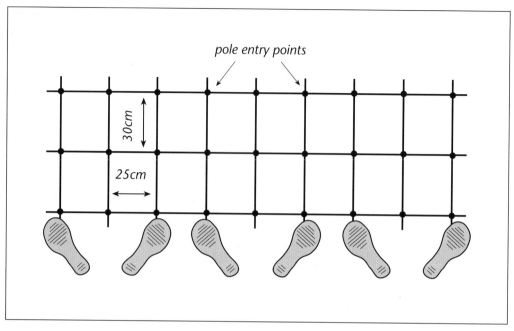

pole entry points

30cm

25cm

Fig. 4.16 Fine probing

of search pattern are normally used.

Coarse probing – This gives a coarse grid of 70 by 75cm, which has only a 75% chance of locating a buried person, but it is relatively rapid (Fig. 4.15).

The search-line stand elbow to elbow, hands on hips to define the spacing. On the command "probe" the probe is inserted between the searcher's feet, and pushed down until an obstruction is felt, or until the top of the probe is at about waist height (probing deeper is wasteful of time).

The controller checks the line of probes and on the command "probe" the line extracts the probes, takes one pace forwards and inserts the probes again. This process continues. Any searcher with a possible find, leaves the probe in place as a marker and informs the shovel party. They will give the searcher a replacement probe and dig at the indicated point. The line must continue to search until the shovel party makes a definite location and it is certain that all victims are accounted for.

Fine probing – Probing at each foot and between the feet, before taking a half

step forward gives a grid of 25 by 30cm (Fig. 4.16). This has a near 100% chance of finding a body (unless very deeply buried) but it is very slow.

To search an area of one hectare, 20 searchers will require four hours for coarse probing and about 20 hours for fine probing. This means that *fine probing is so slow that it is not normally used for locating live persons*. Two consecutive coarse probings give a better chance of effecting a live rescue than a single fine probing and have been successful in achieving live recovery.

Open space coarse probing – McClung and Schaerer, authors of *The Avalanche Handbook*, have described a modification on coarse probing which still gives a 70 by 75cm grid (Fig. 4.17). It is useful if searchers are in short supply or if the debris is too rough to allow elbow to elbow spacing. Searchers space themselves by standing alongside each other, fingertip to fingertip. The probe is inserted twice, once beside each foot, before a pace is taken forwards.

Three point probing – Recent research

by Auger and Jamieson and by Sivardière has indicated that the best balance between accuracy and speed is provided by a further modification of the previous method (Fig. 4.18). Fingertip to fingertip spacing of searchers is again employed. This time, the probe is inserted once between the feet and then once on the outside of each foot before the next forward pace. The insertion of the probe by the feet is deliberately inclined at an angle of about 10° to the vertical. We cautiously recommend this as the method of choice for probe searches.

Areas of Research

Many other methods of locating buried persons have been tried, including radar, gravimeters and metal and heat detectors. None of these has proved to be consistently useful for small, unaided parties in wild country. Some offer encouraging possibilities for organised rescue since they do not require the subject to wear any specific apparatus or transmitter. The use of ground probing radar permitted the recovery of a completely buried fatality on Beinn a' Chaorainn, Glen Spean.

It is now common for ski equipment to incorporate a small RECCO radar reflector or the unit can be purchased at low cost. Many Alpine ski areas and rescue services will have the detection equipment that can locate a buried wearer, usually by the use of a helicopter but, of course, rescue by your companions is not normally an option with this equipment.

Airbag flotation devices which can be triggered if the wearer is avalanched, have been tested and judged promising. The victim is rendered buoyant and will remain on the surface of the avalanche, gaining protection both against the risk of burial and to an extent, against injury by the snow. Unfortunately, at present, the equipment is probably too heavy for use by mountaineers. Another device

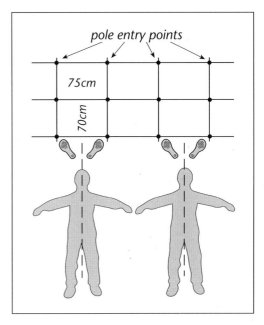

Fig. 4.17 Open space coarse probing

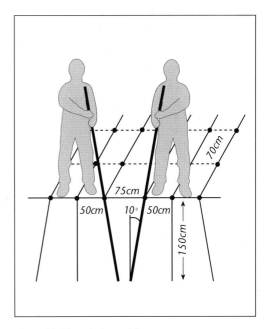

Fig. 4.18 Three point probing

incorporates a simple breathing apparatus into a waistcoat in order to give wearers protection against asphyxiation which may result from the formation of an ice mask during an extended burial.

Fig. 5.1 Ski-mountaineering among avalanche debris on Aonach Mor: push on or turn back?

V   The Grey Zone

"To retrace one's steps, particularly if this entails turning a downhill into an uphill movement, is a manoeuvre which calls for more sterling qualities than are possessed by many a resolute party. The temptation to go on when the danger to be faced is not certain, but only problematical, is such that very few can resist it."

G Seligman 1936

Avalanche incidents and accidents vary in their consequences from the frightening to the tragic and there is no way of knowing at the start what the outcome will be. The following short accounts cover this spectrum, but also span a range of perceived avalanche hazard, so that in some incidents the reality of the situation was obvious to the participants, while at the other extreme, no avalanche hazard at all was anticipated.

In between comes a body of incidents where those involved had probably appreciated that a certain level of hazard existed, but had decided that this was acceptable. The consequences of the accidents do not always reflect the degree of caution exercised by the mountaineers concerned. In the light of one's own experience, it is interesting to consider whether your actions would have differed from those of the avalanche victims.

If anything, these incidents illustrate that avalanche awareness in itself is not enough. Sometimes there is, it seems, a lack of willingness to accept that an avalanche might have disastrous consequences. Perhaps it is the sporting element in the personality of the mountaineer or skier that dictates this. But, ask an audience whether they feel the possibility of being severely injured or asphyxiated in an avalanche is an essential part of the sporting experience for them, and the answer is invariably in the negative.

Still, it may be that a fundamentally gung-ho attitude is a British character trait, if such a thing exists. Certainly, leading climbers from the continent have occasionally remarked that climbers from the UK seem much more willing to gamble with avalanche hazard than those brought up in the alpine winter tradition. If so, it is as well they should be aware of the likely outcome.

Ben Nevis, April 1965

The following lines are extracted from a letter sent to Blyth Wright by the late Philip Tranter, one of the most energetic and prolific personalities to bestride the Scottish climbing scene in the '60s. As the moral to be drawn from the account is obvious, it is offered without further comment. Nevertheless, the reader will deduce from it something of Tranter's overpowering enthusiasm for every aspect of the mountain experience.

"And another thing too, I forgot, Wul and I were avalanched out of No 4 Gully on Nevis on Sunday! Hellish weather, right back in the dead of winter. Rather depressing after the fabulous weather at Carnmore. A vast depth of new snow on old base, perfect avalanche conditions. We set off hoping to try No 2, but soon gave that idea up. Instead waded up to No 4, conferred at foot, saw four avalanches, decided it would be foolish to continue, continued, got 300ft up gully, me 30ft ahead. Were duly avalanched, swept down 500ft. I've heard it said one is supposed to try to swim the stuff, but that was so much rot in that particular avalanche. It took me the whole way down, which seemed ages, just to get a decent effective grip on my axe and start trying to dig it into the hard snow below (I was underneath all the debris).

"Movement relative to the snow (old debris itself), was almost impossible. Like trying to play ping-pong in treacle. Wul, poor sod, lost his axe. His hands were pinned behind him and he couldn't breathe. When we stopped and I crawled out I at first thought I was going to have to use my skill at artificial respiration on Wul, but he came round spluttering and cheerful. Funny thing was, I never even felt breathless. Still, it was all good British fun and enlivened an otherwise rather dreary day."

Ben Nevis, April 1, 1967

Many further accidents have occurred on the well-trodden slopes of Coire na Ciste on Ben Nevis. Because of the nature of the terrain, many of them, like Tranter's, have not had serious consequences. However, two years after the lucky escape recounted above, an accident occurred which could well have resulted in the deaths of both victims.

The two climbers involved, Andrew Philipson and his cousin, David Richardson, were both experienced climbers, Philipson being a member of the elite Alpine Climbing Group. Their equipment also appears to have been good and they were very well clad, a fact which later would be of great significance.

Weather conditions were very bad as the pair climbed the steepening ground towards the foot of *Number Three Gully*, which was their day's objective. It was fairly cold and a strong, gusty wind and much new snow made navigation awkward, to the extent that the climbers were unable to find *Number Three Gully*. They decided that they were too far right and started traversing further rightwards in the hope of finding *Number Four Gully*. The slope at this point is fairly steep, about 40° and one wonders whether the two were

debating the wisdom of continuing. The hazard of avalanche must have been manifest to an experienced party, but no decision to retreat was made.

Events were in any case about to make decisions superfluous, for at about 2pm both were avalanched, carried along the surface for a few seconds and then covered by the sliding mass. Their fall was later estimated at 160m and when the avalanche finally ran to a halt, both of them were buried. Their plight was desperate; no one had witnessed their fall and although new snow contains much air, asphyxia might easily have been their fate. Barring this, death from exposure frequently overtakes the avalanche victim. By great good fortune, however, they were each able to breathe and both, as previously indicated, were well clad. Richardson, for example, wore a string vest, long woollen underpants, a wool shirt, three sweaters, wool breeches, knee-length canvas gaiters, two pairs of stockings and a cotton anorak.

Philipson found himself in a hole about 1.2m beneath the surface, normally not a survivable position. However, the will to live must have been strong, for after nine hours of effort, scraping and scratching at the snow, he emerged almost unhurt into the night air. While no doubt thankful for his own escape, he must have entertained little hope for his friend. Turning his steps downwards, he made for the nearest aid, at the CIC Hut, where other climbers were in residence. Although the hut is close beneath the great cliffs, the way down must have seemed long and, finally to stumble into its warmth, a great release.

The climbers in the hut acted with commendable speed and after phoning the Police in Fort William, set off to search for Richardson. Following Philipson's tracks back to the avalanche tip, they set to without much hope of success. For one person to survive a nine-hour burial was one thing: to expect another to be alive after 11 hours was too much. Nevertheless, soon after midnight, one searcher saw a hand protruding from the

Malcolm Creasey

Fig. 5.2 Heavy snow on Ledge Route, Ben Nevis. Sometimes turning back is as worrying as pushing on

snow. Furious digging revealed someone alive and conscious; Richardson also had escaped.

These remarkable survivals are surpassed only by that of Robert Burnett, recounted in Chapter I and those of the survivors of the Aonach Mor accident in December 1998 (Appendix III). The climbers from the CIC almost certainly saved the second victim by their prompt action, for although the Lochaber Mountain Rescue Team arrived at the CIC at the same time as the stretcher party descending from the vicinity of Number Four Gully, the extra delay might well have been fatal. One could wish that all those who are in a position to do a 'first search' after an avalanche would act with similar despatch and effectiveness.

Stob a' Choire Odhair, Black Mount, November 27, 1938

Ben Nevis has no monopoly of avalanche hazard and many lesser mountains have caused problems for the mountaineer. In the years prior to the Second World War when trains were the primary means of transport, the hills along the West Highland Railway

from Crianlarich to the Black Mount were particularly popular and the pages of the Scottish Mountaineering Club Journal at this time contain several accounts of avalanches.

H MacRobert in his 1938 article Ski-Running, mentions an incident near Cruach Ardrain, where his companion on skis was knocked over by a small windslab avalanche. This was dislodged by MacRobert's skis and completely buried his friend, who was about 30m below. This is the earliest Scottish incident involving skiers of which we have knowledge.

In the same article, MacRobert mentions an "enormous wet snow avalanche on Ben More which carried away one of our members and spread out fan-wise over about 10,000 square yards to a depth of over 10 feet". The member involved was obviously lucky to escape as the mass of snow released on the figures given would be about 15,000 metric tons. It is unusual in such early accounts to have any observational data, even such as the estimates of size given in the Ben More incident. However, the following event, also recorded in the 1938 Scottish Mountaineering Club Journal, is exceptional in the detail given: it is also noteworthy as being still one of the few November incidents on record:

"Traversing a broad ledge on snow at 45°, a large section suddenly avalanched and both men were carried down 300 to 400 feet. The snow was soft and about two feet deep. Rain had been falling for some time and something like a storm was still in progress. The top four or five inches of the snow was saturated and granular and was packing down under the action of wind and rain. Below the snow was powdery. It would appear that the avalanche was caused by the top layer sliding off from the powder snow due to the lateral cutting disturbance made by the traverse. The debris was over 100 feet wide and mostly about four feet in depth."

The persons involved in this incident were JR Wood and ACD Small, of whom Wood was injured in the avalanche but was able to descend unaided.

Even at this distance in time it is possible, from the detailed information given, to see the main factors producing the avalanche; a poor bond between the underlying layers of different crystalline type and size, along with overloading due to the saturation of the surface layer. The mountaineers concerned obviously had a good understanding of the factors governing avalanche release and yet had elected to cross the slope. At that time a snowpit examination of the slope was not normal practice and the conventional view was that Scottish snow was "not much prone to avalanche". Applying modern knowledge and technique, would this incident have been avoided? The only answer is a definite 'maybe!'

Ben Lui, May 12, 1934

The shapely and isolated peak of Ben Lui, standing to the south of the railway line between Crianlarich and Tyndrum, was another mountain easily accessible from the West Highland line in the pre-war years.

Its Central Gully, a fine natural line leading directly to the summit, has long been one of the classic snow climbs of Scotland. Seen face on, it still looks fully steep enough to daunt or to inspire the aspirant snow and ice climber. Today, the mountain is known as the site of several avalanche incidents, including one which in a February blizzard of 1957, carried down four members of an RAF Mountain Rescue Team, resulting in a broken leg for one of the unfortunate climbers.

However, the earliest full account of an avalanche in Central Gully has been left to us by the late Ben Humble. The part which he played in the establishment of the mountain rescue service in Scotland is, perhaps, less well-known than it ought to be. However, his contribution to the literature and photography of Scottish mountains speaks its own story, while his idiosyncratic approach to the hills has been immortalised by abler pens. Humble was an active climber in his younger days and his enthusiasm led him on one occasion, with three companions, to the Central Gully of Ben Lui. The following account is largely a paraphrase of Humble's words.

As the party approached the foot of the gully that morning, they noted much avalanche debris, but once established on the climb, found very fine conditions. It is interesting that from this point there is no further mention of possible avalanche contained in Humble's account. They made good progress towards the large cornice which defended the summit. This obstacle was overcome by digging a six foot tunnel and the climbers reached the summit in brilliant sunshine.

At 2.30pm the descent was begun and as they intended to return by the route of ascent the party roped up meaning to unrope when the summit snowfield had been descended and the top of the gully proper had been reached. They would then unrope and glissade down singly. All four of them were strung out on the upper snowfield, with the last climber immediately below the cornice when, starting just below his position, the whole upper snowfield started to avalanche and all were carried away.

The climber lowest on the slope saw that the slide would carry him not into the gully, but over the rocks to its side. He made a jump and landed on snow which was pouring towards the gully. All the

Rev AE Robertson

Fig. 5.3 Climbers on the classic Central Gully, Ben Lui at Easter 1905. A popular climb in days gone by and the location of some spectacular avalanches

101

others followed. The snow piled up many feet deep, filling the gully and tumbling the first two climbers over at great speed. The last two on the rope succeeded in remaining feet first and on top of the avalanche. Finally, after 500m of helpless descent, all found themselves lying among the debris, well below the start of *Central Gully*.

Thankfully, the climbers gathered their wits and their pieces of equipment. As the slope at this point was gentle, they unroped prior to completing their descent. However, the price for their morning's climb was not yet fully paid. As they stood impotently on the slope, another avalanche broke off from the upper west snowfield and hurtled towards them. Were they to be engulfed by this new peril? The answer, it seemed, was in the negative and they had a moment of relief as the second avalanche ran to a halt a short distance above them.

As it happened, one member of the party had gone back up the slope into the lee of a large rock in order to retrieve a lost ice-axe and so was spared what happened next. The detail of what occurred is uncertain, as accounts are understandably confused, but it seems that the shock of the second avalanche started the original avalanche tip moving again. In any event, the result was that the three remaining members of the party were carried down another 70m or so; again, unbelievably unhurt, after a total descent bordering on 550m. This is still the record for a Scottish avalanche and May 12 is still the latest date in the year on which a party has been carried down by an avalanche.

Unfortunately for our purposes, Ben has not left in his account any indication as to the type of avalanche which figured in this incident. It would be easy to assume that because of the strong sunshine and the time of the year, melting of the upper layers of the snowpack was responsible. However, this tempting extrapolation would be based on insufficient evidence. Wintry weather and accumulation of windslab in May are still quite common and bright

sunshine, even then, does not guarantee high temperatures. Nevertheless, the wet-snow avalanche theory remains by far the most likely.

As a footnote, the total damage in this remarkable incident was one lost ice axe and one rucksack missing. The latter turned up a month later when the snow had melted. It contained a camera with an exposed film which developed perfectly, providing the participants in this event with a pictorial record of their day, which however was unlikely to be as vivid as the cerebral images they retained.

Cairn Gorm, Ben Macdui Plateau, December 8, 1976

Undoubtedly, knowledge and forethought can greatly reduce the chance of being caught in an avalanche. Nevertheless, it is as well to admit that there are some cases in which marginal hazard is perceived, when even a careful examination of the snowpack, combined with a long experience of the winter hills, will not adequately protect the party. The following incidents emphasise this point.

The early winter of 1976 brought fairly heavy snowfalls to the Cairngorms, but by early December, a period of fine, cold weather had set in. For 10 days or so, clear skies greeted lucky mountaineers, although fairly strong winds caused a considerable build-up of new slab in sheltered locations, lying on a pre-existing base of hard névé. Nevertheless, the 10 days from the end of November were without new snowfall.

Glenmore Lodge parties set out on the mornings of both December 7 and 8, in order to bivouac in snow shelters at two different locations. On the 7th, Martin Burrows-Smith set out to spend two nights at the Garbh Uisge Beag with an experienced group of winter mountain leader assessment candidates, while on the 8th, Blyth Wright took a less experienced party of winter hillwalkers to a much less remote site at Ciste Mhearad on Carn Ban Mor overlooking Glen Feshie, for a one-night snowhole.

"Obviously there was a hazard of avalanche from the new slab lying on old

Steve Penny

Fig. 5.4 Probing for avalanche victims

névé and on arrival at Ciste Mhearad, it was indeed apparent that some metres of slab lay on our proposed site, a steep bank of snow about 10m high. I immediately set to work probing the slope with an avalanche probe, finding that there was a uniform resistance to penetration throughout the whole depth of the new slab, indicating a homogeneous layer of slab lying on the old névé. This slab was some 2m thick and in consultation with another instructor who was present, I agreed that the profile of the slope was such that an avalanche of the new slab on the old névé was most unlikely. In this at least we were to be proven correct.

"After having dug some 1.2m into the slope, I was feeling satisfied with the progress of my own snow dwelling, when a shout caused me to stand up. Outside it was all avalanching, and suddenly, irresistibly, I was being propelled downslope. Fortunately, I was on my back and

able to keep on the surface, although the presence of large blocks made burial a real possibility. Then, amazingly, I had stopped, not hurt, able to stand up. Someone was shouting though. One person was missing, buried. Frantic digging revealed the top of a head, then a face, thankfully still breathing. Total injuries, eventually nil, but pride was somewhat ruffled."

This incident caused the instructors concerned some heart-searching, which was not necessarily relieved on arrival at the Lodge to find out that the other Lodge snowhole group had been avalanched not once, but twice. One of these incidents had been at night, when the party was swept 120m in total darkness above their snowhole sites in Garbh Uisge Beag.

Subsequent investigations at the sites of these incidents showed that little or nothing could have been done to predict them by direct examination of the snowpack. The avalanches had run on a buried layer of surface hoar, which although visible once the avalanche had occurred, is generally agreed to be virtually invisible in the snowpack.

On December 14, surface hoar had been visible at Glenmore Lodge, but had not been generally observed on the hill. Similar but different conditions occurred in Winter 1982-83 when the Lodge issued an avalanche warning on the basis of extremely severe avalanche conditions due to buried surface hoar at low level, only to find that high-level locations were virtually hazard-free.

Cairn Lochain, Cairn Gorm, March 10, 1965

Coire an Lochain has already been singled out in previous chapters as the birthplace of great avalanches. Most such avalanches occur in the back of the corrie, in the vicinity of the Great Slab or to the west of it, sometimes filling the whole floor of the corrie with debris metres deep, smashing the thick ice in the lochan and scattering blocks of ice many hundreds of metres.

However, accumulations can be hazardous on the east-facing slope on the western ridge of the corrie, whose mean angle is only 28°, with a maximum near the top of 35°. This is partcilarly so when south-west winds cause a great depth of windslab to gather.

These were the conditions as a large party of eight persons, led by two very experienced winter mountaineers, began to descend the slope from the plateau. One experienced mountaineer was leading and the party following more or less in line, when without warning the firm snow in which they were descending broke away in a huge avalanche the whole width of the slope. The blocks of debris were very large, for this was a hard slab avalanche, with the attendant possibility of severe crushing injuries.

All the ingredients for a tragedy were present, but luck was with this party. Firstly, only three members were carried down, the fracture occurring between the third and fourth members and leaving the others above the crown wall. Secondly, all those avalanched were near the fracture line and so near the top of the avalanche. Thirdly, and quite amazingly, all of those carried away succeeded in remaining on top of individual blocks of debris until the very last stages of their terrifying 200m descent. Other cases are known of similar toboggan rides, but we know of no other case where three persons were permitted to escape by this method. In fact, as the avalanche slowed down, one person did become involved with the tumbling blocks and received crushing and bruising injuries, but was able to walk painfully home.

The mass of snow which avalanched on this occasion was about 9,000 metric tons, the maximum width of the slide path being 400m. Obviously cool heads played a part in the escape of this party, but without the vital element of luck, none would have survived.

Lairig Ghru, Cairngorms, March 30, 1975

In examining the records of avalanche incidents, along with the whole of the related meteorological information, it often comes to mind that, had this information been carefully considered by the parties concerned, they might have acted differently. It is clear that hill-goers do not always do this.

The end of March 1975 was a period of widespread snow instability in the Cairngorms, as evidenced by the small epidemic of incidents and accidents on the 30th and 31st. The following was the most serious of these and took place little more than 1km from Coire an Lochain, where steep slopes fall westwards to the Lairig Ghru. This famous Cairngorm pass has featured in many a drama over the centuries and it is a place of gloomy reputation. Its slopes between the March Burn and the cliffs of Lurcher's Crag offer relatively easy routes to and from the plateau. Although set at an angle of 35 to 40° and bouldery, they do not normally constitute hazardous terrain for experienced and competent persons.

The party which set out on that fine

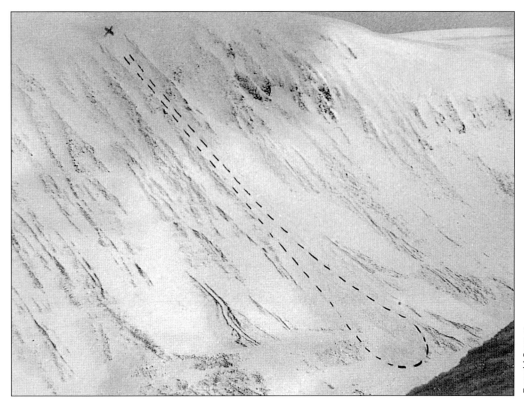

Donald Bennet

Fig. 5.5 The location of the avalanche of March 30, 1975 in the Lairig Ghru, Cairngorms

morning from Corrour Bothy at the south end of the Lairig, was certainly a competent one. As to experience, they comprised some of the more practised ski-mountaineers in Scotland. On the second day of their ski tour, enjoying the much improved weather, what had they to fear as they climbed on foot up these slopes? Certainly, as one member of the party subsequently wrote, "there was no mention, or I believe, even thought, of avalanche", yet they were about to be involved in the most serious avalanche accident yet to affect a skiing party in Scotland.

The details of what occurred as the party climbed out of the Lairig are described in the Scottish Mountaineering Club Journal of 1977, but the bare facts are as follows. The party were avalanched near the top of the slope, something under a kilometre north-west of the March Burn and seven carried down about 200m (Fig. 5.5).

Four members of the party were more

or less seriously injured, including back and pelvic injuries, a compound broken arm and serious lacerations. The uninjured survivors reacted quickly in summoning help and within three hours of the accident, the casualties were evacuated by helicopter. As a helicopter had already been scrambled in order to deal with an avalanche in Coire an Lochain (see the case history in Chapter II), it was possible to divert this aircraft and so expedite the rescue.

One might ask how such an experienced party could meet with an accident like this, particularly in view of the weather history and the snow profile described in the Chapter II case history. They might reasonably not have expected slab of the depth which occurred, although some slab build-up could have been anticipated. The slope which avalanched, a shallow gully rather than an open slope, was 4 to 5m deep, for that was the height of the crown wall. This might have made snowpit observation difficult, if it had been envisaged. A complicating circumstance was that the slope was reportedly covered in sastrugi, which is normally taken as a sign that avalanche hazard is decreasing. Obviously, however, with a very deep snowpack, the surface layers may exhibit sastrugi without the lower layers being affected by the erosion.

It is interesting that one of the party noted a sharp rise in temperature just before the accident happened. It is at least possible in the prevailing conditions of light winds, that as mentioned in Chapter II, this was due to a temperature inversion, with the party emerging from a cold into a warm layer. As a matter of record, the temperature at Glenmore Lodge did not rise above +0.8°C all day. To quote once more from Malcolm Smith's *Cairngorms* guide, "the fact that they (avalanches and cornice collapses) can occur in conditions of temperature inversion, is less well known".

The action of an inversion as a factor in this incident is only a possibility, but it could have provided the final aggravating factor. The party concerned have been particularly generous in publishing accounts of their experience for the possible benefit of others and the accident was a salutary reminder of what may happen even to a competent party when perhaps their guard has been allowed to fall.

Beinn a' Ghlo, January 14 or 15, 1982

Glen Tilt is an age-old route from Atholl to Deeside in the east, or, in a northerly direction via Glen Feshie or the Lairig Ghru, to Speyside. In much the same way as the Lairig, its length splits a mountain range in two, with high summits on either hand. The best known and highest is Beinn a' Ghlo, but there are other worthy goals for the hillwalker and a number of bothies provide basic accommodation. In winter, excellent ski touring is available, but the area does not lack steep slopes which must be treated with care.

These hills, although accessible, are spacious enough for solitary wandering to be enjoyed. Not, however, on January 19 and 20,1982; on these dates 100 searchers were scouring the hillsides, helicopters flew constantly overhead, civilian, police and RAF teams along with SARDA rescue dogs combined in a massive operation, in the hope of finding one missing walker.

This man, a doctor, had set out from home on the previous Thursday, the 13th, and had not arrived back on the Sunday as intended. With only the scantiest information as to his plans, the police found his car on Monday and a huge search was initiated. Weather conditions had been deteriorating over this period, from the fine, cold winter conditions of the week before, and Tuesday's search took place in atrocious weather. It was thought that the missing man might have intended going over Beinn a' Ghlo to the remote Tarf bothy and the day's search took place mainly on the slopes of that mountain. It drew a blank.

By now, hope for the missing doctor was at a low ebb. Even if he had been suffering only from some relatively minor injury, his chances of surviving such a prolonged exposure to bad weather were not good. Nonetheless, Wednesday saw a renewed effort and with better weather, more teams, dogs, and helicopters combed the area.

The day wore on with nothing found when one team from Tayside, searching along the north-west ridge of Beinn a' Ghlo, found some footprints. They were partly melted due to the thaw but were the first possible link with the missing man.

These footprints traversed the side of the hill in a roughly horizontal line. As the search moved along in this direction, the footprints suddenly disappeared. Almost immediately items of equipment were found; a rucksack side pocket, primus stove, and other small items. A few minutes later, the search was at an end. Some distance downslope, the doctor's body was found, almost completely buried in avalanche debris.

This sad find only confirmed the

Dave Cuthbertson

Fig. 5.6 The gentle slopes of Carn Dearg Meadhonach, right, face the cliffs of Ben Nevis over the Allt a' Mhuillin glen, and have been the location of a tragic fatal avalanche

searchers' worst doubts, but all of them expressed considerable surprise that such a tragic event could take place on this insignificant-looking slope. The average angle was about 30 to 35 degrees, although the starting zone, in a shallow gully, may have been slightly steeper. The thaw of the previous couple of days had altered the snow features somewhat, but the main dimensions of the avalanche were clearly visible.

The crown wall at that time was no more than 30cm high and only about 6m wide. The victim was found about 50m below this point, quite near the foot of the avalanche tip, which was approximately 17m wide by 33m long.

What can one learn from this unfortunate case? Clearly the hazards of solo winter mountaineering are again

highlighted. More than that, the danger presented by local steepenings on otherwise fairly gentle slopes is brought out, along with the desirability of keeping to ridge crests in doubtful conditions. Perhaps the doctor had unintentionally diverged from his route or perhaps, like the rescue team, he thought the slope looked harmless; we will never know. However, if he had indeed left his intended route, then the consequence of his actions were surely out of proportion to his 'error'.

Carn Dearg Meadhonach, February 21, 1978

The mountain upon which this accident took place is part of the Carn Mor Dearg range in the Ben Nevis area and overlooks the Allt a' Mhuillin glen and Coire Leis. The following account is condensed from the excellent report prepared by Terry Small, a member of the party concerned.

"On Tuesday, February 21, 1978, a group of five climbers were descending the south-western slopes below Carn Dearg Meadhonach after completing the traverse of the Carn Mor Dearg Arete. They descended from the ridge on to the large easy-angled slopes; conditions were windless, with about one inch of fresh dry snow overlying a firm base for their crampons to dig in. There was no 'balling-up' of crampon points and conditions seemed excellent. The proliferation of rock islands and outcrops on the slope further added to their feeling of security. Forty-five minutes should have seen them to the CIC Hut, some 1,200 feet below at the foot of Coire Leis.

"The group stopped for a chocolate bar, naturally choosing a rocky island to rest on, in preference to the bare slope. The cloud cover began to break up at this point and fine views of Carn Dearg West and Coire na Ciste were obtained.

"Looking across to the south a broad ridge, liberally littered with rock debris, seemed to offer the natural way to the valley bottom, this route was chosen without discussion, it being one of those lines which experienced climbers would naturally choose.

"They left the rest stop and were traversing the slope, at this stage Jason Hunnisett was in the lead, followed by David Meadows, Terry Small, David Wilcoxson and George Jones, each spaced about ten yards apart. The positioning was purely random; no thought of danger was present. A shallow depression was being crossed, caused in part by the ridge for which the party was heading. The events of the next few seconds are not easy to remember in exact detail, but the consensus of the group is thus:

"A shock wave or motion of some sort made them look towards the top of the ridge some 200 to 250 feet above. At the same instant an explosive 'boom', exactly like gunfire coincided with a crack running across the slope 100 feet above the party. The crack was extensive and was probably 100 to 150 feet wide and occurred above the whole of the party. Instantaneously the mass of snow below the break began to slide fairly slowly initially, downwards.

"David Meadows was caught on the edge of the moving slab, which was below the initial wide crack now confined to an area 40 to 60 feet in width, but with quick reaction was able to run off on to firm ground.

"Terry Small, George Jones and David Wilcoxson ran north-westward, contouring the slope in an effort to outrun the crack extending above their heads in the same direction. After a few yards it seemed clear that the direction of flow was actually moving away from them; being channelled by the shallow depression 100 feet below the break.

"They all turned to see Jason Hunnisett in the very centre of the accelerating slab, crouching as if regaining his balance and about to attempt to make for the side. At the same time the slab began to break up into large pieces some ten feet square around Jason and he was lost from sight as the whole mass disappeared into the mist below.

"Looking into the avalanche track as a way down, it showed areas of water ice pushing through the remaining snow layer, and so, after gathering their wits the party decided to descend the slope below them parallel with the avalanche path. In an attempt to minimise any further avalanche hazard they quickly moved from rock to rock on their way down.

"Their feelings and state of mind at this stage can be imagined and their shouts for help while descending were heard by a member of the Pinnacle Club near the CIC Hut, she promptly radioed the police, telling them that there had been an avalanche, and that she feared someone might have been injured.

"Some 500 to 600 feet lower down the slope the texture of the snow showed a marked change, heavy 'balling-up' of crampons resulted in several slips which

Malcolm Creasey

Fig. 5.7 Extensive avalanche debris in Observatory Gully, Ben Nevis

were arrested safely and the whole surface of the snow was covered with golf ball sized 'sun-balls' despite the absence of any sun on the slope that day. Some five hundred feet below this area and a total of approximately 1,200 feet below the avalanche source, they came across the avalanche debris, and after searching they discovered the body of Jason Hunnisett, lying face upwards, head up the slope, some 20 inches below the snow surface. His knee protruding through the debris gave his position. His rucksack, straps torn from the rivets, lay nearby."

The fatal outcome of this accident is all the more tragic in view of the youth of the victim; cruelly ironic, too, when one learns that the party had abandoned plans to climb a gully and had chosen to traverse the Carn Mor Dearg arete "as an ultra-cautious alternative", when the temperature at the CIC hut had been seen to be above freezing.

According to Terry Small's notes, the two days prior to the accident had seen high winds blowing from the north-east, although Tuesday itself was windless. About 2cm of new snow had fallen overnight, but most of the existing snow had fallen in severe, northerly gales three to four weeks before. Here we have a familiar pattern: new avalanche hazard created by a change in wind direction. However, it would seem that the main, significant factor in the release of this avalanche was the exceptionally smooth nature of the bed surface. Large areas of blue ice are mentioned and in fact, the avalanche ran down the path of a frozen burn. The windslab lying on ice was an extremely hazardous situation, but would be impossible to identify without snowpit inspection and clearly the slope was of such an angle (25 to 30°) that few mountaineers would have considered this.

This accident may point out a need for us to be even more careful when cold weather has created ice in streambeds or open slopes, and to bear this in mind when making hazard assessments later in the winter. To hear of incidents such as this can induce a type of fatalism. What can be the use of studying snow and avalanches if any slope at all can be a hazard? The alternative over-reaction of avalanche paranoia is equally unhelpful. We can only make our best judgements based on the knowledge we have gained and hope that our steps do not lead us into a hair-trigger situation such as that encountered by the luckless victim of this tragedy.

Ben Nevis, March 26, 1978

The northern cliffs of Ben Nevis and Carn Dearg are in every sense the crowning glory of the Scottish mountain scene. Few climbers can be unmoved by the sweeping slabs, and the great ridges buttressing the highest summit in the land. In winter, the magnificence of this scene is redoubled, with colourful hangings of green and blue ice decorating the crags. Little hint is given to the visitor on a fine winter's day of the menace that the cliffs can hold. On a normal day, however, with low cloud and spindrift swirling in the gullies the thoughts of the Ben Nevis climber might justifiably be more sombre. Many have remarked that the northern side of the Ben has an atmosphere only to be found elsewhere on the North Face of the Eiger. Significantly, the Ben has an Eiger-like story of tragedy and disaster: the occurrence of the unforeseeable is common-place. Small wonder, then, that Ben Nevis has given birth to some of the most remarkable and destructive Scottish avalanches.

On March 26,1978, there was a fair amount of activity on the Ben. A climber had been hurt in *Observatory Gully* and a RAF helicopter had been called to assist in the evacuation of the casualty. Late in the afternoon the helicopter was returning with the injured climber, passing the cliffs of Carn Dearg when the crew noticed some marks in the snow beneath the cliff. They appeared to be blood stains.

As the helicopter was coming down the Allt a' Mhuillin glen, its progress had been observed by four young Irish hillwalkers. They were below the cliffs of Carn Dearg, some distance above the main path between Lochan Meall an-t-Suidhe and the CIC Hut. They stopped to take photographs of the helicopter as it approached. By no stretch of the imagination were they in what could normally be called a dangerous position. But as the helicopter approached them, a mighty avalanche broke loose from the cliffs above and swept down towards them on a front of 250m. No evasive or defensive action could be of any use in the face of such an overwhelming mass of snow. The tide broke over them and carried them down.

Miraculously, as the avalanche came to a halt, three of the party were still on the surface, though partly buried and suffering from serious injuries. Of the fourth man, there was no trace.

This was one of the largest wet-snow avalanches ever seen in Scotland. We have said that this kind of avalanche is more easily foreseeable, and therefore, guarded against, than a windslab avalanche. But who would expect to be avalanched in such a place?

The injured walkers were quickly rescued and a search initiated for the missing man, although in truth the chances of a live rescue were small. Wet snow contains little air and can set round the victim like concrete, making breathing impossible. Despite the use of dogs, teams of probers and electronic equipment, the missing man was not found until the 28th. His body was located near the burn, some 100m below the point where the avalanche struck him, perhaps the unluckiest of all the Ben's many victims.

Coire an t-Sneachda, December 30, 1986

"There are some days when no steep ground is safe from avalanche hazard – just about every ridge and buttress route has small snowfields on it – and even a very small avalanche can have serious consequences."

A personal recollection by Bob Barton.

It was late December and my week, instructing a winter mountaineering group, had been made difficult by continuously bad weather, high winds and intermittent heavy snowfalls.

On this day conditions were scarcely any better, but the dawn was bright and the winds had eased to 55mph or so as we headed up into the corrie. If we were to climb, today was probably the day. The corrie was a spectacular place that morning with huge downdraughts swirling down the crags and a baleful light emphasising the contrast between the shallow icy snow from November, the whiter than white new drifts and the bold crags of granite.

That there was a considerable hazard of avalanche was all too clear and this was confirmed by the behaviour of the shallow patches of new windslab breaking readily away under my feet. I chose to follow the buttress line to the right of *Jacob's Ladder*, reasoning that we could keep close to the rocks and avoid any significant accumulation areas. So it proved for a couple of pitches; there was certainly windslab but it was only a few inches deep and easily penetrated to the hard snow beneath. However, as we climbed, the weather deteriorated further, with increasing wind and much blowing snow.

I was climbing unroped, my clients, George Williamson, Peter Mansell, David Cash and Mike Green, climbing roped as two twosomes, this being the generally adopted practice of Glenmore Lodge parties at that time. We had reached a sound anchor beneath a small outcrop of rock. Mike and George, the two lead climbers were ready to continue, so I set off first, making an initial traverse to the left onto an apron of snow, perhaps the size of a living room carpet, below another

rock wall. As I did so the thickness of the windslab increased; 15cm, 20cm, perhaps 30cm.

"I don't like the snow here. You stay there while I have a closer look."

I took a couple of steps up, tempted on by the apparent haven of the rocks above and reached up with my axe to probe the snow. As I did so a small slab of snow above me detached. For a moment I was able to resist, but it felt rather like trying to hold several sheets of plasterboard while off balance so, almost immediately, I was knocked over and began to fall, rocketing down the icy snow, head first, on my back.

I quickly grasped my ice axe and began self arrest, but before this could have any effect I shot over an outcrop and crashed onto a lower slope of hard snow, travelling ever faster and still head first. In the impact I had lost my grip on the axe, which now flailed on its sling. I reeled it in and braked again, but once more went airborne over a second, bigger crag to accelerate down yet another snowfield.

Meanwhile, during the few seconds of the fall, as though all normal filters had been removed, my consciousness, my life, had become an intense matrix of parallel paths, each with a different focus and each unrolling at a different pace. One path urgently managed the business of self arrest and survival while another, with great concentration, as though in a vital chess game, monitored progress, ticking off each impact survived, assessing and re-assessing my chances of success. At the same time, another part of my mind was focused closely on each member of my family. Another channel seemed tuned into trivia – my breakfast that morning, the imminent Hogmanay party and so it went on.

A violent impact brought me suddenly to a halt. I had crashed into the boulder field at the foot of the crag and was swamped with two successive waves of emotion; the first of amazement and relief that I was alive and no longer falling, the second of anxiety and guilt for a responsibility abandoned, for I had no knowledge of how my students had fared.

Steve Penny

Fig. 5.8 Inspired flying by RAF Rescue helicopter teams in poor conditions remains a constant source of admiration among all mountaineers

I shouted and tried to stand up to look for them but a dizzying pain in my lower abdomen quickly persuaded me to stay lying on the snow. There was no sign of other life, only the rocks, the snow and the howl of the wind.

I struggled to remove my rucksack, unable to move my right arm, and extracted my radio. "Glenmore Base, Glenmore Base this is Glenmore Bob. Do you read? Over." Miraculously, the radio operated correctly and within a few minutes Roger O'Donovan responded, his lunch-time tranquillity soon to be shattered.

"Roger, I've been avalanched right of Jacob's Ladder and I think that my students are still on the crag. Can you send someone to find them?"

"Yes, I'm OK."

"Yes, they were on a good belay and I think they are probably OK."

"No, I can't walk and I'll need a stretcher."

"Yes, I'm definitely at the bottom of the crag."

"Thanks. Listening Out."

Within a few minutes, my colleagues Iain Peter and Sam Crymble arrived and, a little later, Adrian Liddell. Iain headed up and brought down all my students, who having seen me swept away, were already descending to give assistance.

I was bundled into a bivi-bag and then began the long wait. Sammy, as always, kept up an excellent level of banter, but the weather continued to deteriorate and we were all extremely cold by the time the stretcher arrived. I had been carried a short way down the corrie when Sammy told me that they were trying to get a helicopter in. I had been involved in enough rescues to know that flying conditions were extremely unfavourable, but thanks to some completely inspired flying by the RAF crew, I was soon underneath a hovering Sea King in an amazing maelstrom of noise, whirling snow and yellow metal. Inside, our local doctor, Marjorie Langmuir gave me a quick check over and we sped off to Raigmore Hospital.

At first I seemed to have escaped lightly. Fractures to pelvis, ribs, clavicle and scapula were all expected, given time, to heal. Unfortunately, these multiple fractures had released enormous numbers of fatty globules into my blood and as a result of this my lung function virtually disappeared, necessitating several days on a ventilator, and many anxious days for my family.

There are lessons to be drawn, none of them new, but worth identification nonetheless. The incident emphasises that there are some days when no steep ground is safe from avalanche hazard – just about every ridge and buttress route has small snowfields on it – and even a very small avalanche can have serious consequences.

I should have roped up (or probably, turned back, but even that was not without its own dangers) when I became suspicious of the conditions. On a rope, the consequences of being knocked off would probably have been minor. Guides and instructors are under great pressures (mostly self-imposed) to provide clients with what they have paid for. Several days of 'bad weather alternatives' tend to distort the judgmental processes of the instructor making it even harder to make the right choice.

The damage caused by the fall was also greater than it might have been because in late December the boulder fields were not yet masked with snow. If they had been fully covered I might have fallen further but hit less. I was wearing a semi rigid rucksack containing emergency gear. I believe that this protected me from more serious injury by absorbing repeated impacts during my fall of more than 60 metres.

I could have described each of the contributory factors in advance of my accident – I was not uninformed. The fact that I got it wrong might illustrate my belief that if you regularly go out in full winter conditions, it is very hard to get it right all the time. And that, of course, is one of its joys and compelling attractions.

Fig. 6.1 Rescuers attend to the injured below Great End, Lake District after the avalanche of February 4, 1991

VI   Avalanches in England & Wales

Avalanches show no respect for national boundaries. If the correct combination of snowfall and topography exists, they will occur anywhere. The existence of a significant avalanche hazard in Scotland is now comparatively well known. However, awareness of the level of avalanche hazard in England and Wales seems to be limited to a comparative few, often those with personal experience of avalanche conditions elsewhere.

Information on the incidents that do occur in England and Wales is sometimes hard to come by, and many significant incidents have probably passed unrecorded. Even on the evidence of the limited records, it is clear that a significant hazard can exist in all upland areas of England and Wales, and occasionally, in Ireland too.

The avalanche at Lewes in Sussex, described in Chapter I, is one of the few British locations where an avalanche has actually destroyed a building. This happened not just once, but twice, in the years of 1787 and 1836; the latter being the most serious British incident in terms of loss of life.

At least 26 people have died in avalanches in England and Wales, with at least five incidents involving multiple fatalities. Of the 48 recorded incidents, nine involved one or more of the victims being buried under debris, and of these nine cases, five have involved fatalities. Thus, although burial has not been frequent, when it occurs it has often had severe consequences.

The victims of avalanches outwith Scotland have included climbers, walkers, skiers, shepherds and the good people of Lewes at their firesides. On a number of occasions more than one avalanche incident has occurred on the same day, a phenomenon well known in Scotland.

Perhaps even more than in Scotland, many incidents are confined to a few locations. If snow falls in the Lake District, climbers seem to head to Great End; in North Wales to *Parsley Fern Gully* on Snowdon or to the Black Ladders in the Carneddau and so on. It is noteworthy that all these locations are of north-easterly aspect and thus prone to accumulation of snow in the prevailing south-westerly winds.

These 'black spots' probably feature so commonly in the statistics because they are the obvious choices for winter activities. The conditions that led to avalanches on these cliffs are likely to have been widespread, but more incidents are not recorded at other locations because climbers were only present to trigger avalanches on the popular climbs. This "honey pot" effect appears to have had unfortunate consequences in that, on several occasions, avalanches, which have been triggered by parties above, have caught people beneath. To climb in hazardous conditions is dangerous enough; to follow another party in the same conditions is even more so.

The locations that feature with some regularity are as follows:

- Lake District – Great End (usually Central Gully); eight incidents.
- North Wales – Black Ladders; four incidents.
- North Wales – Parsley Fern Gully; two incidents.
- North Wales – Y Garn; four incidents.
- North Wales – Foel Grach; two very large incidents.

- Cheviots – six incidents in several locations.

The majority of incidents are clustered in a few years, 1979, 1988, 1991, 1994, 'good' winters for climbers and skiers with lying snow and sustained low temperatures. The historical record suggests that the winter of 1886 would have provided outstandingly good conditions for skiing in the Cheviots since three large avalanches were recorded.

A substantial number of avalanches have undoubtedly occurred which have not appeared in mountain rescue statistics, the main source of this data, because no injury occurred. The following is an account by Tony Howard which captures the delight of snatched winter days and the excitement of a close shave in the Peak District.

"In the early seventies I was in an avalanche on the top of Dovestones Quarry. Climbing conditions in the quarry were excellent. I cramponed up from well below the quarry. Having soloed up the edge of Waterfall Climb I emerged onto the upper slope to see that it looked prime avalanche terrain. Perforating it like toilet paper by traversing off to escape the drop below seemed like a bad plan, so I went directly for a small rock tower perhaps 20 metres above and reached it safely, cramponing on hard crust covering soft snow.

"Continuing on, I was just about to plunge my axes with relief into the easing angle where the slope meets the moor when the whole slope cracked off in a big slab avalanche! Probably at least 50 metres either side of me, right along the moor edge across the top of the quarry. I was instantly going backwards, thigh deep in snow and could hear the roar of the lower avalanche edge dropping down the 50 metre vertical cliff to the quarry floor!

"Due to the pressure of snow, I couldn't get my body forward enough to get the axes in, then I went backwards over the small five metre tower, landed with a thud in the snow at its foot, sunk both axes in and the avalanche continued past, mostly over the top of me and down the crag... and left the world to silence and to me.

Which was all a lot more exciting than the traditional family Christmas do I had sneaked out of on a perfect blue sky, frosty winter's day!"

One for the collector of esoteric rarities is the only record that we have of an avalanche in Ireland, on Carrauntoohil in 1986, here described by Denis O'Connell, Pat Long and Deirdre Kelly from their account in the *Mountain Log*. Note again the juxtaposition of unusually 'good' winter conditions and the presence of an avalanche hazard. A graupel layer appears to have been present.

"Conditions were the best yet seen in Kerry with a good build-up of hard snow and ice on the North Face of Carraun. Several lines, often wished for, on the face seemed in good condition, but for our first foray on ice in a year we opted for the far easier outflow stream from the Looking Glass. This was soloed on quite good ice. We then decided to do Curved Gully which appeared to be well banked up and liable to give 1,100 feet of steep but straightforward cramponing. I broke through the crust about two thirds of the way up to a deep layer of 'aerobeads' which flowed from underfoot."

Deirdre writes: "150 feet from the top I met a band of soft, white snow, dug in my axe and looked for a way round it. Next minute, the whole gully seemed to move and I was flying at breakneck speed head first on my back, terrified more by the speed than anything else. I felt the impact of a body, thought somebody had tried to stop me but on I sped, still hopelessly out of control. My shoulder hit a rock and I felt it crack. I knew that if I hit something else I was finished and resigned myself to certain death.

"I had stopped! Everything was so quiet. I did not know what had happened to the others, but I had to find out. It took me some time to work up the nerve to move. I climbed carefully up the gully and out to the right where Pat was crawling off the slope aided on a rope by Denis. Both had lost their crampons and ice axes, though I still had mine. I went down the

Tom Prentice

Fig. 6.2 Climbers in one of the popular Trinity gullies on Snowdon

slope to the Looking Glass calling to our friends on the North Face for help while the others slowly descended. Pat got into his bivi bag while Denis and I looked for a sheltered spot. The bivi bag was spotted by Tom Murphy on the Beenkeeragh Ridge who also could hear our shouts. He descended and alerted the rescue team. This also alerted our friends who then had to descend several hard pitches before reaching us at about 6.30pm. They left all their spare food and clothes and went down for help.

"For us it was a case of waiting and shivering. We did not dare entertain the hope of seeing anyone before dawn so every minute that passed was an achievement and we could hope for nothing more. The relief and joy was indescribable when we heard voices at about 1.00am. It was over! For our rescuers it had just begun."

Avalanche Statistics

This summary of the currently available information on incidents in England and Wales undoubtedly contains inaccuracies and omissions. The authors would value any assistance towards improving the accuracy and completeness of this record, and details can be sent to them at: Scottish Avalanche Information Service, Freepost, Glenmore Lodge, Aviemore, Inverness-shire PH22 1BR.

A more flexible approach to inclusion has been used than that applied to the Scottish data in Appendix III and some of the incidents listed here have resulted in no injury.

(B) = burial, (F) = fatality.

1787		**Sussex, Lewes.** Thaw conditions, buildings destroyed.
1820	Jan 27	**Cheviots, Upper Coquetdale,** (1B, 1F). Shepherd dies under "enormous weight of snow".
1836	Dec 27	**Sussex, Lewes,** (8F). Avalanche from cliff above town destroyed houses. Cold with new snow.
1874		**Cheviots, Fairhaugh.** Shepherd avoids burial in cottage.
1886	Mar 3	**Cheviots, Lord's Seat.** Crushes 14 sheep.
1886	Mar 1	**Cheviots, Wholshope Hill.** Huge avalanche in same valley as 1820 fatality.
1888	Feb 27	**Peak District, Whinstone Lee Tor,** (1B, 1F). Dogs rescue one, other buried "yards deep".
1950		**North Wales, Y Garn,** (1F). Details uncertain.
1957		**North Wales, Y Garn,** (1F). Cornice collapse, four involved.
1963	Jan 1	**Peak District, Chew Valley,** (2B, 2F). Two experienced climbers die in *Wilderness East Gully*. Three involved, very heavy snow.
1965	Nov 1	**North Wales, Foel Fras.** Open slope avalanche 500m wide.
1968	Feb 2	**North Wales, Foel Grach** below refuge. Very large avalanche above Dulyn cliffs.
1976	Dec 4	**North Wales, Snowdon,** *Parsley Fern Gully*. Two swept 210m, multiple injuries.
1977	Jan 21	**North Wales, Black Ladders,** (1B). Three avalanched at foot of cliff after abandoning climb.
1977	Feb 22	**North Wales, Black Ladders,** *Central Gully*, (1F). Two hit by triggered cornice collapse.
1979	Jan 13	**North Wales, Cyrn Las,** *Face Route*. Two carried 70m, recorded on film?
1979	Jan 28	**North Wales, Crib Goch.** One person, fractured ankle.
1979	Jan 28	**Pennines, Ashway Gap,** (1F). Walker avalanched crossing quarry face.
1980	Jan 20	**Lake District, Great End,** (1B). Two, head and neck injuries, probably climbing *Central Gully*.
1980	Jan 20	**Lake District, Helvellyn.** One injured.
1982?		**Lake District Harter Fell.** Five unhurt.
1984	Feb 25	**North Wales, Black Ladders,** (2F). Four carried 300m from below *Central Gully* cornice.
1984	Feb 29	**North Wales, Nameless Cwm.** 10 partially buried. New snow on headwall.
1985	Jan 27	**North Wales, Crib y Ddysgyl,** (1F). *Sinister Gully*.
1986	Jan 28	**North Wales, Black Ladders,** (2F, 1B). *Somme Route*, possibly swept from easy ground at top.
1986	Feb 14	**Peak District, Crowden,** (1B). Skier in wet slab avalanche at 400m.
1986		**Ireland, Carrauntoohil.** Three hit in *Curved Gully*, shoulder fracture.
1988	Feb 7	**Lake District, Scafell Crag.** Climber carried 260m, fractured ribs.

Bob Barton

Fig. 6.3 A notorious avalanche blackspot – Great End, Lake District, in classic conditions during 1974

1988	Feb 7	**Cheviots, Bizzle Crag**, (2B, 2F). Five skiers.
1988	Feb 2	**North Wales, Y Garn**. *B Gully* avalanches as party climb *C Gully*, five involved.
1989	Feb 4	**North Wales, Foel Grach**. Large, full depth, wet slab.
1991	Jan 13	**Lake District, Great End**. Four people in two avalanches.
1991	Jan 13	**Lake District, Helvellyn**. Two with broken legs after slab/cornice collapse in *Nethermost Gully*.
1991	Feb 10	**Peak District, Kinder** (1B, 1F). Two walkers trigger slab below cornice in Crowden Brook; 1.2 metre deep, asphyxia.
1991	Feb 4	**Lake District, Great End**. Six in slab/cornice collapse after heavy snow, fractured pelvis etc.
1991	Feb 15	**Lake District, Great End**. Slab below cornice in thaw.
1991	3 Mar	**Lake District, Great End**. Four in possible spontaneous avalanche in *Broad Gully*, fractured pelvis.
1993	Feb 2	**North Wales, Glyder Fawr**. Four carried 35m.
1994	Feb 20	**North Wales, Snowdon**, (1B). Climber buried to neck in *Parsley Fern Gully*, uninjured.
1996	Feb 8	**Lake District, Birks, Grisedale**, (1F). Lone walker carried 60m by slab, head injuries.
1999	17 Jan	**Lake District, Great End**. Four hit by windslab in busy *Central Gully*, two injured.

Fig. 7.1 *Studying snow crystals under a lupe glass. It is preferable to wear gloves*

VII The SAIS story

A personal account by Blyth Wright

For many years, it had been thought by some of us involved both in mountain training and mountain rescue, that it would be helpful to create in Scotland a system of avalanche forecasting modelled on the provision in alpine countries. Early work was done by Eric Langmuir while Principal at Glenmore Lodge, as well as by Ben Beattie, who was an instructor at the same establishment. Ben's death on Nanda Devi in 1978 set back avalanche work in Scotland by several years. Rod Ward added to this work in the 1970s, when based at Glenmore Lodge during his completion of the first avalanche-related PhD in Scotland. Hamish MacInnes, resident on the other side of the country in Glen Coe, also made a significant contribution.

Various prominent figures in the field of avalanche science visited this country and gave us the benefit of their opinions. Notable among these was André Roch, formerly of the Swiss Federal Snow and Avalanche Research Institute at Davos. André, aged 71 at the time of his visit in 1978, was in the view of many, the ideal expression of the mountaineer – avalanche scientist. His first ascents in the Alps, such as the North Face of the Triolet, still command respect, while his capacity for communicating his knowledge of snow and avalanche related topics made him almost a cult figure, particularly in North America.

It was generally agreed that Scotland had a very special avalanche problem, largely related to the extreme volatility of the mountain weather regime compared to alpine conditions. The attempts at forecasting made by the early workers, based on methods in use in the Alps and elsewhere, did not give good results. This was later found to be due to over-reliance on observations performed at fixed-site snow study plots, as well as a failure to appreciate the necessity of continuous daily observation. Because of the marked variability of avalanche hazard with altitude in Scotland, it was found essential in most conditions to carry out observations in or near actual avalanche starting zones.

In the mid 1980s, it appeared that we were facing a fairly sharp escalation of the seriousness of the problem. Fatalities, including the death of one of Scotland's most promising young climbers, brought the subject of avalanche accidents and their prevention, into the media spotlight again. To many of us, though, it still seemed unlikely that the scale of the problem would be seen as great enough to attract the public funding which would be required to address it. However, in this we had under-estimated the degree of public concern. The issue had entered the political domain and it became evident that the establishment of an avalanche forecasting service enjoyed a considerable degree of cross-party support in the House of Commons.

Forecasting Service Established

In the winter of 1988, a decision was made at ministerial level in The Scottish Office that a pilot avalanche project would go ahead the next winter. This was to take place under the aegis of the Scottish Sports Council (SSC), which seemed appropriate given the expertise which existed at the Council's National Sports Training Centre

Mountainsportphoto.com

Fig. 7.2 The accurate recording of snowpack data is an essential element in avalanche prediction

at Glenmore Lodge. An administrative structure was rapidly evolved, with the backing of many interested agencies and at the same time the Scottish Mountain Safety Group was created, to advise the SSC on the progress of the Scottish Avalanche Project, as the initiative was to be called, as well as on other mountain safety-related matters.

It was decided that the project would operate initially in Glen Coe and the Northern Cairngorms, two of the main problem areas. In the case of the other prime avalanche accident venue, Ben Nevis, daily access to the avalanche starting zones was deemed to be too difficult for the meantime. Teams of three observers were established in each of the two areas, in order to give adequate daily coverage. Experienced mountaineers, guides, instructors, mountain rescue team members and similarly

qualified practitioners were selected rather than theoreticians, as a high degree of mountaineering skill would be necessary in order to retrieve the information from difficult mountain locations in all winter weathers. They would receive the necessary training in observation and recording techniques, based largely upon the training which Glenmore Lodge staff had received in France and Switzerland.

In the first season, Eric Langmuir as chairman both of the Scottish Mountain Safety Group and the Scottish Avalanche Project, bore overall responsibility. In Glen Coe, Hamish MacInnes acted as supervisor, while I discharged the same function for the Northern Cairngorms during my somewhat scanty spare time. The latter difficulty was addressed when, for Winter 1989-90, the Scottish Sports Council agreed to my secondment from my job as an instructor at Glenmore Lodge, to act as the full-time Co-ordinator of the project during the winter months. At first, due to pressure on accommodation at the Lodge, this required me to work from home, which at the time was unsuitable. The Co-ordinator then occupied a succession of progressively more adequate offices at the Lodge, starting with the 'famous' garden shed and ending, for the meantime, with the present relatively spacious premises. Without the willing co-operation of Glenmore Lodge and other council staff during this time, the strain placed on the system would have been virtually insupportable.

The project was supported by the Meteorological Office via Glasgow Weather Centre, and observers were in the privileged position of being able to speak directly to duty weather forecasters. In the first two seasons, apart from display on local bulletin boards, the Met. Office's Mountaincall recorded message service and a similar service called Climbline, were the mainstay of distribution for the bulletins (or Snow and Avalanche Reports, as they were called.) Two national newspapers, *The Herald* and *The Scotsman* also printed the daily reports, but we were in general rather disappointed with the coverage of reports in the media. We little realised how much work had to go in to earning the wider coverage which assiduous co-operation with the media would bring. Credibility would have to be earned and that would not be an overnight phenomenon.

It should not be thought that in the early years the project enjoyed universal support from Scotland's mountaineering community, or indeed that the SAIS does so now. There were those who saw providing reports as an intrusion, while some mountaineering professionals saw possible liability problems in the event of accident. The experience of fighting front and back in trying to deal with the avalanche problem became familiar. There is no doubt that some cast envious eyes on the budget which had been

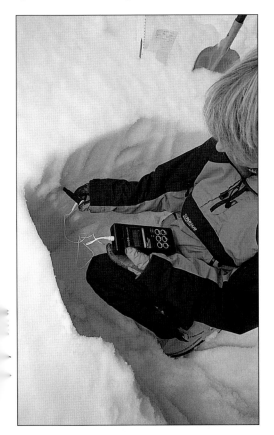

Fig. 7.3 Determining the temperature gradient between snow layers in a snowpit

allocated to SAIS, feeling it could be more usefully spent on other aspects of mountain safety. There were two answers to this: firstly, if the money had not been assigned to avalanche work, it would not have been assigned to other mountain-related activities. It would simply have disappeared. Secondly, I felt that we had identified a problem which could be alleviated by certain action, which required to be funded. We had successfully presented our case and if others could identify similarly deserving projects, then it was open to them to try to do the same.

Gradually, however, as it became apparent that the provision of reports was not intended to threaten the freedom of choice of those going to the hills, and that individuals within the service saw themselves as among the custodians of the Scottish mountaineering tradition, this problem receded.

The mountaineering credentials of our observers, some of them climbers of international repute, were also crucial in this process. In addition, as technology has increasingly become part of the operation and a rising generation of computer literate and information friendly mountaineers takes to the hills, this trend is reinforced.

In the early days, the methodology of observation had not evolved far from the techniques used by Langmuir, Beattie and Ward. Daily surface snowpits were dug and crystal size and type, wetness and hardness, as well as shovel test values were observed. It has to be said that the recording of this information in those early days, was less than systematic. Weekly ram penetrometer profiles were also performed and although the point of carrying out this exercise, sometimes in iron-hard snow-ice or névé escaped some of our observers, the data gave us the first apparent evidence of the process of temperature gradient weakening taking place over a period of time in the Scottish snowpack (Fig. 7.3).

From the start, a five-point rising scale of avalanche hazard, was used, from Category 1 (Very Low), to Category 5 (Very High). The Category 5 designation was based on the conditions which existed in

Glen Coe on February 6, 1988, when several accidents occurred and an 'all altitudes, all aspects' hazard existed. These conditions, which I witnessed on the day, were unique in my experience and it was envisaged that the implementation of Category 5 would be very rare. Our use of the five-point scale meant that much later, when in winter 1994-95 it was decided to change to the new five-point common European Avalanche Hazard Scale, little adaptation was necessary.

It has to be admitted that in the first two seasons, the project was involved to a large extent in 'now-casting'. In other words, a hazard category was issued only for the day of observation, while the outlook or forecast day had no category assigned, although the text would specify the likely development of the avalanche hazard.

When, for the 1990-91 season, I insisted on the implementation of the hazard category for the forecast day, this met with considerable resistance from the observers, who were not confident about their ability to meet this requirement successfully. However, results soon showed that it was not only possible, but appreciated by the public. In particular, newspapers became much more interested, as journalists had previously felt that our reports tended to put the emphasis on yesterday's news.

There was also a feeling among observers that assigning a hazard category to the forecast day would lead to the situation where users might read only the category, without reading the text.

Recognising this potential problem, it was agreed that for the 1994-95 season only the verbal description, e.g. 'High', would be used in the outlook or forecast section of the report, leaving out the number. As the winter progressed, it became evident that we were in the middle of Scotland's worst ever season for avalanche fatalities and I unilaterally rescinded the arrangement. My reaction may well have been subjective, as there really was nothing to show cause and effect, but as all the European avalanche services had by then adopted the same system, there has never since been much temptation to go back (Fig. 7.4).

Along with the appointment of a full-time co-ordinator in winter 1989-90 came an enhancement of the scope of the forecasting provision. The opening of the Aonach Mor ski area made possible an extension of the service to cover Lochaber. Although it was still envisaged that daily observations on the Ben Nevis snowfields were impracticable, the opening of the ski lifts enabled rapid access to slopes of the same orientation on the East Face of Aonach Mor, at altitudes which were comparable to Coire na Ciste on the Ben. It was hoped that the Aonach Mor sites would be sufficiently similar to the Ben Nevis sites to act as analogues in most cases. Experience rapidly proved this to be true, although visits to the Ben were made as often as deemed to be necessary.

This provision filled the major gap in our coverage, but other developments were also in hand.

SNOW AND AVALANCHE REPORT LOCHABER

AVALANCHE HAZARD 1500 HRS TUE 3/2/98
Snow showers and strong Westerly winds have continued to load sheltered areas with fresh snow. This snow has formed as soft unstable windslab and is poorly bonded to the underlying snow layers. Main accumulations exist at the tops of NE, E and SE facing slopes and gullies above 1000m. In these locations the avalanche hazard is High (Category 4). Soft unstable cornices have also formed above these aspects. Avalanche incident reported in Coire an Lochain, Aonach Mor.

AVALANCHE HAZARD OUTLOOK WED 4/2/98
Snow accompanied by strong Westerly winds will continue overnight and during Wednesday. Areas of unstable snow will continue to form, with greatest accumulations being at the tops of NE, E and SE facing slopes and gullies above 1000m. Avalanches will occur in these locations. The avalanche hazard will be High (Category 4). Cornices will continue to form and be prone to collapse.

CLIMBING CONDITIONS

SNOW DISTRIBUTION: Fresh snow falling above 800m.
ICING: Freezing level remaining at around 800m.
COMMENT: Soft unstable snow present at the tops of many gullies.

Fig. 7.4

Alan Hinkes

Fig. 7.5 Checking the scarp slope below the cornice on Aonach Mor

Lochnagar on the royal estate of Balmoral was well-known as the site of several avalanche accidents and presented itself as the next location most deserving of attention. It was felt, however, that the magnitude of the problem did not at the time justify a full-time presence, but that a weekend coverage might be appropriate. A different approach would be tried, with observers present one day per week, on Fridays, and using a 48-hour weather forecast to produce reports covering Saturday and Sunday.

Finding mountaineers resident on Deeside who could commit themselves to this task proved difficult and ultimately much of the work was done by Eric Langmuir and myself. This involved several hair-raising journeys from Strathspey on snow covered roads. In the event, the exercise did not prove productive, as the 48-hour weather forecasts were not sufficiently detailed for the purposes of avalanche forecasting and one or two near disasters resulted.

In the ensuing two seasons of 1989-90, observer presence on both Friday and Saturday ensured a much more satisfactory operation and results improved dramatically. After that, however, the Lochnagar presence was deemed not to be cost effective and was withdrawn, not to be reinstated until the South Cairngorm operation was introduced in winter 1996-97.

The forecasting operation was not the only concern of the Scottish Avalanche Project. Along with forecasting came a wider effort both to raise the awareness of the avalanche problem in Scotland and to enhance the level of technical knowledge of snow and avalanche-related matters. This was done by poster and leaflet campaigns, lectures to mountaineering and ski clubs, and assiduous use of the opportunities presented by our now very considerable media profile. Glenmore

Blyth Wright

Fig. 7.6 The original Heriot-Watt University Automatic Weather Station on the summit of Cairn Gorm

Lodge also improved its programme of avalanche courses. In co-operation with the providers of the Lodge's courses, a syllabus for an SAIS approved two-day course was evolved and SAIS attendance certificates issued. In the opinion of some, the raising of the public awareness of the avalanche problem in Scotland and indeed the UK, has been the major achievement of the whole operation, although this would not necessarily be my own view.

Another very important strand of the effort was involvement with academic institutions. This arose naturally, from requests for data to assist with academic projects, but grew to such an extent that it has now become a major feature of the operation, enabling the avalanche service to access resources which would otherwise never have been available. In particular, the work undertaken by Ross Purves in the course of his PhD research project over the

three winters from 1992-93 to 1994-5, gave new insights into snow temperatures and demonstrated the possibility of automatic monitoring of snowpack temperature and depth in the wet/cold Scottish mountain environment. Interestingly, the influence of solar warming much earlier in the winter than we had hitherto believed possible, was also shown. There were many spin-offs from this work, not least the continued links it brought with Heriot-Watt University and the Department of Geography at the University of Edinburgh (Figs. 7.6 & 7.7).

Prior to the winter of 1990-91, the two-year pilot scheme of the Scottish Avalanche Project was judged to have been a success and the operation adopted as a service of the Scottish Sports Council. It was renamed, somewhat cumbrously, the Scottish Avalanche Information Service and would run for a three-year period before further review.

The European Dimension

A very important development at this time lay in the establishment of much improved links with avalanche services in other countries, particularly continental Europe. This was initiated by the Swiss Federal Snow and Avalanche Research Institute at Davos, in the person of Dr Othmar Buser. He had been given the task of developing the NXD Nearest Neighbours numerical avalanche forecasting model and was interested to see whether it could be applied to our Scottish climate regime.

This was opportune, as for winter 1990-91 we were improving the recording of the data in our daily surface snowpits, including daily snow temperature profiles, specifically with reference to the requirements of possible future forecasting models.

Fig. 7.7 Ross Purves installs a snow temperature station on the Cairn Gorm plateau above Coire Laogh Mor. Installed in early winter, the station was then buried by snow and transmitted half-hourly snow temperature readings to the SAIS office at Glenmore Lodge

A visit was arranged and in November 1991 Othmar Buser came to Scotland. This was the first of several visits, during which versions of the NXD model were configured for all three of the then SAIS areas. Some interesting problems presented themselves. For instance, the Swiss model contained no input for the effect of rain on the snowpack, a fairly important consideration in Scotland. However, these problems were gradually overcome and NXD became a useful addition to the resources available to SAIS observers. A British Council grant enabled some reciprocal visiting and SAIS observers benefited from first-hand experience of developments at the Davos Institute. One of Buser's colleagues at the Davos institute, Dr. Robert Bolognesi, also visited Scotland. Bolognesi, with experience of working in both the French and Swiss systems, is one of the world's top experts on computer avalanche forecasting models. He brought with him his latest brainchild, NX.LOG, a rules-based model which we hoped to trial in Lochaber. Unfortunately, it turned out to depend too heavily for our purposes on explosive control of avalanche paths and we retained NXD as our forecasting model.

As it happened, Bolognesi's visit took place in February 1995 during the 'Black Winter' described in Chapter VIII. The avalanche search in Coire na Tulaich in Glen Coe was at an advanced stage, with huge excavations covering most of the corrie. His outings with our observers in the three areas also took place in realistic conditions and he left well impressed both with the scale of the avalanche problem in Scotland and the measures being taken to combat it.

The French avalanche service, under the auspices of Météo France, was also most helpful and very generously gave us their state-of-the-art ADIPRA data management programme. SAIS, or rather its collaborators, later evolved custom programmes similar to ADIPRA.

Information technology in many of its aspects has become a major feature of the SAIS operation. Aside from computer forecasting and data management, modern telecommunication systems have become a vital element. This grew from a Met. Office insistence that SAIS improve the system of transmission of reports to them. As they were prepared to delegate their Scottish IT manager, Gavin Owen, to do this, they met with no strong objection. SAIS had, of course, to find resources to supply each area base with the necessary computer and peripheral equipment, but this was ultimately begged, borrowed or, if necessary, bought. Many things were learned about the black art of tele-communications as applied to sometimes cranky Highland phone lines, but a working system was evolved and Gavin Owen's programmes remain the basis of SAIS communications.

This has had other spin-offs, including the more professional printing of reports for local display and the much improved transmission of reports to the media via electronic mailboxes.

However, perhaps the most significant addition to the capability of SAIS which this permitted was the transmission of reports to a website at Glasgow University. In the winter of 1993-94, the SAIS website, created by Mark Sanderson and now maintained by Norman Davis, was the first avalanche service website in the world to feature daily avalanche bulletins, (see Appendix V). Subsequently, this website has proven of immense value, not only in the dissemination of the reports, but also in enabling communication with the public, so that feedback as well as supplementary information on avalanche occurrence may be received and ideas for improvements to the service implemented.

Following a full-scale review of SAIS, commissioned by the Scottish Sports Council in 1996, two further additions were made to the areas covered by SAIS. A personal change for me at this time also occurred when I took early retirement from my instructional job at Glenmore Lodge. My continued role as SAIS co-ordinator was then on a contract basis.

Expanding Coverage

As a result of the review, it was decided to reinstate coverage on Deeside, but to broaden the geographical scope, so that Glen Shee and occasionally Beinn a' Bhuird might be covered. Recent visitor studies, as well as subjective opinion, indicated that climbing on Lochnagar and mountaineering in other parts of the area was no longer only a weekend phenomenon. The diffuse nature of the topography meant that two bases were necessary and these were found in Ballater and Braemar, through the generosity of the education authority and police respectively. Although qualified mountaineers were now available on Deeside, it was decided that for an initial period the operation would be staffed by persons familiar with SAIS working methods.

The other new area was Creag Meagaidh above Loch Laggan, which had emerged in recent years as justifying provision. It had been the scene of a number of serious avalanche accidents and Lochaber Mountain Rescue Team had made a formal request for coverage. However, it presented several serious practical difficulties.

It lay wholly within a national nature reserve and it was by no means guaranteed that its owners, Scottish Natural Heritage, would be agreeable to the operation. The SNH base at Aberarder, on the way in to Coire Ardair, would be the ideal, or perhaps the only possible base. Fortunately, SNH were happy to accommodate us, thereby eliminating the first major problem. However, Aberarder proved to be a telecommunications black hole and it would require all our hard-won expertise to achieve a workable system there.

The other major problem was logistical. Coire Ardair, the main climbing corrie, was a substantial hike from Aberarder and in deep snow conditions the problem of access would be considerable (Fig. 7.8). It also emerged that the path in to the

Tom Prentice

Fig. 7.8 Deep snow makes access to Coire Ardair of Creag Meagaidh, problematical. Instead, avalanche observers on skis head for readings in nearby Coire a' Chriochairein

corrie was threatened by avalanches at one point.

However, as with Aonach Mor and Ben Nevis, more accessible sites were found which gave good correlation with conditions in Coire Ardair. Coire nan Gall of Carn Liath was one of these, and included an excellent view of Coire Ardair from the summit. Thus, visits to Coire Ardair could be combined with observations at other sites.

Recruitment of observers presented a further difficulty. Lagganside was sparsely inhabited, with few, if any, suitably qualified mountaineers. Fortunately, Fort William and Roy Bridge to the west proved a fertile recruiting ground, as did Kingussie to the east, with probably a larger population of qualified mountain guides than any other village in the UK. Strangely,

the first avalanche casualty seen by SAIS observers on Meagaidh was a dog, a Labrador found dead in avalanche debris in Raeburn's Gully, alone and miles from anywhere.

Future Developments

What are the prospects for SAIS in the new millennium? On the organisational side, a further renewal of contracts may see new individuals involved. More broadly, the European dimension will become increasingly important, as harmonisation of procedures and joint research increase. SAIS presence at major meetings of the European avalanche services is now routine. The status of SAIS as a service of the Scottish Sports Council, linked to

Jerry Rawson

Fig. 7.9 Traversing Liathach in full winter conditions. Improved access and better information have led to more winter climbers in Torridon, more avalanche incidents, and calls for SAIS forecasting to be extended

the Scottish Office, has greatly eased acceptance into these forums. Our links with agencies outside Europe may grow and on a couple of occasions observers have attended the International Snow Science Workshop, held in the USA every two years. We have been honoured to welcome leading avalanche workers from Canada and the USA to Scotland over the past two years.

From the point of view of areas covered, there may be developments. However, it should be understood that a case has to be made for every extension of

the service, as there are inevitably budgetary implications. Any extension can only take place on the basis of a demonstrable avalanche problem in the area, evidenced by a significant number of avalanche accidents. What number might be classed as 'significant' is obviously open to debate, but it would require to be of a comparable magnitude to that which existed at Creag Meagaidh or Lochnagar.

Torridon has been heavily backed in some quarters as a candidate for SAIS coverage. Certainly, the area has seen some very regrettable accidents in recent years.

However, it is still true that the numbers do not compare with the other areas mentioned, even if the whole of Ross-shire is included. It is possible that things may change. Road travel is easier and the opening of the Kessock and Skye bridges have significantly affected patterns of mountain usage. Climbing fashions change too and the icefall climbing on the back of Liathach is now well known to climbers from south of the border. All of this will inevitably affect the accident rate in the areas which have effectively become less remote (Fig. 7.9).

A partial answer to this problem may lie in the refinement of computer forecasting techniques. A current research project, benefiting from a SSC grant, aims to use data obtained by SAIS observers and from automatic summit weather stations in two areas (Northern Cairngorms and Lochaber) to create a forecast for a third area (Ross-shire). The initial feasibility study for this was done by configuring an experimental version of NXD, results from which appeared to be encouraging.

Development and testing of the new model is being carried out at the Department of Geography in the University of Edinburgh. If tests are successful, field trials will take place with the co-operation of guides, instructors and other mountaineers in the Ross-shire area over the winter of 1999-2000.

At the moment, no avalanche forecasting agency in the world issues forecasts based solely on computer modelling. The human input is deemed necessary in order to eliminate any aberrations. However, given sufficient provisos and especially if reference to local observation is possible, then a useful aid to decision making may result. In this way it may be possible to extend provision to regions where a full SAIS presence cannot be justified.

A further area being explored at the Department of Geography lies in the three-dimensional visualisation of avalanche hazard. Two successive research projects within the department's MSc in GIS (Geographical Information Systems) have been devoted to this. The idea for this research came from an examination of one or two avalanche accidents in which the victims appeared to have accessed the avalanche forecast, but had failed to act upon it. It was felt that if the individuals involved had been able to see the report in the form of a graphic, they might have retained the information better.

In the model, a map is draped over the 3D representation of the mountain area and in turn, the zones subject to avalanche hazard are draped over this in colour. The avalanche hazard drape is automatically updated as the observer types in details of altitude, angle and orientation of the hazardous slopes. It is possible for the operator to 'fly through' the virtual mountain area and to follow a chosen route, noting whether the proposed climb or itinerary crosses any of the hazard zones. Ultimately, the 3D model could reside on the SAIS website, with data for the new overlays being transmitted to the site daily.

There are difficulties and perhaps dangers in presenting the public with such a 'virtual reality' game. For instance, potential run-out zones cannot yet be depicted. However, trials will shortly take place and the results are awaited with interest (see colour plates).

Despite the increasing contribution being made by technology, the backbone of the SAIS effort has been and will remain the work of the observers, who have carried out a very daunting task in bringing back systematic information from Scotland's winter mountains in all weathers. Also, in writing this, it has not been possible to thank the many organisations and individuals who have gone to immense trouble to assist the work of SAIS. Finally, it should be remembered that the Scottish Sports Council (now known as **sport**scotland) continued to fund the service at times when great demands were being made on its budgets, and that many SSC departments have made important contributions to the work.

Fig. 8.1 Rescuers attending to an injured climber after the March 25, 1995 avalanche on Cinderella, Creag Meagaidh. The climber's four companions wait below (see Appendix III)

VIII   1994-95: The Black Winter

A personal account by Blyth Wright

Winters in Scotland vary enormously from one season to another. One winter may be very cold, another may be very snowy, another snowless. Yet another may be characterised by high winds. Almost the only generalisation it is possible to make is that it is unlikely that consecutive winters will be similar.

However, in the two winters of 1993-94 and 1994-95, we seemed to have an exception to this. Both winters were relatively snowy and exhibited periods of fairly intense avalanche activity. Nevertheless, despite these similarities, their outcomes as regards accident statistics were very different. In the first winter, 65 persons were carried down by avalanches in Scotland and although five fatalities occurred, generally speaking there were many lucky escapes: people were walking away from their avalanche experiences. In Winter 1994-95, an equal number of incidents occurred, but the crucial difference was that, to a much greater extent, the victims were not spared.

The winter started quietly enough, with some avalanche activity reported on Creag Meagaidh and the Cairngorms by RAF Mountain Rescue Teams and instructors from Glenmore Lodge near Aviemore. Then, in January, came a number of incidents. On the January 4, avalanches occurred throughout Ross-shire, with sites including Fuar Tholl, The Saddle and Meall a' Chrasgaidh in the Fannaichs. In the incident on The Saddle, a party descending triggered a large slab, while in the Fannaichs an accident resulted in a spinal injury to one victim.

The broad-scale nature of the continuing hazard was shown when, on the next weekend, RAF teams reported the debris of a huge avalanche on Ben Lui near Tyndrum, the classic avalanche site described in Chapter V. It was no surprise, therefore, to hear of an avalanche accident the following Thursday in an even more southerly location, on Beinn Ime at Arrochar. In this a young climber was badly injured descending a gully. I was acquainted with the victim of this incident and was glad the injuries had not been still more serious.

Over the next few days further avalanche activity was reported, mainly in the Cairngorms, but with no further human involvement. Then, on January 21, came evidence of the persistence of the hazard in Wester Ross, with word of a fatal avalanche accident on Liathach, on a popular ice climb in Coireag Dubh Mor called *Poacher's Fall*. This was sad news and also rather strange, as it was almost a year on from a previous avalanche fatality on the same mountain, which had attracted widespread publicity. The victim in the latest accident was a young trainee mountain guide. His companion was also partly buried in the debris but not too seriously injured. Earlier that day there had been another avalanche incident on Liathach, when two climbers had been avalanched out of *Hillwalk Gully* in Coireag Dubh Beag, fortunately without injury. This gully had, in fact, been the scene of the avalanche accident the previous winter.

The further fatality on Liathach resulted in considerable media coverage. This was now normal on all such occasions, but the lack of SAIS provision in the area was becoming an issue. I could only point to the fact that the Torridon area fell a long way behind other contenders such as Lochnagar and Creag Meagaidh if further provision were to be contemplated.

Contact with the media over this

Steve Penny

Fig. 8.2 Tarah from the Search and Rescue Dog Association searching avalanche debris on White Coomb in the Moffat Hills, March 5, 1995 (see Appendix III)

winter was almost continuous and on the whole, very helpful. It probably represented about 30% of my workload, but, apart from the necessity of giving an SAIS response in these circumstances, it provided the opportunity to gain publicity for a message, not only on the avalanche problem in Scotland or elsewhere, but also on other mountain safety-related matters. It was my experience that, if an honest attempt was made to satisfy the legitimate enquiries of the media, they were generally quite happy to co-operate in this way. It is quite true to say that this process has gained a huge amount of free mountain safety propaganda in the UK, which could never have been afforded had it been necessary to pay for it.

At any rate, up to this point in the winter there was little to indicate that anything abnormal was developing. We had seen one or two avalanche accidents, apart from the event on Liathach, but there was no way of knowing whether a typical Scottish thaw might take place, stripping the hills of their snow cover, or whether the build-up would continue. Certainly, nothing in the past records prepared us for the next three weeks, which were in some ways the most disastrous in the annals of Scottish mountaineering.

It became fairly obvious over the next few days, both from what was recorded by SAIS observers and the reports we received from the public, that avalanche activity continued to be widespread throughout the Highlands. As yet, however, there was no indication of avalanche activity elsewhere.

As January passed into February, melt-freeze cycles with little new precipitation, particularly as the second week of the month approached, led to a general stabilisation of the snowpack. Climbing conditions were relatively good and no doubt, those intent on spending the mid-term holiday winter climbing in Scotland, were looking forward to their experience.

On Friday, the SAIS observers in the Northern Cairngorms assessed the avalanche hazard as Category 2 (Moderate). However, overnight snowfall was forecast and the Avalanche Hazard Outlook posted for Saturday was Category 4 (High). It may be that the pre-existing relatively favourable conditions had lulled mountaineers into a false sense of security, but the fact is that when Saturday came some climbers were less than judicious in their choice of routes.

The first accident in what was to become a nightmare month for rescue services, occurred in the area of the Goat Track in Coire an t-Sneachda of Cairn Gorm, noted in Chapter I as the site of the accident to Jack Thomson's party. In all, five climbers were carried down, four sustaining injuries, including a broken pelvis and a broken leg. SAIS avalanche observers were on the scene and quickly helped organise the rescue. This was not part of their job, but it is expected that they will do the necessary in these circumstances.

This accident, dramatic enough for those involved, was nevertheless only a foretaste of what was to come. The next accident, which took place on Lochnagar on February 14, was an agonising tragedy which touched many of my friends and colleagues. The avalanche, involving a member of the growing community of climbers resident in Aviemore, occurred as the two members in the party were in the process of negotiating the cornice at the top of *Parallel Buttress*, a classic Grade V climb.

Only a thin layer of surface slab detached itself as the leader stepped on to it, but it was sufficient to cause him to lose his footing and fall about 70 metres, until the rope held him. Rescue attempts by his companion, himself an expert in improvised techniques, proved futile.

Only a fully-equipped rescue team could be of any help and as ill luck would have it, the weather that night deteriorated very rapidly. By daylight the wind had reached a speed of 130mph and despite the Braemar team fighting its way through the blizzard to reach the accident site, it was too late. In fact, given the victim's situation and the nature of his injuries, it is unlikely that he survived for long.

This accident, happening to such a competent party, came as a great shock to many people. It showed again that avalanches are no respecters of personalities. I knew the victim only as an acquaintance, but the grief among many of my friends and colleagues was palpable. Again the media spotlight turned on the lack of SAIS cover on Lochnagar and the next accident did the same for another area lacking such provision, namely Creag Meagaidh.

Meagaidh, occupying a special position in meteorological terms, half-way between the maritime influences of the West Coast and the sub-Arctic conditions of the Cairngorms, first emerged from relative climbing obscurity in the late 1950s and early 1960s. A succession of favourable climbing winters at that time saw the first ascents of many of the great classic lines of today. The famous Laggan Inn with its non-stop hospitality was in its heyday and many legendary names gathered there, bent on new routes as well as revelry.

Although avalanches in the main gullies, or Posts of Coire Ardair had been noted by the great pioneer of Scottish winter climbing, JHB Bell, the '60s passed without avalanche incident on Creag Meagaidh. Only with much increased popularity in the '70s and '80s did the first serious avalanche accidents begin to occur. The first recorded avalanche fatality took place in *Easy Gully* on February 21, 1991. The buried victim was retrieved by other climbers, but regrettably not in time. Ironically, another climber had survived such a burial at the same spot a month before, on January 19, 1991.

The 1995 event occurred on the Inner Coire face of Coire Ardair, near *Diadem*, when two men suffered head and leg injuries. Conditions at the time were hazardous, as further evidenced by the fact that four climbers on their way to assist the victims were also avalanched. These rescuers were uninjured, but one of the two original victims died some time later in hospital.

Many other avalanche events were reported around this time, some in unaccustomed locations such as Beinn Dearg (Ross-shire), the Loch Lochy hills and the Angus glens: it was evident that a broad-scale hazard was persisting for an unusually long period. Airborne-powder avalanches were reported on Beinn a' Chaorainn, Ben Nevis and a few days later, on Meall a' Bhuiridh. This last event was triggered by an off-piste snowboarder, the first such recorded incident in Scotland.

Weather conditions had been variable, with much poor visibility and a search had been taking place over the days prior to the Meagaidh accident for a mountaineer who had gone missing after falling through a cornice above the North-East Buttress on Ben Nevis. Although this accident was not attributable to avalanche, the search had to be abandoned because of extreme avalanche hazard and the victim, buried in the snow, was not found until some time later.

Next came an event which was the worst avalanche tragedy in Scotland since the McArtney accident on Ben Nevis in 1970. The site was Coire na Tulaich on Buachaille Etive Mor, where the easy summer route of ascent gains the main summit ridge to the west of Stob Dearg. In winter, the route presents little technical difficulty in good snow conditions, but the corrie's status as a terrain trap in avalanche conditions is unparalleled. Any avalanche releasing on the upper slopes is likely to funnel into the narrow defile formed by the burn lower down. SAIS observers have noted at least one avalanche which swept the full length of the corrie to reach the River Coupall in the floor of the glen. A fatal avalanche accident had occurred here the previous winter, on February 27, 1994.

The avalanche forecast for Wednesday, February 22, 1995 envisaged a Category 4 (High) hazard, mainly on north-east to south-east facing slopes above 700 metres. Much of Coire na Tulaich is of a north-east orientation, with the corrie headwall steepening up from around the 700 metre contour.

A party of three, a father his son and the son's friend, had gone into the corrie without the intention of proceeding far. By evening, they had not returned and Glencoe Mountain Rescue Team was called out. The members of the team, with the Glen Coe SAIS observers among them, were well aware of the perilous nature of their search. As they lined out across the lower, narrow part of the corrie, the deputy team leader Davy Gunn was posted as look out with a radio higher up, in what was deemed to be a position as sheltered as possible from avalanches releasing on the upper slopes.

Suddenly, the searchers were startled to hear his voice over their radios, yelling out a warning. A huge avalanche had just passed him and was bearing down on his colleagues below. They ran, trying desperately to make height up the steep sides of the gully, away from the deadly trap beneath them. Just as suddenly, it was over: miraculously, no-one had been caught. The search was abandoned for the night.

The detailed search which took place over the ensuing weeks, with RAF teams lending support, involved trenching the debris over the whole corrie, to a depth of many metres. Sadly, the victims had still not been found when, two weeks later, the Buachaille was to deliver its next hammer blow.

During the intervening period, avalanche hazard had remained high in the Glen Coe area. Similar conditions had prevailed in Lochaber and although the Northern Cairngorms had seen some periodic stabilisation, as the weekend of March 4 and 5 approached, increased hazard was forecast. The stage was set for the blackest avalanche weekend ever on the Scottish mountains.

On the Saturday, I was having a day off, a relatively rare event for me in winter. The media frenzy which had accompanied the events of the previous weeks had died down somewhat, but could be sensed simmering quietly in the background. As I busied myself with domesticity in my home in Aviemore, I looked from time to time towards the hills and noted, as the afternoon progressed, that the wind was picking up, as forecast, from the south-west. From about that point, it all started to go wrong.

Curious as to the developing conditions on the hill, I called the duty Cairngorm SAIS observer on his mobile phone. Evidently, I had called at a bad moment, but gleaned the information that there had been an avalanche accident involving a large party on the headwall of Coire Laogh Mor, just outside the Cairngorm ski area. There were injuries, some serious and a mutual friend, the leader of the party, was among those hurt. I left the observers to their rescue work and prepared to head for my office at Glenmore Lodge in order to write the avalanche report myself.

I found out more about the accident: eight people had been involved and there were at least two stretcher cases. A mobile phone had expedited the rescue and climbing helmets worn by the party had undoubtedly prevented much more serious injuries. Freshly-formed windslab and the overload caused by the presence of a large party on the slope, offered themselves as the explanation for the event. In any case, conditions in the Cairngorms were now rapidly deteriorating. Only an hour or so after the Coire Laogh Mor accident, two mountaineers descending from Cairn Toul into Coire Odhar above the Lairig Ghru, triggered a large slab avalanche on the north-east aspect of the corrie. As they had been proceeding cautiously, facing in to the slope and moving slowly down on the front points of their crampons, they avoided being carried down.

As I went out to dinner that night, I received a call from one of our observers in Glen Coe. Three more climbers were missing on Buachaille Etive Mor. They had been seen by a member of the Glencoe Mountain Rescue Team who was abandoning a climb due to the high avalanche hazard. They had been proceeding up *Curved Ridge*, a relatively easy winter route, but lurking at the back of

my mind was the recollection that an avalanche accident had occurred on the open snow slope above *Curved Ridge* in 1982.

The failure of the climbers to return was disturbing, but there did not seem at that stage to be undue cause for alarm. Many a party has sat out a winter night on the Glen Coe hills without coming to harm. Later that evening, I was rather more perturbed to be told that two young climbers visiting friends on the staff at Glenmore Lodge had failed to return from a climb in the northern Cairngorms. They had left no word of their intended route, but a search would start next morning.

In my office next day, further reports filtered in. There had been an avalanche accident on Helvellyn in the Lake District at Red Tarn. The climbers involved were from the RAF Stafford Mountain Rescue Team and it appeared that one victim had been seriously injured. All the apparatus of a major rescue effort was now assembling at Glenmore Lodge. Cairngorm Mountain Rescue Team, along with RAF teams and Glenmore Lodge staff were assisting in the search for the two young climbers in the northern Cairngorms. Dogs and handlers from the Search and Rescue Dog Association were at the ready.

The weather was favourable and two RAF helicopters operated a shuttle service to the Cairngorm corries and plateaux. Speculation as to the likely whereabouts of the missing pair initially favoured the Northern Corries of Cairngorm, but no trace was found there. This major search, carried out in often hazardous conditions, went on for four days.

Later that afternoon, I received a phone call from Andy Nelson, one of our SAIS observers in Glen Coe and a member of the rescue team there. "We've just taken three bodies off the hill in Glen Etive", was his message. The three missing climbers had indeed been avalanched at the top of *Curved Ridge* and taken a 300-metre fall. Although partly prepared for this news, I began to be overtaken with pessimism as to the result of the search in the Cairngorms.

Dave Cuthbertson

Fig. 8.3 Good conditions on the exit gully to Curved Ridge, Buachaille Etive Mor. While the ridge is objectively safe, some fatal avalanches have occurred on the exposed exit slopes

By 4.30pm I had transmitted all the day's snow and avalanche reports to media recipients and to our website at Glasgow University. I was preparing to go home when the phone rang. The caller was a search and rescue dog handler from the Borders. Like Andy Nelson, he wasted no time in coming to his point: "I've just dug a body out of an avalanche on White Coomb." It seemed that this appalling weekend had an unlimited store of grisly surprises.

Even then, I had not learned everything. Only the next day did I receive information on another accident in Glen Coe, fortunately not fatal. However, it was unusual for Scotland, in that it involved skiers. On Saturday, the two victims had been ski-ing off-piste in a gully on Creag Dubh on Meall a' Bhuiridh, when both were carried down. One was partly buried, but survived, although hospitalised. The other victim was less seriously injured.

I have to say that taken along with other difficulties that winter, this accumulation of avalanche problems had left me somewhat shell-shocked. The situation was quite unprecedented. Six people were lying out on the Scottish hills, presumed dead. There had been twelve avalanche fatalities, more as it turned out than had occurred in Canada that winter. This was not a happy position in which to be at the beginning of March, with no sign of a let-up in avalanche conditions.

As fate would have it, however, there were to be no more avalanche fatalities that winter, although, of course, I had no way of knowing that at the time. The bodies of the missing victims were eventually found, including the two climbers in the Cairngorms, who as it turned out, had been avalanched as they descended in the Twin Burns area in Coire an Lochain.

At the end of March, I attended an annual meeting of avalanche professionals at Leukerbad in Switzerland. They were certainly aware of the events in Scotland that winter. Strangely enough, the fact that there had been so many fatalities seemed to remove any lingering doubts over the existence of a serious avalanche problem in the UK. The meeting at Leukerbad, which brings together all those involved in computer-assisted avalanche forecasting in Europe, was a very welcome respite. I was to some extent able to recover from my paranoia and not to worry too much over what further disasters might be occurring in my absence.

As it happened, one further avalanche accident had occurred while I was in Switzerland. It involved five people, on *Cinderella* on Creag Meagaidh: there were no very serious injuries.

It is difficult in retrospect to know what conclusions to draw from the experience of such a winter. It is possible to be philosophical and say that the number of fatal accidents as such was not exceptional. It could be said that the depressing statistics are largely attributable to three accidents involving multiple fatalities. It does appear that the ease with which it is possible to arrive in avalanche hazard zones on Buachaille Etive Mor is a particular problem. This gave rise to the current efforts to use three-dimensional modelling as a possible way of reinforcing avalanche hazard information.

The experience also begs the question that if such events can occur, is it worth while making the effort to provide the information? My firm belief, which I believe is borne out by the figures, is that it is. The work done by SAIS serves to abate the number of accidents attributable to avalanche. The winter of 1994-95 showed some of the potential for tragedy which exists on the hills in a winter of substantial snow accumulation and that is the important fact to remember. As to the possibility of a recurrence, it is interesting, though probably unscientific, to note that such a peak in avalanche fatalities is usually followed by three or four winters of lesser activity, but that so far a line drawn through the peaks of the graph shows a linear increase. Fortunately, this increase is greatly exceeded by the increase in participation in winter mountain activities.

Appendix I

Avalanche Classification

Several systems of avalanche classification exist. The mountaineer and skier do not require full scientific rigour; a simple five-point system is adequate.

In rescue operations it is also of value to know the nature of the debris: i.e. dry or wet; distinct blocks or mainly homogenous; contaminated or uncontaminated (with rocks, earth).

Size of Avalanche

Various systems of describing the size of avalanches exist. In Scotland, the dimensions of the slide path and debris are described. For the sake of interest, the Canadian system of size classification is shown below.

The largest known Scottish avalanches, such as the 1800 Gaick event (see Chapter I), would probably rate between 3 and 4 on the Canadian scale.

Canadian Snow Avalanche Size Classification System and Typical Factors

Size	Description	Typical Mass (tonnes)	Typical Length
1.	Relatively harmless to people	<10	10m
2.	Could bury, injure or kill a person	100	100m
3.	Could bury a car, destroy a small building, or break a few trees	1000	1000m
4.	Could destroy a railway car, large truck, several buildings, or a forest with an area up to 4 hectares	10,000	2000m
5.	Largest snow avalanches known; could destroy a village or a forest of 40 hectares	100,000	3000m

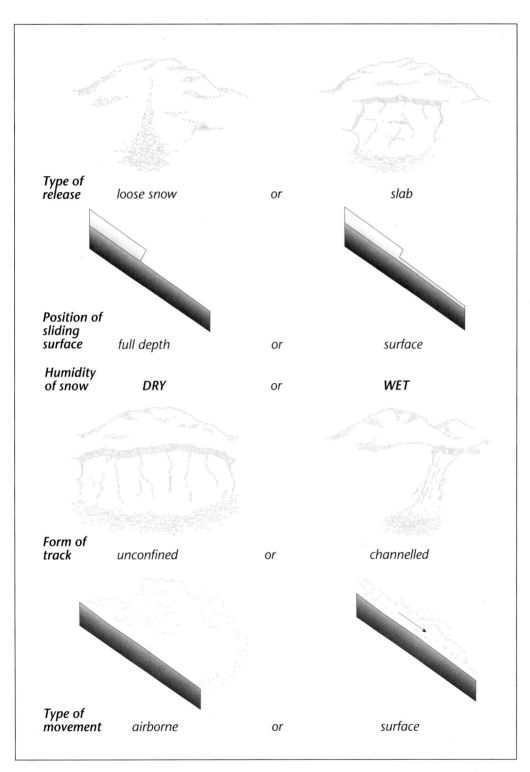

Type of release   *loose snow*   *or*   *slab*

Position of sliding surface   *full depth*   *or*   *surface*

Humidity of snow   **DRY**   *or*   **WET**

Form of track   *unconfined*   *or*   *channelled*

Type of movement   *airborne*   *or*   *surface*

Avalanche classification

Appendix II

European Avalanche Hazard Scale

Degree of Hazard	Snowpack Stability	Avalanche Probability
1 Low	The snowpack is generally well bonded and stable	Triggering is possible only with high additional loads[2] on a few very steep extreme slopes[4]. Only a few small natural[6] avalanches (sluffs) possible
2 Moderate	The snowpack is moderately well bonded on some[1] steep[3] slopes, otherwise generally well bonded	Triggering is possible with high additional loads[2], particularly on the steep[3] slopes indicated in the bulletin. Large natural[6] avalanches not likely
3 Considerable	The snowpack is moderately to weakly bonded on many[1] steep[3] slopes	Triggering is possible, sometimes even with low additional loads[2]. The bulletin may indicate many slopes which are particularly affected. In certain conditions, medium and occasionally large sized natural[6] avalanches may occur
4 High	The snowpack is weakly bonded in most[1] places	Triggering is probable even with low additional loads[2] on many steep[3] slopes. In some conditions, frequent medium or large sized natural[6] avalanches are likely
5 Very High	The snowpack is weakly bonded and largely unstable	Numerous large natural[6] avalanches are likely, even on moderately steep terrain

[1] Generally described in more detail in the avalanche bulletin
[e.g. altitude, slope aspect, type of terrain, etc.]

[2] Additional load: high – e.g. group of skiers, piste machine, avalanche blasting.
Low – e.g. skier, walker

[3] Steep slopes: slopes with an incline of more than $30°$

[4] Steep extreme slopes: those which are particularly unfavorable in terms of the incline, terrain profile, proximity to ridge, smoothness of underlying ground surface

[5] Aspect: compass bearing directly down the slope

[6] Natural: without human assistance

Appendix III

Avalanche Accidents in Scotland

The following list is not exhaustive and there are undoubtedly errors. The authors would value any assistance towards improving the accuracy and completeness of this record, and details can be sent to them at; Scottish Avalanche Information Service, Freepost, Glenmore Lodge, Aviemore, Inverness-shire PH22 1BR. In the period 1925-45, there were one or two further accidents for which no details exist.

Only accidents involving bodily injury or a mountain rescue call-out are included. Climbers and walkers have been involved in many more avalanches over the years, and some are described in this book, however they are not listed below, because there were no 'injuries' and no call-outs. Doubtful cases and instances of collapsing ice-pitches are not included, but cornice collapses are. Undated incidents are not listed. (B) = burial, (F) = fatality.

1938	Nov 27	**Stob a' Choire Odhair, Black Mount**. Two walkers carried 100 to 130m by slab. One injured, descended unaided (see Chapter V).
1948	Jan 18	**Sgor Mor, Cairngorms**. Avalanche hospitalised four walkers
1949	Mar 14	**Ben Nevis**, *Number Five Gully*, (1F). Party of four. Fatality concussed, died in CIC hut
1949		**Lochnagar**, *Raeburn's Gully*. Two roped parties hit by cornice collapse.
1950	Dec 12	**Ben Nevis**. Avalanched in 'a gully'; fractured leg.
1952	Apr 6	**Cairn Gorm, Coire an t-Sneachda**, (1F). Party of three carried over *Alladin's Buttress*; probably windslab. One killed, two slightly injured.
1952	Apr 26	**Cairn Gorm, Coire an Lochain**, (2F). Three avalanched near top of climb; two killed, third broken leg.
1953	April 1	**Ben Nevis**, (2B, 2F). Six day search for missing climbers. Bodies found April 19 roped together near foot of *South Castle Gully*.
1957	Feb 23	**Ben Lui**. Party of four avalanched near summit in blizzard conditions; one broken leg.
1959	Mar 8	**Ben Nevis**, *Number Two Gully*. Two avalanched near top; new snow on old, hard snow. Dislocated hip and chest injuries.
1960	Jan 30	**Stob Coire nan Lochan, Glen Coe**. Two avalanched to point above lochan in heavy snow and high wind. One had head injuries and broken jaw.
1960	Feb 14	**Stob Coire nan Lochan**, *Forked Gully*. Two avalanched in deep, new snow; one had fractured spine and head injuries.
1961	Dec 4	**Aonach Eagach, Glen Coe**, (1B, 1F). One of party of three in powder snow avalanche just below spot height 3162m. Avalanche area extended 230m; body found next day, completely buried.
1962	Jan 7	**Buachaille Etive Mor, Glen Coe**, *Crowberry Gully*, (1F). Three fell 330m in avalanche; one killed, two injured. Two rescuers avalanched 50m, OK.
1963	Dec 24	**Ben Nevis**, *Gardyloo Gully*. Two fell 330m into *Observatory Gully* in windslab avalanche.
1964	Dec 28	**Beinn a' Bhuird, Cairngorms**, (3B, 2F). Three walkers descending SW slopes towards Quoich Water buried by large avalanche. One walker not buried raised alarm; survivor alive after 22hr burial (see Chapter I).
1965	March	**Cairn Gorm, Lurcher's Meadow**. Three of eight carried 300m by a hard slab avalanche 400m wide, while descending from the plateau. Close proximity to the line of fracture saves them; severe bruising.
1965	Dec 27	**Cairn Gorm, Coire Cas**. Party of two descending headwall avalanched by thick slab when half way down and partly buried; torn ligaments. Wind drifted snow accumulating previous week.
1967	Jan 27	**Mam Sodhail, Glen Affric**. While roping companions down 45° slope, snow avalanches 15 to 20m on either side of party. Leader's ice axe belay failed and he fell about 30m hitting boulder. Scalp wounds and severe bruising to head, chest and shoulders; others uninjured.

1967	Apr 1	**Ben Nevis**, (2B). Two carried 160m on surface of new snow avalanche below *Number Four Gully*, then buried. One freed himself after 9hrs and descends to CIC. Companion found affer 10hrs burial; had hand free. Exposure, slight frostbite (see Chapter V).
1968	Jan 3	**Cairn Gorm**, (2B). Search party avalanched in **Coire Raibert**. One buried but dug out by others and party retreated to the Shelter Stone. Injured helicoptered out next day with torn ligaments. Another search party avalanched next day.
1968	Feb 6	**An t-Sron, Glen Coe**. Three thought to have taken wrong course when descending in bad visibility. All carried down by windslab avalanche; two escaped but third swept much further. Not badly injured.
1968	Mar 18	**Ben Nevis**, *North Gully*. One carried 100m by cornice collapse. Rescue party avalanched by snow from *Number Four Gully*.
1969	Feb 19	**Cairn Gorm, Coire Cas**. Nine members of skills training course avalanched on west side of corrie at 11.30am. Help from other parties and ski patrol; six hospitalised, two serious.
1970	Jan 18	**Ben Nevis**, *Italian Climb*, (3B, 3F). Four climbers in wet slab avalanche near top of route. One not attached to rope at time survived. Others found dead in debris at foot of climb.
1970	Feb 7	**Buachaille Etive Mor**, *Great Gully*, (3B,1F). Four carried 70m by wet snow avalanche. Three buried, two dug out, but third could not be found. Unconcious when found, buried 1.5 to 2.5m – could not be revived.
1970	Feb 16	**Ciste Dubh, Cluanie** (1B). Party climbing SE shoulder, avalanched 100m after encountering new snow on snow ice at about 900m. Three dug themselves out and after five minutes found fourth, (finger sticking out of snow), unconscious with head injury. Others, one broken ankle, one head wound.
1972	Feb 12	**Corrie Fee, Glen Clova**, *B Gully*. Two avalanched in thaw conditions. Fractured femur and arm and facial injuries.
1972	Feb 12	**Aonach Dubh a' Ghlinne**. Party carried 160m in new snow avalanche. Snow had fallen 24 hours previously. Minor injuries caused by ice axe.
1972	Feb 1	**Lochnagar**, *Raeburn's Gully*. Leader knocked off by small powder avalanche; broken leg.
1972	Apr 16	**Lochnagar**, *Raeburn's Gully*. Party of three avalanched by cornice; one badly gashed leg.
1973	Dec 1	**Ben Nevis**. Party of three carried 160m by slab avalanche en route to *Number Three Gully*. Fine, cold; one stretcher case, broken arm. Others, bruising and cuts.
1973	Dec 19	**Cairn Gorm, Coire an t-Sneachda**, *Alladin's Couloir*. Instructor carried 160m; injured knee.
1973	Dec 23	**Cairn Gorm, Coire an t-Sneachda**. Two carried 100m; slight injuries.
1974	Mar 17	**Cairn Gorm, Coire Laogh Mor**. Two instructors in soft slab avalanche: one abdominal injury, one broken tib. and fib.
1974	Apr 7	**Cairn Gorm, Coire an Lochain**. Two hit by cornice avalanche; one minor head injury, one broken ankle.
1975	Jan 19	**Ben Nevis**, *Hadrian's Wall*. Leader avalanched and slightly hurt; rescued next morning.
1975	Jan 19	**Ben Nevis**, *Tower Gully*. Climber avalanched; broken ribs and ankle.
1975	Jan 19	**Beinn a' Chreachain, Bridge of Orchy**. Three climbers soloing gully carried 160m by large powder avalanche from above. Two stretcher cases, one cracked ulna, one broken ulna and ribs, both ice axe lacerations.
1975	Jan 19	**Stob Coire nan Lochan**, *Broad Gully*. Party of two descending start minor avalanche; one fractured ankle, one suspected rib injury.
1975	Mar 30	**Cairn Gorm, Coire an Lochain**. Two traversing top of **Great Slab**, when large slab broke away; ankle and knee injuries.
1975	Mar 30	**Cairn Gorm**. Eight skiers avalanched on N side of Lairig Ghru near **March Burn**. Three injured - evacuated by helicopter called for previous incident (see Chapter V).
1976	Feb 14	**Cairn Gorm, Coire an t-Sneachda**, *Red Gully*, (1F). Knocked from steps by small avalanche at foot of route. Unable to brake with axe and hit boulders; died in hospital.
1976	Mar 12	**Cairn Gorm, Coire an t-Sneachda, Goat Track**. Skills training party; broken leg and other injuries.

Blyth Wright

Few British mountains can generate avalanches like Ben Nevis. An impressive avalanche boulder below Number Five Gully, Ben Nevis. A school party of five escaped unhurt in this incident

1976	Mar 12	**Cairn Gorm, Coire an Lochain**, (1F). Party en route to assist with above; six injured, one died in hospital (see Chapter I).
1976	Mar 13	**Cairn Gorm, Coire an t-Sneachda**, *The Runnel*, (1F). Climber fell 35m after avalanche; held by second but killed.
1976	Mar 14	**Lochnagar**, *Raeburn's Gully*. Two soloing, one hit by small avalanche and fell to foot of climb; broken femur.
1976	Mar 14	**Bidean nam Bian, Glen Coe**, *Central Gully*. Wet snow avalanche when descending. Swept 230m, passing over 10m rock face to corrie basin; fractured femur, fractured clavicle and ribs.
1976	Nov 14	**Cairn Gorm, Coire Cas**. Two carried 180m by full-depth powder avalanche on back wall; one injured, carried down by companions.
1977	Feb 3	**Ben Nevis**, *South Castle Gully*, (1B,1F). Two fell 260m in cornice avalanche; one severely injured right arm, other buried 2m and found dead.
1977	Feb 15	**Ben Nevis**, (1B,1F). Two in area of *Garadh Gully*. One climbed, other turned back. Climber returned to CIC, but no trace of companion. Finally found buried 2m in avalanche.
1977	Apr 20	**Ben Nevis**, *Point Five Gully*, (1F). Climber 3m back from edge when cornice collapses.
1977	Mar 23	**Cairn Gorm, Coire an t- Sneachda**, *Central Gully*. Carried to about 30m above lochan; broken lower left leg.
1977	Mar 29	**Ben Nevis**. Two avalanched in **Coire Eoghainn**; one head injury, one leg injury.

1977 Dec 28 **Cairn Gorm, Coire an Lochain.** Two avalanched below *The Vent*; one injured leg.
1978 Jan 21 **Cairn Gorm, Coire an t- Sneachda.** Two avalanched at foot of cliffs; head injuries and broken knee. Snowing.
1978 Jan 21 **Cairn Gorm, Coire an t-Sneachda.** Two thought to be in Central Gully, soon after previous incident. First had head and pelvis injuries, second exposure. Snowing.
1978 Jan 21 **Lochnagar,** *Raeburn's Gully*, (1F). Two swept 230m by slab; one killed (no helmet - head injuries), other with chest and back injuries.
1978 Feb 19 **Cairn Gorm, Coire Laogh Mor.** Hillwalkers avalanched by 400m slab; one injured. Another party in avalanche on back wall of Coire Cas earlier same day.
1978 Feb 21 **Carn Mor Dearg,** (1B,1F). Instructor carried 400m by large windslab avalanche. Buried and although dug out quickly, could not be revived.
1978 Mar 26 **Ben Nevis,** (1B,1F). Four walkers caught in huge wet snow avalanche **on path** from CIC hut to Lochan Meall an t-Suidhe. Three injured (one fractured skull); one buried and found dead on 28th.
1978 Dec 19 **Cairn Gorm, Coire an Lochain.** Five carried away by one metre slab avalanche on Great Slab, two injured.
1978 Dec 26 **Braeriach, Coire Bogha-Cloiche,** (2B, 2F). Bodies of two walkers missing on 25th found in large avalanche.
1979 Feb 28 **Cairn Gorm, Coire an t-Sneachda.** Climber carried 70 to 100m by slab, about 100m across and 15 to 60 cm thick, below *Fiacaill Couloir*; cracked pelvis and lower leg.
1979 Mar **Lochnagar,** *Parallel Gully A.* Leader of party of three knocked off by snow from direct finish. Sunny weather, possible cornice collapse. Held on belay, injured shoulder, lowered off.
1979 Apr 8 **Ben Nevis,** (1B, 1F). Two at *foot of Italian Climb* hit by small slab from above Garadh Gully. Fatality buried 1m near foot of avalanche - asphyxia. Weather conditions "good but mild", 1°C. Snow flurries, soft, dry snowfall 24 hours earlier.
1980 Jan 19 **An Coileachan, Fannaichs.** On first ascent of *Downward Bound* in Garbh Coire Mor, leader avalanched (dry slab) on last pitch. Both climbers fell to bottom; one broken nose.
1980 Jan 20 **Lochnagar,** (1B). Two carried 130m by powder avalanche *below Parallel Gully A.* One rescued by climbers (collapsed lung, broken rib), other buried, but found alive after 8hrs 30mins burial (fingers of one hand showing). Unconcious, hypothermia, femur fracture, frostbite. No new snow falling, but windy. Two accidents in Lake District this day.
1980 Feb 21 **Ben Nevis,** *Number Three Gully Buttress.* Party of two pick buttress as gullies liable to avalanche (good weather but mild), but both swept from top of first pitch by small avalanche. One cracked a leg bone, other uninjured, went for help.
1980 March 9 **Stob Coire nan Lochan,** *Twisting Gully.* Two caught in small avalanche from above at foot of route. One with head and shoulder injuries, other uninjured.
1980 Mar 16 **Cairn Gorm, Coire an t-Sneachda,** *Aladdin's Buttress.* Two in soft slab avalanche below buttress; one hurt. Debris about 20m wide.
1980 Mar 17 **Creag Meagaidh,** *Raeburn's Gully.* Party of seven or eight in gully. Small slab avalanche took three down, but two stopped after 7m. One fell 160m; broken pelvis and ribs.
1980 Mar 17 **An Garbhanach, Mamores.** Three walkers about to traverse below cornice, when it collapsed, carrying them 160m. Descended to Steall, then two stretchered out; severe bruising and broken ribs.
1980 Nov **Cairn Gorm, Hell's Lum.** Climber avalanched below crag; injury to hip joint.
1981 Feb 11 **Creag Meagaidh,** *Cinderella.* Six in dry slab avalanche on route. Two instructors sustained broken legs, two others hurt.
1981 Feb 21 **Lochnagar,** *Parallel Gully A.* Three in slab avalanche, one fell 85m; rib, chest, leg injuries. New snow on old snow-ice.
1981 Feb 21 **Stob Coire nam Beith,** *Central Gully.* Two avalanched; one slightly injured, other head iniuries, serious. Hard frost, no new snow.
1981 Oct 28 **Ben Nevis,** *Number Three Gully.* Five carried 300m by avalanche in gully vicinity; one fractured ribs and injured wrist.
1982 Jan 5 **Ben Nevis,** *Point Five Gully.* Approaching gully, one climber carried away, OK. Other left above 2.5m crown wall; assisted by other climbers. Debris reached over Allt a' Mhuillin at foot of *Observatory Gully.* Heavy snow and blowing (also night before).

1982 Jan 14/15 **Beinn a' Ghlo, Glen Tilt**, (1B, 1F). Solo hill-walker missing for five days. Body found on 25th, buried in slab avalanche on NW side, only hand protruding (see Chapter V).

1982 Jan 18 **Bidean nam Bian**, (1B). Two climbers in **Lost Valley**, carried down by large avalanche. One badly bruised, other buried up to chest, but dug out by companion after 30mins.

1982 Feb 15 **Ben Nevis, The Castle**, (2B, 2F). Five avalanched in area of *Castle Gullies*; two dead, another seriously injured.

1982 Feb 15 **Ben Nevis**, *Gardyloo Gully*, (1F). Four avalanched; one dead, one fractured femur.

1982 Feb 15 **Ben Nevis**, *Number Two Gully*. Climber avalanched; two broken arms, but walked down, then airlifted by helicopter.

1982 Feb 15 **Creag Meagaidh**, *Raeburn's Gully*. Three avalanched; one broke leg in 160m fall, others uninjured.

1982 Mar 8 **Buachaille Etive Mor**, *Curved Ridge*. Three traversing snow to descend route, when two avalanched 80m.

1982 Mar 17 **Ben Nevis, Coire Leis**. Cornice fractures 5m back from edge on descent to Carn Mor Dearg Arete. One fell a short way, other 300m; broken ribs and internal injuries.

1982 Dec 27 **Ben Nevis**, *Number Three Gully*. Four carried 130m in windslab avalanche from near top of route. One spiked through knee by crampon, others cuts and bruises. No windslab at foot of gully and generally good snow conditions.

1983 Jan 2 **Ben Nevis**, *Bob Run*. Climber fell 230m when slab gave way, 15m from top of route; no fractures but chest and facial injuries.

1983 Jan 29 **Driesh, Glen Clova**, *Easy Gully*. Large area of ice veneer came away from underlying snow. Ankle injury to one person; 30m fall arrested by axe braking and grabbing handrail.

1983 Feb 17 **Ben Macdui, Shelter Stone Crag**, *Pinnacle Gully*. One of party of four caught in windslab avalanche and falls 300m tearing knee ligaments.

1984 Feb 25 **Sron na Creise, White Corries**. Two downhill skiers lost off-piste when weather closed in. Next morning searchers saw one person "shoot out" of an avalanche in a gully near top of peak. The other had been above the avalanche.

1984 Feb 24/25 **Mullach Clach a' Bhlair, Glen Feshie**, (1B, 1F). Two days of extensive searches for missing walker among debris and high avalanche danger. Several avalanches near searchers, some triggered off by them, over 1000 metres wide. Body found in **Coire Domhainn** on Apr 29 on uphill side of drumlin; victim had survived Ben Nevis avalanche of Jan 2nd 1983.

1984 Mar 24 **Aonach Dubh, Glen Coe**, *No. 6 Gully*. Two swept 200m by avalanche of loose, wet snow; one uninjured, other broken leg and ankle. Snowing, strong E wind.

1984 Mar 25 **Ben More, Crianlarich**. Three unroped climbers traversing steep slopes on N face triggered off a large avalanche, probably windslab. All three swept down; one uninjured, two with skull and leg fractures.

1985 Jan 8 **Ben Nevis, Red Burn**, (2B, 2F). Two buried on descent from summit, said to be windslab (snow being blown strongly into rescuers' faces as they ascended the hill). Bodies found by dogs at GR145720, first after 30mins at 2.5m, second after 1hr at 1.3m.

1985 Mar 31 **Ben Wyvis**, (1B,1 F). Solo cross-country skier buried under 1.8m wet snow avalanche in **An Cabar** area. Found by dogs after helicopter search on April 1.

1985 Dec 31 **Cairn Gorm, Coire Cas** (1B,1F). Headwall buries climber who'd returned to look for ice axe lost while glissading same slope 24 hours earlier. Avalanche debris 150m wide - victim found by dog 6m from the E side of it, head about 60cm down and completely buried.

1986 Jan 2 **Bidean nam Bian**, *Central Gully*. Dry slab avalanche about 50m wide carried two climbers 70 to 100m. One stopped, one fell over crag; dislocated shoulder.

1986 Jan 4 **Stob Coire nam Beith**, *North West Gully*, (2B, 2F). Three avalanched and fell 300m. One completely buried, killed. Another buried, legs visible, but could not be pulled out by survivor, who sustained broken leg.

1986 Jan 21 **Ben Nevis, North Gully**. Soloist in party of five climbing cornice when it collapsed (windslab avalanche). He fell to the bottom of *Number Four Gully* together with others in two ropes of two. Soloist sustained pelvic fracture and chest injury; one other broke leg and ankle, another had broken nose and walked down. Two uninjured.

1986 Jan 21   **Ben Nevis**, *Number Four Gully*. Some 30mins after above incident gully avalanches, sweeping two of the five 70m and partly burying both of them, including the soloist. Stretchered.

1986 Mar 3   **Skye, Sgurr Nan Gillean**, *Pinnacle Ridge* (1B, 1F). Intending to do Tourist Route, but on Pinnacle Ridge due to low cloud and bad weather. Descending Coire Riabhach, deceased slipped and broke leg. Helped by companion to easier ground and put in sleeping bag in a snowhole. Rescue attempts called off that day due to extreme weather. Found next day (pm) by dog and probing under 60cm of snow. Victim had been avalanched to well below snowhole.

1986 Mar 3   **The Saddle, Glen Shiel**, *Forcan Ridge*. Party of three avalanched 130m while descending W facing slope of 30 to 35°. One back injury, other two OK, walked off. Another party dislodged an avalanche on other side of ridge, same aspect, about same time, but not carried down.

1986 Mar 20   **Ben Macdui**. Instructor and two others avalanched by soft slab, possibly from above, to left of ice-craft area below **Garbh Uisge Beag**. High winds (153mph gusts on Cairn Gorm summit) and 5m visibility. Snow falling.

1986 Mar 25   **Stob Coire nan Lochan**, *Twisting Gully*. Two swept down by collapsing cornice; one bruised back, other strained ligaments.

1986 Mar 26   **Lochnagar**, *Parallel Gully A or B*, (2F). Two roped climbers found at bottom, partially covered by avalanche debris. Believed large cornice gave way at top of climb. Rescue teams witnessed three other avalanches.

1986 Mar 27   **Beinn Alligin**, (1F). Walker killed in 300m fall and two companions suffered broken legs and hypothermia in avalanche, possibly on Horns of Alligin.

1986 Mar 28   **Stob Coire Easain, Loch Treig**. Climber fell through cornice and carried 100m by avalanche into upper part of **Coire Laire**; cuts and bruises.

1986 Apr 15   **Sgurr Alasdair, Cuillin**. One of party of five in *Stone Shoot*, carried 100m by slab avalanche; broken leg.

1986 Dec 30   **Cairn Gorm, Coire an t-Sneachda**. Instructor fell about 130m when avalanched to right of *Jacob's Ladder* while soloing above roped party. Soft slab, snowing, strong wind; broken pelvis, scapula (see Chapter V).

1986 Dec 31   **Ben Nevis**, (1F). Descending from plateau, two found in *Five Finger Gully*, probably swept down by slab avalanche; one fatal, one chest injuries. Found by climbers descending between *Five Finger Gully* and *Surgeon's Gully*.

1986 Dec 31   **Sron na Creise**, (1F). Victim leading party down unnamed gully on the W slopes of the N ridge, avalanched 30m, then channelled down gully and buried; probably windslab. Dead when found by SARDA dog 3hrs 15mins later.

1987 Jan 1   **Ben Nevis**, *Five Finger Gully*. Two walkers seeing New Year in on summit, lose map, take a westerly bearing and come down Five Finger Gully. One dislocates shoulder in small slab avalanche and bivvies in poly bag, other goes for help. Night search by Lochaber MRT in dangerous avalanche conditions.

1987 Mar 14   **Creag Meagaidh**, *South Pipe Direct*. Rope of three hit by avalanche. First belay came out and two climbers fell until held on their ropes by the belay of the third, who was not in the avalanche. One had a fractured clavicle and the other slight injuries; third, uninjured, walked down.

1987 Mar 24   **Ben Nevis, Red Burn**. Three walkers suffered cuts and bruises when avalanched in Red Burn.

1987 Dec 15   **Cairn Gorm, Coire Cas**. Party of six avalanched on headwall by slab 1m thick, about 300m wide. One injured leg in tumbling fall - badly bruised but assisted down by companions.

1988 Jan 21   **Sgurr a' Mhaim, Mamores**. Party of three avalanched, one hurt neck and shoulder injuries.

1988 Jan 31   **Buachaille Etive Mor**, *Great Gully*. Three climbers avalanched; cuts and bruises.

1988 Feb 6   **Gearr Aonach, Glen Coe**, *Rev Ted's Gully*. Two climbers avalanched; one suffered bruising, other broken pelvis.

1988 Feb 6   **Buachaille Etive Mor**, *Easy Gully*, (1B,1F). Climbers decending from Rannoch Wall carried about 250m. One buried and dead on recovery, other broken elbow.

1988	Feb 6	**Aonach Dubh, Glen Coe.** Climber avalanched just *below Yoyo* on N Face and carried 160m; gashed eye.
1988	Feb 8	**Ben Nevis.** Climber avalanched as he began a climb on *Tower Ridge*; back injury.
1989	Feb 19	**Ben Nevis**, *Observatory Gully*. Three climbers finished *Tower Scoop* and traversed to *Observatory Gully*, when *Tower Gully* avalanched and carried all down; one broken ankle.
1989	Feb 28	**Sgurr na Ciste Duibhe, Glen Shiel**, (1B, 1F). Hill-walker carried down and buried in large slab avalanche, **Coire Dhomhdain**.
1989	Mar 18	**Lochnagar**, *Central Buttress*, (1F). Six climbers moving up snowslope above route to plateau, when slope avalanched, and carried four down. All injured. Avalanche also hit two climbers in Shallow Gully; one died of injuries.
1989	Dec 16	**Cairn Gorm, Coire an t-Sneachda**, *Spiral Gully*. Three climbers avalanched, two carried down, one broken leg.
1989	Dec 16	**Cairn Gorm, Coire an t-Sneachda**, *Jacob's Ladder*. Four climbers carried down; one sustained ice axe injury to hand.
1990	Jan 4	**Cairn Gorm, Coire an t-Sneachda**, *The Runnel*. Two avalanched and carried down two others; one broken arm.
1990	Jan 4	**Cairn Gorm, Coire an t-Sneachda**, *The Runnel*. Three avalanched from cornice; two seriously injured (head, back, internal), other broken ankle.
1990	Jan 4	**Beinn a' Bhuird.** Two about to leave **Coire na Ciche** due to unstable snow conditions, caught in large airborne-powder avalanche coming out of *Twisting Gully*. One took cover behind boulder, other carried away and sustained broken femur. Dust cloud, air blast (see Chapter I).
1990	Feb 11	**Ben More.** Walkers following in single file on north side near summit, carried 160m in slab avalanche; one serious ice axe puncture wound.
1990	Apr 14	**Ben Nevis, Coire Leis.** Three walkers in slab avalanche to right of abseil posts; one facial injury.
1990	Dec 25	**Braeriach.** Climbers approaching cliffs in **Coire Bhrochain**, avalanched by dry slab; one fractured pelvis and jaw.
1991	Jan 13	**Aonach Dubh**, *No. 6 Gully*. Two avalanched from top; one broken arm, other head cuts.
1991	Feb 3	**Stob Coire nan Lochan.** Walker approaching **East Ridge** tries to out-run slab avalanche; broken ankle.
1991	Feb 3	**Beinn Fhada, Glen Coe**, (1B, 1F). Two of party of seven carried down by slab avalanche in easy access gully on **Lost Valley** side. Fatality carried into bergschrund; other uninjured.
1991	Feb 3	**Seana Bhraigh, Strath Mulzie**, (1F). MRT leader conducting training session at bottom of cliffs in **Luchd Coire**, caught in shallow slab avalanche and carried into boulders.
1991	Feb 9	**Beinn Udlaidh, Glen Orchy.** Climber in gully knocked off by large spindrift avalanche and fell 100m; broken ribs, torn ligaments both ankles.
1991	Feb 9	**Bidean nam Bian.** Party of nine ascending towards Bidean – Stob Coire nan Lochan col on Coire nam Beith side. Leader avalanched and carried about 100m with five or six others. Injured person (broken upper arm) buried, but dug out by companions. Slab ran on faceted crystals above snow-ice layer.
1991	Feb 11	**Stob Coire nam Beith.** Three walkers avalanched *near Hidden Gully* and carried over crag; all injured, none serious. Strong temperature gradient in snowpack.
1991	Feb 21	**Creag Meagaidh**, *Easy Gully*, (1B, 1F). Two climbers descending gully trigger avalanche and carried to bottom. Other, non-serious injuries.
1991	Mar 2	**Cairn Gorm, Coire an t-Sneachda**, Aladdin's Couloir. Two avalanched; one with knee and ankle injuries.
1991	Mar 2	**Ben Nevis**, *Orion Face Direct*. Leader avalanched by dry slab on last pitch and fell 70m, held by second; broken femur.
1991	Nov 11	**Stob Coire nam Beith.** Party of three on descent route from ridge, *near Hidden Gully*, carried down by dry slab avalanche. Two seriously injured.
1992	Feb 15	**Cairn Gorm, Hell's Lum**, *Escalator*. Preparing to climb scarp slope at top of route, leader triggered dry slab avalanche and fell full length of rope. Leader sustained lacerations and bruising, second rope burns.

1992   Mar 26   **Ben Nevis,** *Comb Gully Buttress.* Climbers moving together on second pitch avalanched and fall about 160m; one with severe bruising, other concussion.

1992   Mar   **Ben Nevis,** *Tower Scoop.* Instructor in cornice-triggered avalanche; broken ankle.

1992   Apr 4   **Cairn Gorm, Coire an t-Sneachda,** *The Runnel.* Cornice collapse avalanched two; head and leg injuries.

1992   Dec 5   **Ben Nevis,** *Number Five Gully.* Climber fell 35m in cornice collapse.

1992   Dec 5   **Ben Nevis,** *Observatory Buttress.* Climber avalanched at top of route and held by second, but both injured (chipped vertebra, broken hand, bruising), so abseiled off.

1992   Dec 21   **Ben Nevis, Red Burn** (2B, 1F). Two of party of three carried down and buried (one complete, other partial) in dry slab avalanche releasing from northerly aspect of the gully. Strong temperature gradients present: avalanche ran on facets.

1993   Dec 11/12   **Stob Coire nam Beith,** (2B, 2F). Two missing climbers found buried more than 5m deep.

1993   Dec 22   **Cairn Gorm, Coire an t-Sneachda,** *The Runnel.* Two avalanched from near top of route; facial and other injuries.

1993   Dec 28   **Sgurr na Fearta, Coire na h-Eilde, Achnashellach.** Walker carried down by wet slab avalanche; injuries to hand, legs and hips.

1994   Jan 2   **Beinn a' Chlaidheimh, Letterewe.** Two of three carried 80m in dry snow avalanche while ascending slope on west side of summit.

1994   Jan 16   **Liathach, Torridon,** *Hillwalk Gully,* (1F). Guided party of four avalanched near top of route; two others injured.

1994   Feb 3   **Buachaille Etive Mor,** (1F). Two climbers in *Crowberry basin,* descending due to hazardous conditions, hit by small avalanche from above. One ice axe braked, other fatal head injuries.

1994   Feb 16   **Glen Doll, Cairngorms.** Walker injured in avalanche.

1994   Feb 27   **Buachaille Etive Mor, Coire na Tulaich,** (2B, 1F). Two climbers off-route on descent caught in large dry slab avalanche. One freed himself after half an hour, dug out but could not rescuscitate companion.

1994   Apr 4   **Sgurr an Lochain, Cluanie.** Guided party of five carried down in cornice collapse; two with leg injuries rescued next day.

1995   Jan 4   **Meall a' Chrasgaidh, Fannaichs.** Ascending after deciding slope too dangerous, two walkers from party of seven were carried down by dry slab avalanche; one spinal injury, one minor injuries.

1995   Jan 12   **Beinn Ime, Arrochar.** Climber descending gully carried down by avalanche; fractured pelvis.

1995   Jan 21   **Liathach,** *Poachers' Fall,* (2B, 1F). Two climbers carried 400m by cornice collapse and avalanche. One with head free rescued by other climbers, other fatal. Another avalanche incident in Hillwalk Gully this day, no injuries.

1995   Feb 11   **Cairn Gorm, Coire an t-Sneachda,** *0.5 Gully.* Five avalanched by dry slab in descent, four injured; fractured pelvis, leg, wrist, bruising.

1995   Feb 14   **Lochnagar,** *Parallel Buttress,* (1F). Leader on last pitch avalanched by shallow snow. Due to extreme weather, he could not be reached in time by rescue team.

1995   Feb 18   **Creag Meagaidh,** (1F). Two climbers avalanched off Inner Coire face *near Diadem;* both with head and leg injuries. Four going to their assistance also avalanched, but OK. One of original victims died in hospital.

1995   Feb 22   **Buachaille Etive Mor, Coire na Tulaich,** (3B, 3F). Three walkers in bottom of corrie buried by large avalanche coming from above, not found for several days. Searchers had near miss from another large avalanche that night.

1995   Mar 4   **Buachaille Etive Mor,** *Curved Ridge,* (3B, 3F). Three climbers unroped on snowfield at top of route when carried away by a small slab avalanche and fell 300 to 400m. Bodies found below Waterslide Wall.

1995   Mar 4   **Cairn Gorm, Coire Laogh Mor.** Eight members of winter skills training group carried down in dry slab avalanche on back wall of corrie; four injured, two seriously. Mobile phone used for callout.

1995   Mar 4   **Meall a' Bhuiridh, White Corries.** Two skiers in avalanche in gully near **Creag Dubh,** one partly buried.

1995	Mar 4	**Cairn Gorm, Coire an Lochain**, (2B, 2F). Two climbers descending into west side of corrie carried down by dry slab and buried. Found May 27. Avalanche accident also on Helvellyn this day.
1995	Mar 5	**White Coomb, Moffat Hills**, (1B, 1F). Walker buried in large wet slab avalanche; dog find.
1995	Mar 25	**Creag Meagaidh**, *Cinderella*. Five avalanched in possible cornice collapse; three hospitalised.
1995	Dec 30	**Beinn Eighe, Coire nan Clach, Torridon.** Two walkers descending corrie carried down by loose dry snow avalanche; both sustained broken legs.
1996	Feb 8	**Am Bodach, Aonach Eagach.** Four members of Glen Coe MRT ascending from east when triggered soft slab. Two carried down 50m, two 150m; cuts and bruises.
1996	Feb 1	**Aonach Dubh**, *Dinner Time Buttress*, (1F). Guided party traversing shelves to left to avoid amphitheatre above, judged to be avalanche prone. Guide was unroped, investigating route but triggered dry slab and fell 200m over cliff.
1996	Feb 17	**Ben Nevis**, *Number Two Gully*. Leader fell on to runner when avalanched and sustained broken shoulder. Joined by another party of three for self rescue attempt, but leader of this party also avalanched when 3m from top of gully. All five carried down; two further casualties with crushed vertebrae.
1996	Apr 4	**Cairn Gorm, Coire an t-Sneachda, Goat Track.** Two members of winter skills party of seven carried down in shallow slab avalanche; one broken ankle.
1996	Apr 4	**Creag Meagaidh**, *The Pumpkin*, (1F). Four climbers fall when slope above the climb avalanched.
1996	Nov 24	**Cairn Gorm, Fiacaill a' Choire Chais.** Two walkers descending went off side of ridge in whiteout and were carried down in soft dry slab avalanche 1m deep. One with back injury, other muscular injury. One partly buried.
1997	Jan 11	**Cairn Gorm, Coire an Lochain**, (2B). Two from party of three walkers ascending west side of corrie in twin burns area, when both carried down in a large slab avalanche to the lochan and buried to a depth of 1.5m. Impact with iced-up loch opened crevasses in snow debris exposing them to an air supply. Self-extrication after 6hrs 15mins burial. Arrived back in time to meet MRT setting out (see Chapter I).
1997	Feb 2	**Creag Meagaidh**, *Cinderella*. Two of party of five carried down by small cornice or scarp avalanche. One knee and ankle injury, one broken femur. Mobile phone used for callout.
1997	Feb 9	**Creag Meagaidh**, *Cinderella*. Six casualties with various injuries including spine/neck, broken leg, ankle, arm.
1998	Jan 14	**Ben Nevis**, *Gardyloo Gully*. Two climbers from party of five carried 250m down Observatory Gully from bottom of route by dry slab. Both had bruising, one knee laceration.
1998	Feb 1	**Cairn Gorm, Hell's Lum**, *Escalator*. Two climbers moving together up scarp slope above route fell to bottom of crag when shallow slab avalanched. One punctured lung, one suspected leg fracture.
1998	Feb 7	**Aonach Mor**, *Lemming Ridge*. Guide belaying at top of route when cornice collapsed, triggering slope below. Held on client's belay; chipped elbow.
1998	Nov 5	**Stob Coire nam Beith**, *Central Gully*. Two in slab avalanche; one escaped, other sustained broken lower leg.
1998	Dec 7	**Cairn Gorm.** Walker sustained head injury in avalanche, location uncertain. Found by climbers who alerted rescue.
1998	Dec 29	**Aonach Mor**, (7B, 4F). Guided party of seven all buried by small avalanche in *G and T Gully*. Three survive around 14 hrs burial.
1999	Feb 21	**Carn a' Mhaim, Cairngorms**, *Silver Chimney*. Two members of MRT avalanched while on training exercise; one with two broken legs, other lacerations.
1999	Mar 13	**Ben Nevis**, *Point Five Gully*, (1F). Party of two fell from top part of route. Possible shallow slab avalanche or large spindrift sluff; failure of axe belay.
1999	Mar 13	**Cairn Gorm, Coire an t-Sneachda, Goat Track.** Two descending climbers triggered large slab avalanche and fell 150m; one with ankle injury.

Appendix IV

Avalanche Accident Blackspots

These locations are not necessarily more hazardous than any others in the Scottish mountains, but are notorious mainly because of their popularity. This list shows the number of accidents at, and comments relating to, specific locations. However it should not blind mountain-goers to the possibility that any slope may have the potential to avalanche.

Raeburn's Gully (Lochnagar)	5	None recent. Airborne powder avalanche site
The Runnel (Cairn Gorm)	4	Approach, scarp, cornice hazards
Great Slab (Cairn Lochain)	4	The classic Cairngorm site and not just in Spring
Cinderella (Creag Meagaidh)	4	New contender
Coire Cas headwall (Cairn Gorm)	4	One very big accident
Goat Track (Cairn Gorm)	3	A popular descent route
Coire Laogh Mor headwall (Cairn Gorm)	3	Two with multiple injuries
Gardyloo Gully (Ben Nevis)	3	Victims fall a long way
Tower Gully (Ben Nevis)	3	Dangerous run-out
Number Two Gully (Ben Nevis)	3	Exit bowl has many slope aspects
Number Three Gully (Ben Nevis)	3	Not always a suitable descent
Number Four Gully (Ben Nevis)	3	As above; approach problematic also
Number Five Gully (Ben Nevis)	3	Site of earliest mountaineering avalanche fatality
Castle Gullies (Ben Nevis)	3	Airborne powder avalanche site
Red Burn (Ben Nevis)	3	Two fatal; beware N-facing side also
Coire na Tulaich (Buachaille Etive Mor)	2	Both fatal; notorious avalanche trap
Twin Burns area (Cairn Lochain)	2	Victims carried to lochan in both accidents

Many other sites show two accidents

Appendix V

Further Information

Books
Snow Structure and Ski Fields, Seligman, (1936 Macmillan). A wonderful record of pioneer work by a true enthusiast.
The Avalanche Handbook, McLung and Schaerer (Cordee), ISBN 0898863643. A comprehensive manual; a worthy successor to the US Forest Service publication.
Avalanche Safety for Skiers and Climbers, Daffern (2nd Edition, Diadem Books), ISBN 0906371260. A well-received book with some coverage of Scotland and some good illustrations.
Snow Sense, Fredston and Fesler (4th Edition, Alaska Mountain Safety Center, Inc.), ISBN 0964399407. Accessible and complete coverage.
Mountaincraft and Leadership, Langmuir (3rd Edition, Scottish Sports Council, MLTB), ISBN 1850602956. Includes chapters on snow and avalanche. The author did much pioneer work on the Scottish snowpack and masterminded the pilot Scottish Avalanche Project.
International Mountain Rescue Handbook, MacInnes (3rd Edition, Constable), ISBN 009094753601. Update of the standard work by the progenitor of avalanche forecasting in Scotland.

Websites
Scottish Avalanche Information Service   http://www.sais.gov.uk/
Cyberspace Snow and Avalanche Center   http://www.csac.org/
Canadian Avalanche Association   http://www.csac.org/
Snow Crystal Research   http://www.lpsi.barc.usda.gov/emusnow/
Snow and Avalanche Research Davos   http://www.slf.ch/slf/slf.html
European Avalanche School   http://www.avaschool.com

Association Nationale pour l'étude de la Neige et des Avalanches (ANENA)
http://www-pole.grenet.fr/POLE/Alpes-Montagnes/annuaire/ANENA.html

Research Papers
The stability index and various triggering mechanisms, Paul M B Föhn, Avalanche Formation, Movement and Effects (Proceedings of the Davos Symposium, September 1986), IAHS Publ. No. 162, 1987.
Infiltration of water into snow, H Conway and R Benedict, Water Resources Research, Vol 30, No 3, pages 641-649, March 1994.
A branch grain theory of temperature gradient metamorphism in snow, Richard A Sommerfeld, Journal of Geophysical Research, Vol 88, No C2, Pages 1484-1494, February 20, 1983.
The layered character of snow covers, SC Colbeck, Reviews of Geophysics, Vol 29, No 1, Pages 81-96, Feb. 1991.
The sintering process in snow, Rene O Ramseier and Charles M Keeler, Journal of Glaciology, Vol 6, No 45, 1966.
Evaluation of the shovel shear test, Peter Schaerer, The Avalanche Review, Vol 7, No. 6, March 1989.
Snowpits, Bruce Tremper, The Avalanche Review, Vol 7, No 6, March 1989.
Rutschblock precision, technique variations and limitations, JB Jamieson and CD Johnston, Journal of Glaciology, Vol 39, No 133, 1993.
Snow in strong or weak temperature gradients. Part 1: experiments and qualitative observations, R Perla, Cold Regions Science and Technology 11, (1985), 23-35.
The Stuffblock: a simple and effective snowpack stability test, Ron Johnson and Karl Birkeland, Proceedings of the 1994 International Snow Science Workshop.
Merging data analysis and symbolic calculation into a diagnostic system for natural hazards, Robert Bolognesi and Othmar Buser, The International Emergency Management and Engineering Conference, 1995.
Transport and sublimation of snow in wind-scoured alpine terrain, JW Pomeroy, Snow, Hydrology and Forests in High Alpine Areas (Proceedings of the Vienna Symposium, August 1991). IAHS Publ. no. 205, 1991.
Snow stability during rain, H Conway and CF Raymond, Journal of Glaciology, Vol. 39, No. 133, 1993.
Avalanche forecast by the nearest neighbour method, Othmar Buser, Monika Butler and Walter Good, Avalanche Formation, Movement and Effects, (Proceedings of the Davos Symposium), 1986. IAHS Publ. no. 162, 1987.
Two years experience of operational avalanche forecasting using the nearest neighbours method, Othmar Buser, Annals of Glaciology 13, 1989.
Automated measurements of snow temperature profiles in the Cairngorm mountains, Scotland, RS Purves, JS Barton and DSB Wright, Meteorological Applications 2, 199-207, 1995.
A method to allow avalanche forecasting on an information retrieval system, RS Purves and M Sanderson, Journal of Documentation, vol. 54, no. 2, March 1998, pp. 198-209.

Index